Becoming Conscious is a result of thirty years of Dr. Joseph Howell's research and practice in psychology and spirituality. In this groundbreaking work he presents the ancient Enneagram's often-forgotten passageway to consciousness. Also presented is how the Enneagram is consistent with the messages of Jesus Christ.

"Yes, I want to become a conscious being but I can't meditate all day or go to an ashram … I've got a job and a family … Don't busy people like me get to find meaning, happiness, and an end to our pain?" Dr. Howell clearly answers this question and many more with everyday examples and interviews with people of all ages and walks of life.

Becoming Conscious gives a practical method for self- realization. Follow its passageway to the new consciousness and the peace it provides. This sacred journey awaits you.

Dr. Joseph Howell received a Bachelor of Arts degree from Samford University, a Master of Arts degree in religion from Yale Divinity School, and a Doctor of Philosophy degree from the University of Virginia in a combined professional and scientific program of clinical child and family psychology. He was also a fellow in clinical psychology in the Department of Psychiatry at Harvard Medical School.

Dr. Howell was assistant professor of family medicine with the University of Alabama in Birmingham School of Medicine for ten years. He coauthored Physician Stress.

For the past twenty-three years, Dr. Howell has been in private practice and is a member of the American Psychological Association. He teaches and speaks at conferences on the Enneagram and other subjects related to spiritual transformation, consciousness, and self-realization.

Active in the Alabama Episcopal Diocese and their local parish, he and his wife, Lark, are the parents of Ben and Lauren and live in Anniston, Alabama.

www.drjoehowell.com

Becoming Conscious:

The Enneagram's Forgotten Passageway

Joseph Benton Howell, Ph.D.

BALBOA.
PRESS
A DIVISION OF HAY HOUSE

Balboa Press books may be ordered through booksellers or by contacting:

Balboa Press
A Division of Hay House
1663 Liberty Drive
Bloomington, IN 47403
www.balboapress.com
1-(877) 407-4847

Because of the dynamic nature of the Internet, any web addresses or links contained in
this book may have changed since publication and may no longer be valid. The views
expressed in this work are solely those of the author and do not necessarily reflect the
views of the publisher, and the publisher hereby disclaims any responsibility for them.

The author of this book does not dispense medical advice or prescribe the use of any
technique as a form of treatment for physical, emotional, or medical problems without the
advice of a physician, either directly or indirectly. The intent of the author is only to offer
information of a general nature to help you in your quest for emotional and spiritual well-
being. In the event you use any of the information in this book for yourself, which is your
constitutional right, the author and the publisher assume no responsibility for your actions.

Any people depicted in stock imagery provided by Thinkstock are models,
and such images are being used for illustrative purposes only.
Certain stock imagery © Thinkstock.

ISBN: 978-1-4525-5715-1 (sc)
ISBN: 978-1-4525-5716-8 (e)
ISBN: 978-1-4525-5717-5 (hc)

Library of Congress Control Number: 2012916283

Printed in the United States of America

Balboa Press rev. date:09/17/2012

*…. it is the spirit in a person,
the breath of the Almighty, that
gives them understanding.*

Job 32: 8

TABLE OF CONTENTS

PREFACE

In the mid nineteen eighties, I read an article shared with me by a friend about an ancient system of nine personalities. As a clinical psychologist, I was fascinated with how the nine types resembled categories of human behavior outlined in modern psychology. Each type was described in its healthy and unhealthy mental status. More than that, I was intrigued that this mysterious typology could also contain a spiritual pattern for healing the maladies of each type.

Shortly thereafter, I embarked on a personal quest to learn as much as possible about this miraculous system. My first course in the Enneagram was at the Jesuit Retreat House in Cleveland, Ohio. It was there, that the learned teachers Maria Beesing and Patrick O'Leary unfolded its amazing basic concepts. I will always remember one special evening during the first days of this study. Our teachers instructed us students, who numbered about forty, to separate into groups according to our types. The method by which we were to "find" our type included the following directions:

"Go down the adjacent long hallway of small rooms. Notice that the door of each room is affixed with one numeral. Go into the room with the number on its door, of what you believe your type to be. Then sit down and talk to the people there who have chosen the same room. If in the atmosphere and discussion you feel a sense of belonging, this is most likely your type. In a room that is filled with persons of your type, you will resonate with the topics chosen, their presuppositions about life, the concerns they think about daily and their approach to dealing with all facets of living. Try sitting in several rooms until you have found for sure, your people".

Following the instructions, I visited a couple of "chat rooms" in which I was sure I would feel a sense of kinship. But I did not have that feeling of familiarity I was prepared by our teachers to experience. I left both of those rooms. There was a third type I was not thrilled about, but was quite fascinated by. I thought I'd 'drop in' on these folks, just to observe their discussion. As soon as I opened the door I felt like I was sitting around the kitchen table with my own family of origin. The atmosphere, the topics of discussion, the daily preoccupations, the areas of concern, the hopes, dreams...they were so deeply familiar. I did not ever dream there were others who shared some of my deepest fears and hopes in such similar ways! This experience brought the power of Enneagram types "home" for me. Type did not appeal to me because of its classification aspect, but because of its vital link to the most miraculous part of the Enneagram: that type reveals to each person, their own personal passageway to healing and wholeness.

After this experience I was fortunate to come to know Don Riso, who was beginning his ground-breaking lecturing and writing career. He graciously accepted an invitation to present the

Enneagram at the medical residency program at which I served as an assistant professor of Family Medicine in Anniston, Alabama. I am indebted to C. Neal Canup, M.D. and to his openness to new ideas which made this event possible. House staff and faculty were enthralled by Don and the Enneagram. He came a second time for another more advanced workshop. Thanks to Don many participants brought the truths of the Enneagram into their medical practices and into their personal lives.

As my teaching and clinical practice grew, and as I integrated the truths of the Enneagram into my own life and work, the beneficial results were evident.

Becoming so familiar over the years, with the types and their energies, in my clinical work, I was able to "recognize the person" almost within the first interview. This recognition fostered the patient's positive response to therapeutic intervention. This was amazing and became second nature to me.

I was at the same time, applying the Enneagram to my own spiritual growth. In this personal application, I found the Enneagram to be completely consistent with my spiritual principles, and my Christian faith. In fact, for me, the Enneagram echoed and underlined in a different language, the concepts taught by Christ. This powerful integration of ancient Middle Eastern spirituality and Christianity, both of them ways of life from the same part of the globe, became my worldview. Thereafter, my Enneagram studies were from many teachers who all greatly added to my foundation.

In teaching the Enneagram for many years across the country, I have passed through various phases of emphasis. In the beginning, I focused mainly on the healthy and unhealthy psychological characteristics of type. Then I shifted the major focus to the spiritual and transformative aspects of the system. The role of prayer in spiritual development became an essential aspect of my teaching.

Several years ago, I was introduced to the lectures and writings of Eckhart Tolle, Richard Rohr, and Ken Wilbur. Their contributions to consciousness-raising are monumental. These wise teachers, each say in their own way, how essential it is to shed the false self in realizing one's true nature and in stopping needless human suffering. It was after studying these concepts I saw how the Enneagram could be an actual <u>starting point</u> for becoming conscious. Then I discovered how it contains a method by which consciousness can "flower" in us, over and over. It is evident that as long as people and collectives remain in the false self, greater consciousness cannot be achieved. It is also clear that current escalating global concerns are making a loud call to become conscious as fellow dwellers on Earth. The call is to be aware of our true nature as divine beings. The call to consciousness also awakens us to the reality of hunger in this world, the needless deaths occurring daily, changes in earth's climate, the ultimate exhaustion of earth's fuels, the cycle of emotional and physical violence, and of the ability humanity now has to end itself, and all other life. It is possible for humanity to awaken in enough numbers, to affect a global shift in awareness. Many experts say that this shift in global consciousness is already occurring. One of the most powerful tools to create consciousness one-by-one, is the Enneagram. Transformation of many individuals can occur if a clear passageway to consciousness such as that inherent in the Enneagram, can be "re-membered" and taken. This book's goal is to interpret the Enneagram's step by step, passageway to consciousness. Herein are many interviews conducted with various people. Names and identifying data have been changed for privacy.

The person who has contributed most to the birth of this book is my wife, Lark who is the practical know-how behind so much. Her creativity, patience and love are beyond all measure, and I am so grateful to you, Lark for this and for your love.

I am so very thankful to Kim Wade for her generous willingness and excellent computer skills that are above and beyond what I could have asked for in doing this project.

I would like to express appreciation to three persons who helped form my life path in the beginning years. The first was my mentor at Yale Divinity School, the late Henri Nouwen. As my faculty advisor, as well as my academic teacher, Henri helped me to integrate spirituality and psychology into a professional career. And greater than that, he helped me to see that there is really no separation between the two fields. The second person is the late George G. Ritchie, M.D. whose mentoring when I was a graduate student at the University of Virginia, and later as a healer, will always be my touchstone. The third person is Raymond Moody, Ph.D., M.D., whose collaborative relationship of nearly four decades and whose essence continue to be a deep inspiration to me. I am also grateful to Cheryl Moody who cheers me on.

A huge thank you goes to The Reverend Susan Sloan for insisting that I write this book. Her wisdom, friendship and strength are invaluable. I also am indebted to my dear friend The Reverend George Cox, for his loving and ongoing support in this project and in life itself. His gifts are precious to me and as I carry them, I promise to pass them on.

I would like to express my gratitude to Nikki Chenault for whose love, innovative ideas, artistic expression, and spiritual courage are amazing. A heartfelt thanks goes to my friend, Katharine Smith for contributing her time and fantastic abilities to this work and to the conferences. Thank you, Livy Abele for years of peer collaboration and friendship both of which are in this work and my life.

My soul-felt appreciation goes to artist and friend, Provie Musso, whose tremendous creative energy has breathed new life into countless persons including me, for decades. Reverends Kelly and Dale Clem have been there since the beginning for me in mind, presence, and spirit. I am grateful to you both for how you are living embodiments of faith.

Deep gratitude goes to Dorothy and Clif Dixon for their prayers, their outreach, and their commitment to helping others and especially to Dorothy for her persistence. A person who has flowered in this work and who has supported it for years is Susan Murphy – thank you. To Bryan Freeman, M.D. goes appreciation for taking the challenge and embracing the consciousness in it. Likewise, I would like to thank Rev. Dr. Roland Brown for his ongoing ministry that includes these truths.

I must add that I have so much gratitude for the love and support from Beverly Casey. Thank you, Wendy and Bud Owsley for your enthusiasm and for living out your truths…so beautifully. I would like to express my appreciation to Avis and Will Gunter for their participation and love in putting this information out there. I also thank Esta and Daniel Spector, Ph.D. for their light, tears, and laughter, and especially to Dan for his help in reviewing the manuscript.

Jennifer and Stewart Moore represent the hope of the future and shining stars for me. Clay McKinney you are the best. Thank you for being the music beneath the wings of this project and the conferences. Thank you. And finally, I would like to express love and appreciation to my friend, Sue Tidwell, whose searching soul led her to the Enneagram which she so generously shared with me.

July, 2012
Anniston, Alabama

In gratefulness…to Lark

INTRODUCTION

The Enneagram has its beginning in mystery. No one knows exactly where it comes from, yet it is thought to have its origins in the Sufi tribes of the areas between Pakistan and Afghanistan, around twelve hundred years ago.

The Enneagram literally means nine points (ennea – Greek for nine and gram- Greek for mark, points or configuration.) The Enneagram was most likely given its Greek name by those who learned it from the Sufis. The Enneagram is basically a study of the flow of energy. It is much larger in scope than its particular use in understanding personality. This system based in mathematical concepts, reveals the movement and foundational principles of knowledge, including theology, music, philosophy, architecture, law, science etc.

In the study of personality, the Enneagram is primarily designed for self-inquiry. By discovering one's Enneagramatical personality, one can come to know one's many layers of self in a very personal and particular way. It is not simply a typing system as are some personality theories; rather it is a system of becoming enlightened as to one's deepest strengths and weaknesses. Then it goes much further. It points out exactly how the strengths can become more stable and more dynamic, and how the weaknesses can be brought to consciousness and even healed.

There are nine rudimentary personality types in the Enneagram (defined in Chapter Two) just as there are nine basic types of energy in the universe. When one discovers his or her own energy, then they can discover their very unique personality. As in most bodies of knowledge, the Enneagram builds upon information from its foundational aspects all the way to its more complicated forms of revelation. Each step must be accomplished before the next can begin.

The ancients, who first devised this system, did not write it down. They used only the Enneagram "map" as a visual aid. The actual knowledge was perceived as mystical and was passed down in the oral tradition only to the select pirs or wise persons of the tribe. For this reason it was sacred knowledge used by only the few pirs, or recognized religious authorities of the tribe. It has been written down relatively recently, given its long history. Oddly enough, even today the Enneagram is said to be understood best when presented orally.

The Enneagram is such a profound spiritual tool of enlightenment, that it is used in spiritual direction and for other theological and sacred learnings. This is its best virtue: - it leads us to consciousness.

Chapter One
The Enneagram of Personality – A Passageway to Consciousness

A passageway to becoming conscious is nearer than we can imagine. We can follow this passageway only by knowing the deeper aspects of ourselves as revealed by powerful spiritual truths. A profound reflection of these truths, the Enneagram, reveals to us our true self which miraculously opens the passageway to the land of conscious being.

In opening the gate of this transformational passageway we become familiar with our personality type as depicted on the Enneagram. By seeing far more deeply into our own being, we discover on the Enneagram of Personality the particular obstacles that block our type's ability to become conscious. These obstacles can be removed only through faith and spiritual transformation. Like lightening and thunder awakening us to a greater alertness, the Enneagram's wisdom sheds light upon what a dark night would have hidden. Revealed in a flash are our personality, its inherent imprisonments, and amazingly we also see our pathways to freedom! Let us now discuss this phenomenal process.

In our new awakening, we discover that our personality includes "traps" of compulsive thoughts and behaviors, which repeatedly delude us into making the same mistakes which bring on much suffering. This unconscious repetition of the same thoughts and actions seemed to bring hope and satisfaction. Now, however, it is evident to the greatly suffering person, that these patterns bring overwhelming pain, instead of fulfillment. John Sanford spoke to this when he said "…the outer shells of the personalities of many people conceal a hollowness, an emptiness longing to be filled, with an accompanying agony of the soul". (1) The personality driven by the ego can not be healed by ego alone. The Enneagram points out that we have identified with the ego who has fixated upon certain behaviors and thoughts that dominate and trap the person in unconsciousness. To turn and enter consciousness, the ego fixation must be replaced by something more powerful.

The Enneagram's wisdom blows away the shrouding smoke of unconsciousness by revealing the startling truth that <u>our personality is not really our truest self</u>! Personality is but a mask, a "social vehicle" in which we move among other masked personages. It and its ego can even mask one's true nature from oneself. Just imagine, the suffering we have born simply because we have lived as a personality that is not who we actually are! When this false self is unmasked, we are free to reclaim something that is holy, beautiful, and powerful: our deepest nature, our soul's essence. Living out of this real self, the suffering caused by unconscious living vanishes. Ego suffering is irrelevant now, because the world is seen through new eyes and heard with new ears of consciousness. Jesus spoke to the eyes and ears of spirit as they are used in perceiving reality. "He that hath ears to hear, let him hear (Mark 4:9) (2) and "the eye is the lamp of the body. So if your eye is healthy, your whole body will be full of light. (Matthew 6:22) (3). These new senses of consciousness enable the person to perceive life not as a self among a conglomeration of separate selves, but as a living pulsating part of a greater unity of humans who all have this true deeper nature. To live as one's true nature (or essence), instead of as a personality of ego, completely reframes the reason for living and puts suffering in a new light.

When living unconsciously, life is seen primarily through the lens of ego. This lens views the world as a subsidiary of self. People are seen as extensions of self or as oppositions to self. Examples of the unconscious self include viewing oneself as a role, status, material worth, external appearance, and as a self-created story. In short, when living unconsciously, the self is seen as separate from the whole, and as the product of its' own story. This perception of life ultimately leads to great suffering in that the self, the extensions of self and the story of self, could never really heal loss, illusion, and the suffering they bring.

From Self to Consciousness

Knowing one's personality type can light the way out of this needless suffering. How is this possible? By way of answering this question, let us presume that the false personality is like a piece of masking tape. This sticky tape covers a luminous crystal which symbolizes consciousness. If one can unmask (untape) the crystal, the brilliant clarity of consciousness will shine.

We can begin the unmasking process by peeling back one small corner of the tape. In scraping our fingernail across an edge of the tape, a tiny corner is loosened and is now free; we can feel it between our fingers. Pulling this tab of tape away from the crystal, begins the removal of the rest of the tape in its entirety. One corner of the tape was the starting point for a total unmasking.

3

This corner of the tape represents the discovery of our personality type and the type's ego fixation. Lifting away the first block to consciousness is the beginning of becoming conscious. It is the beginning of letting the light in and out.

There is a seamless yet fine line of spiritual reasoning that leads us through the passageway to consciousness. The following shows the sequence of challenge and transformation which link by link, forms a chain of consciousness.

The Chain of Consciousness

> In knowing ourselves, we can know
> our false self.
> In being conscious of our false self,
> we can see our ego.
> In seeing our ego, we can know its
> compulsions, traps, and illusions.
> In knowing our ego's compulsions,
> traps, and illusions, we can see the
> cause of our suffering.
> In seeing the cause of our suffering,
> we can shed our ego and false self.
> In shedding our ego and false self,
> we can know our true self, our
> essence.
> In conscious awareness of our
> essence, we can be that essence, free
> from the old sufferings.
> In being our essence free from the old
> sufferings, we can perceive others'
> true natures.

In perceiving others' true natures, we can know we are from the same source.

In consciousness that we all have a common source, we can be aware that the source is divine love.

In knowing we are from divine love, we can embrace the sanctity and interdependence of all life.

In being aware of this sanctity and interdependence, we can see the common shared needs for sustenance, healing, and illumination.

In being conscious of humanity's shared needs for sustenance, healing, and illumination, we can have compassion.

In having compassion, our fears of "others" can be diminished.

In diminished fearfulness, we can abandon violence to sustain, heal, and illuminate our fellow humans.

In sustaining, healing, and illuminating our brothers and sisters, we can love them and understand the connection of all life to its planet home.

In loving others and understanding the connection of all life to our planet home, we can become conscious of our planet's need for restoration and preservation.

> In being conscious of our planet's need
> for restoration and preservation, we
> can experience its divine essence.
> In experiencing our earth's divine
> essence, we can be truly thankful
> and become more conscious of its
> Creator.
> In being thankful and becoming
> more conscious of the Creator,
> we can understand our specific
> purpose.
> In understanding our specific
> purpose, we can live consciously.
> In living consciously, we can flower
> in consciousness.

This chain of reasoning takes us to consciousness, link by link. Helping us make a giant leap, the chain's first link is to know ourselves. Our having been "fascinated" by learning our personality type leads us to our true identity with its cosmic implications. In exploring our personality we can predict that more descriptions, nuances, and characteristics could be added to self, but instead, we are led to shed this self. We discover that the personality of self is really not the real us at all. We find that there is a truer self far more essential and deep than our superficial personality and its ego. It is the removal of, not the adding to, the false self that exposed the true self. In living in our true nature we are aware of and connected to all life. We see the limited centricity, short-sightedness, and futility of being driven by the ego, and identification with it. "Self" is redefined in a new and inestimable way. Living out of this "new self" carries vast implications for all life. It means being conscious. Consciousness brings life to its fullness. Without consciousness life on this planet will end.

What is True Consciousness?

What does true consciousness look like, and how do we know we have reached it? Consciousness, as we have seen, is an awareness that our vibrations, the energy we emit, our thoughts, feelings, attitudes and behavior profoundly affect ourselves, our loved ones, our neighbors, the world, the collective consciousness, the collective unconscious, and the cosmos.

As this awareness grows, it increases its sensitivity to the reality that we are more than physical beings. In fact we become more and more aware that we are filled with an emanating life force that is far more 'us' than is our body. We are aware that this life force is invisible, immeasurable, and within everything on the planet, including animals, plants, the planet itself and beyond.

True consciousness is awareness that all life and material substance share this same life force, and that there is a super intelligence within that energy that sustains it, protects it, brings it to its fullness, holds within it the blueprints of its design, and enables that life force to transform into new life or into another form.

True consciousness is also the awareness that all human life manifests from this Divine Intelligent Life Force. This force is love and is good. Though each human life is unique, a common alikeness in all humans is that their life force comes from the same Source of All Being. Consciousness naturally acknowledges that there is an inter-connectedness of all life which requires cooperation and interdependence between all life, and an interdependence of all life with its planet home.

True conscious living accepts and understands that agendas for self promotion and gain for our life as a separate entity, without consideration of the whole, is egocentricity. This comes from a narrow, unconscious and ultimately destructive view of self and others. Conscious persons are aware that such self promotion, at the expense of other life, is a product of the unchecked ego and its fixations. Consciousness is awareness that this is true of any collective ego as well, such as that of groups or nations.

It is known and understood by those who are truly conscious that the ego persists in trying to satisfy its wants and to defend itself against those it fears. It is known that all persons are susceptible to such inclinations as part of the experience of being human. It is through the process of becoming conscious that human self-centeredness and fear of others can be transcended. There are those who know this and those who do not. Those who do not know this will act from ego. Those who do know this will be compelled to live in true consciousness.

True consciousness knows and understands that the unconscious ego ultimately blocks the dominion, superiority, intentions and intervention of divine intelligence in the human experience. True consciousness knows that this intelligence is perfect, that it exists in our bodies, and that it intrinsically propels and governs the body as well as the earth and the cosmos. Those who are aware of this understand that unconscious ego demands want absolute authority over the body, mind, soul and psyche. Ego strivings want nature to go along with ego's overarching purposes. For the people of the unconscious, the ego is supreme. Others, nature, and God have tertiary and subordinate roles, although they may be "exalted" as all important.

True consciousness is aware that there are those who are aligned with divine intelligence and there are those whose primary alignment is with their own ego. Those who are blinded by their ego and its supposed needs cannot see how alignment with, and subordination to, divine intelligence could satisfy them. True consciousness assents to the fact that the blindness of the individual ego is the same with collective egos of families, groups, and nations.

True consciousness is also open to the fact that reality is a mystery to which we must surrender. To oppose the mystery is to assert ego's will. To align with the mystery enables one to join the divine plan and to use its force to better the person and the world. No one human or collective of humans can fathom the expanse of creation. Divinely conscious persons are aware that this mystery is unfolding, and that it is the real story. Those who are unconscious let their egos make up their own stories about life and the life of the world. Divinely conscious people know that the ego story is temporary and cannot offer transcendence or ultimate meaning.

True consciousness understands that awareness of the unconscious ego will be the starting point for finding another way to live. This new way to live invites harmony with the planet instead of conflict inside of self, inside of families, between groups, and between nations. Truly conscious persons know that any positive changes that are brought about are changes in consciousness first. True consciousness is knowing that a critical mass of people who recognize our common source, our common alikeness and the common sanctity of all life, will bring about a global shift in consciousness. This global shift could mean a mindset of peace on this planet.

True consciousness is the awareness that when we are able to shed our egos and live out of our essence, the basic selfishness and short-sightedness that affect humans will be diminished. Truly conscious persons know that the cycle of violence is born of ego's will. True consciousness knows that to stop the cycle of violence, we must place more energy into finding our true essence and living out of it, rather than putting energy into self and ego agendas.

True consciousness does not divide the world into dualities. For the conscious person there is no "we", versus "they", "black" versus "white", or "good" versus "bad". True consciousness knows that all is truly one and that there is light within darkness as well as darkness within light.

True consciousness is aware of the global escalation of violence among collective egos. True consciousness is aware that this is the first time in the history of the planet that its human inhabitants have the capacity to destroy the planet and all life upon it. This fact among truly conscious persons sensitizes them to the need for the unconscious egos of individuals and collectives to be brought to consciousness. They know this can best be done by raising the consciousness of people one by one. They know this must be done for life to continue.

True consciousness is aware that appearances are not necessarily what is real, and that life built on illusion will inevitably crumble. True consciousness includes the understanding that one must look past the egos and false selves of others to communicate with their essences (their true selves) even if these others are unaware of their own essence. True consciousness does not use gender, sexual orientation, race, religion, ethnic group, or any other label to define a person's soul. True consciousness knows that true essence and spirit are channeled through being fully present to the moment. Conscious persons know that the past and future cannot be experienced except in the present moment. Only in this instant can we live.

True consciousness knows that the only permanent thing is the transcendent life force within us. True consciousness knows that the life force is spirit from the One Source of All Being, and that it is the underlying word or logos of all things seen and unseen.

True consciousness is not trapped in a static dogma, but reflects the movement, adaptability, and constant change of the body, the planet, and the cosmos. Therefore true consciousness is open to the unseen, to its divine mystery, and to the unforeseen ways that divine intelligence may continue to manifest its message and its will. Being open includes receptivity to all holy methods of discerning the divine message. Such methods include dream interpretation, natural spirituality, prayer, meditation, worship, various other religious and spiritual experiences, the arts and physical portals such as yoga, Ti Chi, fasting, etc.

True consciousness is living in totally receptive awareness of each instant, each breath, each blink of the eye, each distant and nearby song of the birds, each caress of wind upon one's cheek, each holy being in one's midst, including one's holy self, and the expression of God.

The Enneagram of Personality describes how we function in the world, before and after reaching consciousness. The following diagrams illustrate the names and numbers of each type in the Ennagram of Personality (Figure 1), the Traps each type falls into (Figure 2), the Virtues of each type (Figure 3), and the Passions of each type (Figure 4).

Figure One
Enneagram of Personality

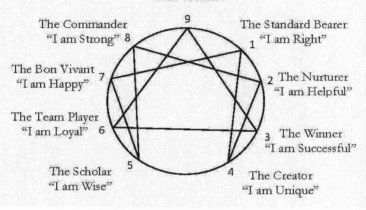

The Harmonizer
"I am Peaceful"

9

The Commander   The Standard Bearer
"I am Strong" 8   1 "I am Right"

The Bon Vivant 7   2 The Nurturer
"I am Happy"   "I am Helpful"

The Team Player
"I am Loyal" 6   3 The Winner
                       "I am Successful"

The Scholar 5   4 The Creator
"I am Wise"   "I am Unique"

Figure Two
Enneagram of Traps

Self Abasement

9

Justice 8   1 Perfection

Idealism 7   2 Service

Security 6   3 Efficiency

Knowledge 5   4 Authenticity

Figure Three
Enneagram of Virtues

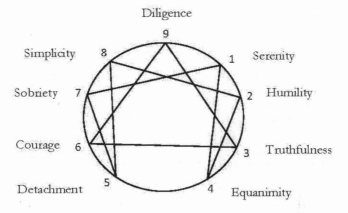

Diligence
9

Simplicity   8   1   Serenity

Sobriety   7   2   Humility

Courage   6   3   Truthfulness

Detachment   5   4   Equanimity

Figure Four
Enneagram of Passions

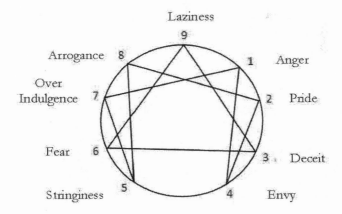

Laziness
9

Arrogance   8   1   Anger

Over Indulgence   7   2   Pride

Fear   6   3   Deceit

Stringiness   5   4   Envy

Chapter Two
The Types

Categorizing human behavior is not a new thing. People have always done it. It is much easier to label people than to truly understand them. This gives the ego a sense of satisfaction by placing people in a category that fits its perception of the world. Categorizing is frequently expressed in the following commonly heard phrase, "Oh, you know, he's just that type". "He" is assigned to a group type almost as if type is the reason why "he" is the way he is. Type, in and of itself, is not a major cause of personality. It is simply a grouping of similar personalities who all got there by their own physical, mental, emotional, and spiritual pathways. The actual first cause or etiology of type has to do with our biological and spiritual origins.

Coming into this world, we are almost a pre-packaged entity, freeze-dried if you please, so that when we are placed in the "water of life", we 'expand' into our fullest self. Of course, the condition of the "water" (the environment) affects us, and our interaction with it, shapes us and forms us. The biological and spiritual blueprints arrive in us at birth. The following prayer by George Appleton acknowledges this phenomenon and describes it as the seed placed inside us at our making.

A Gathering Prayer

Give me a candle of the spirit, O God
As I go down into the deep of my
Own being.

Show me the hidden things. Take me
Down to the spring of my life, and
Tell me my nature and my name.

Give me freedom to grow so that I
May become my true self – the
Fulfillment of the seed which you
Planted in me at my making.

Out of the deep I cry unto thee,
Oh God. Amen. (1)

George Appleton

The genes we inherit seem to be the most powerful determinants of personality. Psychological studies over many years have proven this at rates of statistical significance. For example, studies of identical twins separated at birth and raised apart from one another in completely different environments, show how strikingly similar they turn out to be. Never having contact with one another, these twins develop similar personalities, and even many of the same major preferences, as well as mental and physical diseases. Nothing can account for this similarity except for the genetic make-up shared by the twins. (2)

When it comes to the spiritual givens a person is born with, there is less clarity or scientific evidence. If indeed twins are born with the same genetics, and if it supposed that we are born with our spiritual essence, one would suppose that the twins' spiritual essence would be similar. If this is true their Enneagramatical types would also be the same. However this does not seem to necessarily be the case.

What is emerging is the knowledge that every human being, whether sharing genes or environment with others, is a unique expression of creation. Though biology and environment are great determinants of personality, the soul also comes with its own propensities. Carl Jung addressed this concept when he wrote, "The initial creature existed before man was, and the terminal creature will be when man is not." Psychologically speaking this means that the "child" symbolizes the pre-conscious and the post-conscious essence of man". (3) The soul is living on a much deeper level than personality and therefore expresses the essential nature (or essence) of a human being. The following type descriptions are not descriptions of the soul's essence. These are personality characteristics that persons in each type share with one another to a greater or lesser extent.

The following type descriptions are quite general, and are presented as portals to entering a fuller understanding of types. When reviewing each type description, keep in mind that there are many intervening variables beyond "type". To label someone as a type is a misuse of the wisdom of the Enneagram. People cannot be experienced in their wholeness if they are seen just as a "category." The transcendent nature of the person can never be reduced to a label. Several other dimensions of how a human being simply is, must be considered. The Enneagram is most effective in the processes of self-discernment and understanding. Self inquiry is the first step toward self-realization and consciousness. To use the Enneagram to categorize, judge, limit, control, demean, or even to idealize self or others is to miscarry this most precious revelatory gift.

Dimensions of the Enneagram that must be considered in self discernment for the purpose of conscious living are:

1. Basic Type
2. Ego Fixation, Trap, Avoidance, Passion, Virtue
3. Instinctual Subtype
4. Wings
5. Level of Integration/Disintegration
6. Level of Suffering
7. Temperament According to Life Situation; Mental and Physical Status
8. Level of Expressed Essence, the Holy Ideas, Spiritual Fruits
9. Stage of Consciousness Emergence
10. Level of Consciousness

Figure Five
The Three Centers

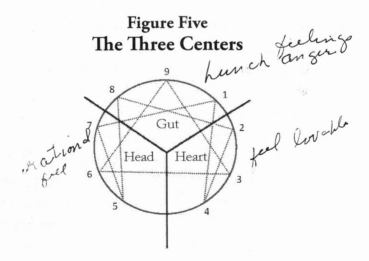

The Three Centers and The Types Within Them

There are three major centers within the Enneagram. These are the gut, the heart and the head centers. (See Figure Five) The types are organized in groups of three within the three major centers of the Enneagram. Types Eight, Nine and One are the gut center. Types Two, Three and Four are the heart center. Types Five, Six and Seven are the head center.

The centers help in one's determination of type because they give a broad area to which one can begin to narrow down their focus to a specific type. For example, if one knows that they are more prone to go with their "gut" on an issue rather than to go with their heart or head, then that person would do well to look within the three types that are in the gut center. Persons in the gut center come from an instinctually intuitive place. If a person usually makes choices based on her heart (or her feeling/emotional depths), she should look toward the heart center's three types. If the person usually uses mental constructs (using the mind to address issues of loss, fear, etc.) to deal with the issues of life, the head center is the place to look for her type.

The gut center most primarily expresses the anger or rage of being in a body and not in control of reality. The Nine of this center deals with his anger by "going to sleep" or numbing himself to the undercurrents of the rage. On the other hand, the Eight of this center deals with the anger and rage by becoming powerful, strong and in control. The One of the gut center deals with its rage by trying to restore perfection through being right.

The heart center's types express the issue of being unloved and being unloveable. For the Three of this center, this issue is handled by being successful to win love. For the Two, love is sought by meeting others' needs. For the Four, love is sought through alluring uniqueness and creativity.

In the head center's types the issue expressed is fear. This is fear of not having a place, a life or a function. At its worst, it is fearful of annihilation. The Six goes about this dilemma by being loyal to a protective authority or system to find security. The Five feels that the issue of fear is one primarily of inner emptiness, solved by keeping full. For the Seven, fear is dealt with by over-indulgence, distraction and escape.

THE NINE TYPES

Type One: The Standard Bearer
Type One says to the world, "I am right".

Ones are our discerners, who are able to make the right call most of the time. The Standard Bearers among people, Ones are extremely aware of doing things "the right way". An often quoted saying, applicable to the type One personality is, "If it is worth doing, it is worth doing right". Type Ones are usually very hard workers who believe that work is good and play must be earned. They are seldom found being lazy or inactive. They hold themselves to the same high standards that apply to everyone else. This means they can be critical of others, and especially of themselves. They are trapped in seeking perfection. This causes tremendous suffering.

A natural inclination for this type is to zero-in on any flaw. Because their tendency is to have things perfect, they spend lots of time monitoring things, circumstances, and people. They can end up resenting others in the end, because no person seems to be able to "get it just right". Ones can see problems in advance, and are usually prudent with resources. They tend to follow the letter of the law. Their talking style is in a teaching motif as they, who are in the know, feel duty bound to instruct others about what's what.

The One makes a good judge. Often people solicit the advice of a One when they need to know the correct decision to make.

Ones can easily become resentful when people do not do as they advise. They may say to themselves in response to people who make the wrong choices against their advice, "I am so discouraged; no matter how hard I've tried to show them what to do, they insist on making mistakes…" When Ones are particularly discouraged they may say "No matter what I say or do, everything is going to hell in a hand basket". Ones avoid anger because it is wrong to be angry. Instead they internalize the anger, and it oozes out as resentment.

When Ones find levity and optimism, they can lighten up and live out of a balance between perfection and the real world. People can be around them more easily when they are understanding of shortcomings rather than judgmental of them.

Type Two: The Nurturer

Type Two says to the world "I am helpful".

Twos are the people who will give a gift and meet a need naturally. They're very good at finding out what other people's needs are, but their avoidance is their own needs. The Two is zeroing-in on a person to find out what that person's needs are. If they can find out what a person lacks, they'll supply it. If someone lacks eggs, they will know where there is a chicken coop. If someone needs their house painted, they know five house painters. If someone is sick, they're going to bring food. Whatever the person needs, they've got it covered because they are compelled to be helpful. The Two may tend to flatter you, but the heartfelt sense of wanting to give you something is usually behind this "verbal gift".

Just remember that the Twos want to be loved and to enjoy relationships. They must continually reassure themselves that they are needed. In their craving for love, Twos forget their own innate loveableness even though it's there without their giving and helping. They delight when they've been of service because they are reassured that they are needed, yet they are trapped in that service. To be needed is their major conscious need. They are often oblivious to their own needs. They resist acknowledging they have needs that others can fulfill. Fiercely independent, Twos want to be the giver not the receiver.

Twos, once they find a balance, make extremely good friends and family members because they love relationships, depth, connection, and intimacy. When integrated, they are attuned to what others need or want yet they are not blinded to their own needs.

Type Three: The Winner

Type Three says to the world "I am successful".

The Three's drive is to be successful and to <u>avoid failure</u>. The pride of the Three is, "I am successful and efficient". The Three wants to ascend the ladder of success and win the trophy. Whatever the game may be, they do not want to lose. Whether it is a conversation, a business deal, a political race, or even a video game, they avoid failing. Threes don't want a game to end without their winning because winning bolsters their ego. They need to be admired, wanted, and therefore, loved. Winning means they are successful and therefore loved. Threes are not sure of their loveableness, therefore they must find love through being successful (like Twos want love through their giving).

The daddies in the park say, "Great! You're wonderful Jill. You made a homerun"! Or, "Great son, you aced it; you're a good guy. You scored". There is a hidden meaning in such comments

– that if one doesn't achieve, they are not such a "good guy" or so wonderful. "If you're a success, then you are acceptable", says a Three who achieves for love.

Threes make wonderful administrators because they like to bring things together, delegate jobs, send people out and then bring them back together to measure the success. This is also an efficient way to accomplish their goals.

Threes are peacocks who show their colorful feathers in a way that they feel is most beneficial. When two Threes meet, the exchange can be highly competitive, either outright or subtly. There are many different aspects to the Three, and no description fits each. Threes have been called chameleons because they can change their appearance and manner to adjust to a situation while being perceived as they think that situation dictates. Threes tend to be able to 'tweak' their verbalization and image so that they gain approval from those around them. Their talking style is called "propaganda" or "advertisement", as they are adept in marketing themselves or whatever they are "pushing". All of this comes from an overriding desire to feel loved. Harboring a huge lack of self-acceptance, on a deep level of being, Threes feel that they must "come up with" a way to feel loved. As the Three disintegrates, he or she becomes more desperate for that love because the absence of it is felt acutely. At this point Threes have the capacity to "relax" their sense of fairness. To compete they may tend to misrepresent their accomplishments, or at the worst, use deceit to appear successful.

Compelled to be in a mad rush to succeed, Threes are caught in a trap of efficiency. This trap is maladaptive for them, as they end up being in a frenzy to get more and more accomplished. They hope this will bring them more and more admiration. Translated to the bottom line, the Three has to be efficient for the sake of being loved.

Type Four: The Creator

Type Four says to the world "I am unique".

Picture with me, if you will, a vision of Jackie Kennedy walking from one room of the White House to the other, looking out the windows. There she is, on top of the world's political, social and economic ladder as she looks out the window, down the mall, takes a big breath, sighs and says to herself, "I wish John and I were alone together". She's feeling the beautiful draperies with her fingers, admiring the material and how well they are made, sighs and laments "I don't own these...I don't own anything and I don't have anyone". Someone comes to her and says, "Mrs. Kennedy, it's time to get ready for the state dinner tonight". She replies, "I'll be there in just a minute". When the door is closed, she sighs again and says to herself, "I'd like to be in the attic painting". She is one who sees life through different kinds of glasses because she says, "I am so very different from most people...I am not meant to be in a camera's eye...I am best suited for something else. I just don't know what. I am so very misunderstood...I don't even understand myself...I envy those who do, yet it seems I am envied by others".

When a Four plays that role of uniqueness out all the way, nothing can satisfy him or her. For Fours, if they become content, they feel it makes them common. There are many Fours who resist being labeled a Four, simply because the label means it's a category into which others may fall. Having any linkage with the common sea of humanity simply goes against their grain. Their defense against the world is, "That doesn't apply to me. I am different from *that*". And hence, they are unique; set apart. They avoid being common.

Fours are not going to present themselves as peacocks but as more subtle birds with hidden, exceptionally beautiful, plumages.

Usually something about a Four's appearance is going to be different or unusual. For example, it might be a basic black dress with a fuchsia sash or a neutral suit with a unique necklace. For a male it may be the one-of-a-kind quote on the back of his T-shirt or, a tie that has an unusual weave. Their <u>avoidance is ordinariness</u>.

Fours are given to melancholy because they perceive their past as complicated and tragic. They seek to understand their past, but seem to like that it is somehow incomprehensible. There is this undertone of, "Oh me...oh, nothing is good enough. When will I find what I am looking for"? They envy those who they think have found "it". They are usually looking for a special person who has all the answers, who can bring them out of confusion to give their life meaning. The disintegrated Four is looking for a partner who will complement them (as colors complement other colors). Fours are trapped in authenticity – they search for their real life – the life they want to begin living...someday...somehow. By themselves, they yearn for someone to give them clear direction.

Fours find a balance when they know the right direction to take with their life and passion. Being lovers of the beautiful, the misunderstood, and neglected, they go for causes that help these facets of society. For example, they may work for abandoned children, animal welfare, or saving endangered species, etc. Fours are full of heart and art. Without them we would have very few "different takes" on life.

Type Five: The Scholar

Type Five says to the world "I am wise".

Five's <u>avoidance is emptiness</u>. Fives would much rather be in their own room reading books than sharing what they've read with anyone else. Their fear of their own inner complete emptiness drives them to seek more and more fulfillment. They usually choose to fill themselves with knowledge, and this becomes their trap.

In gaining as much knowledge as they can, Fives can't do that with a lot of other people. Therefore they are usually given to being introverts. Fives need to be with other people sometimes, because their wisdom will never be felt unless someone sees it. So they let out just a little, enough to let everyone know that they've got something that could be given. This wisdom of theirs, shared or unshared, fuels the ego fixation to accumulate knowledge. The more knowledge for the Five, the more "me" there is for them, and the less empty they perceive themselves to be.

Fives are the keen observers of all. They are compelled to take in as much information as possible. This is because they have lost a feeling of inner fullness and the certainty that they will be filled. They live their lives balancing on a precipice. With every step they take they are fearful of falling off. If they fall to the right, they will go into the world and be devoured by the crowds, noise, and demands. If they fall to the left, they will be alone, away from people with no one except their own thoughts.

Fives love to collect. Frequently, they collect information. This is now done easily with computers. Many collect information to have a sense of being an authority on a certain topic. This "special knowledge" may give them a feeling of being loved and needed and quell their fear driven anxiety of being discounted. Collecting can escalate into the material. As information is hoarded, so are things such as books and objects that represent their inner selves.

Fives are outstanding teachers and mentors. Those Fives who have integrated in personality functioning have learned to move in the world and share their knowledge. Fives who are not so healthy and conscious may sit on their largesse and deteriorate. Their fear of not having enough to fulfill them has paralyzed them. They are trapped in their own knowledge, its analysis and their fantasies spun by living in their heads.

Type Six: The Team Player

Type Six says to the world "I am loyal".

Sixes can be consumed with fear. Then have a pervading anxiety of being excluded, abandoned, ridiculed, or taken advantage of. A Six is fearful that he or she is going to suffer at the hands of another. For this reason, Sixes avoid deviances which they consider unacceptable to the group at large. This avoidance may come from early childhood experiences, and is the reason for the closeness to a group. "If I am in a group, I can hide. If I am in a group, I can be one of the "good ol' boys or good ol' gals", or I can be part of this establishment, not an object of attention for anyone to take potshots at me. I am responsible, but I am so connected to others (the pack) that I share my responsibility". Sixes are team players.

The hallmark of the Six is the need for an authority figure. This authority compensates for the strength and power the Six feels they do not have within. The authority also protects the Six from those who would shun them because of their deviance. The authority figure is there because the Six needs security from someone who is older, wiser, or more powerful. Sixes "hire" various authority figures all through life to protect them, to guide them, to be their mentor, their friend, or their father-mother-confessor. They must find that in life there is neither real security nor perfection in the authority figure.

The Six's ego compulsion is termed "ego cowardice" because fear is a primary motive behind most choices. This fear is engendered by a pervasive self-doubting because of his or her perception of being defective. Being deviant, or different from the perceived norm, is tantamount for the Six to being a reject, deformed, wrong, and unloveable. Deviance is so feared that a Six can greatly over-compensate for it by appearing as a "regular" or even fearless person. Being regular is enhanced by their being attractive, warm, and charming. These attributes are developed to hide their <u>deviance which is their avoidance</u>. Sixes have an unspoken fear of being punished, or banished for their deviances. In the most extreme form they fear being put to death for deviances weaknesses, or transgressions.

Some Sixes are counter-phobic. Instead of hiding as a regular person, they over-compensate with a defense in the form of being blustery or forcefully strong. Sometimes they come across as daredevils or intimidators. In psychological terms, this defense mechanism is called a reaction formation.

Sixes are seemingly tireless in achievement. This is to make sure they are seen as valuable and essential to the group. They do not want to be excluded, but included. When Sixes integrate, they become self-reliant.

Type Seven: The Bon Vivant

Type Seven says to the world "I am happy".

Sevens love joy and happiness. <u>Their avoidance is pain</u>. Some people have said that we live in a Seven society, because avoidance of pain is such a theme of our culture. Many Sevens avoid pain with substance abuse, technology, and with constant activity. Sevens hardly ever sit and reflect on pain because it hurts. They are told by our society that hurting is not good and must be avoided at all cost. Sevens are seemingly always searching for the ideal happiness that traps them in an unending quest. Their trap is idealism.

Sevens do this in a beautiful way: in their heads. No one can ever take some one's mind away, so Sevens capitalize on that. As a member of the head center, when met with pain, they beautifully transform the situation by vaporizing it into something wonderful. For example, you can be talking with a Seven and say, "Oh, woe is me! The Internal Revenue Service has sent me a message that I'm going to be audited. This is terrible! I can't stand it. I could have made a mistake. I'm going to be taken off to jail hand-cuffed." The Seven will put their arm around you and say, "Let's go see a movie." And for some reason, you do! They have this way of elegantly enveloping people in a vaporization of pain because they're experts at it. They do it themselves. They know exactly how to transform the negative into the positive.

Sevens are also gregarious people. They love relationships, not as much for their emotional depth, but for the good feelings that abound in the fun of it. They are usually very sensual people, very visual, focused on color, texture, design, externals, and the feel of a room or an environment. They are very sensitive, for example, to whether the colors in a room bring it life. They cannot live in drab surroundings, bad design, or lack of aesthetics. Sevens' surroundings are part of who they are. Their home or office is part of them because they feel that they are reflected in their environment. Many Sevens do not process information well because of their distractibility and selective attention. Painful things on television are quickly turned off. News items that are about death, pain, or suffering don't hold their interest. They would rather read the comics. They don't usually discuss sad news items. If they do, they focus on its redemptive themes. They are epicureans, love good food, and love to eat, drink and be merry. When they go to a restaurant, they love it if they may get a conversation going with another table and turn it into some kind of special evening. It's a life in which there's always more than what is needed. After the extras there has to be even more. More is better, and having too little is deprivation.

We live in a Seven society. We are exposed to a constant media blitz that encourages more, bigger, and better. This gets Sevens into trouble because they live in perpetual fear that they will not be able to get more or do more. *But,* they easily transform their fear into hope. They have hope that one day they will get what they desire. "Well, next time I am in town, I'll go to that restaurant. I'm so disappointed, *but next time,* I'll get there". Or, "Gosh, I didn't get that dress that I wanted this time, but I bet I can get it at such-and-such a time". Or, "I'll bet I can get a better bargain on it somewhere else". In their own minds, they go ahead and acquire that dress, that meal, or that experience. It's all done mentally and acquired through hopeful fantasy. When Sevens slow down and become integrated, they know how to deal with pain. They process it and do the necessary suffering for growth to occur.

Type Eight: The Commander

Type Eight says to the world "I am strong".

Eights desire power and strength, and they are very powerful and strong. They are leaders, movers, and shakers. They have a strong sense of what is just and a definite vision of how to make things that way. Their <u>avoidance is weakness</u>. Eights are strong because they are afraid of weakness in themselves. In fact, they are full of rage that they have any limitations. The stronger they can portray themselves to be, there is less risk in exposing their vulnerability. They live life large, having a penchant for power and a lust for what they want. Seeking justice for their causes empowers Eights, yet it traps them into seeking justice for themselves and for others they want to protect.

Eights spend a lifetime proving that they are strong. The unhealthy way they do that, is exemplified in the life of Saddam Hussein. Unhealthy Eights are much like Hussein, a power hungry person who was tyrannical and homicidal in securing power. Their sense of justice becomes toxic as they elevate themselves to be the judge, jury, and executioner. Healthy Eights have faced their weaknesses, know them, understand them and acknowledge having a weak part in themselves. An example of the healthy Eight is Golda Meir, the fourth Prime Minister of Israel. Because of understanding the necessity of compassion, healthy or conscious Eights like Meir reach out to others in a very strong way. They help others and seek justice for the weak. They minister to the weak because they've found their own weakness within and have ministered to it.

Eights want to be leaders. They can manipulate people and circumstances to own the entire situation. They want to be the top of the pyramid, chairman of the board, supervisor, or president. Their arrogance gives them a very strong idea of "we and them". Eights say, "There are people out there who are against us and we're going to get them before they get us". With Eights there is a lot of oppositional behavior. This is the way they can flex their muscles and be assured of their identity. If you meet an Eight where the aisles come together in a store and you don't know which way to go, the Eight waits for you to fumble around and get out of the way so they can walk through.

Knowing these people, you realize that's just the way they are. Even the Eights who have faced their weaknesses still seem to have a regal, powerful air about them. Learning to deal with humility is one of the hardest things for them to learn. They are the Fortune 500 people who build bank buildings, malls, and highways. They are politicians and strong people of a community. They know how to gather resources and people together, in a phenomenal way. They attract people through rousing passion, getting them to understand that there is justice and injustice. Integrated Eights understand the nature of power and the essential nature of compassion.

Type Nine: The Harmonizer

The Nine says to the world "I am peaceful".

Nines say, "Well, I'll do it later", or "So, big deal. The bill did come but, you know, I was going to pay it…guess time slipped away. It's no big deal, I'll get the water cut back on tomorrow". For the Nine nothing is all that big or bothersome. They are the balancers of extremes and the harmonizers between factions. They can see the flip side to everything.

The Nine is wonderful at negotiating. When people are arguing, if you bring a Nine into it, that's great! They can help reach agreements because they see both sides. It is the gift of having the perspective of all sides of an issue. When someone comes in all upset over something, the Nine understands why he or she feels the way they do and can tell him or her another way to look at their problem. After listening to the Nine, the person will calm down and say, "Well, I never thought of it that way". The Nine can reframe the difficulty by saying, "It is in rough times like this when we know we are alive". And we think in response, "Hey, that's right! If we can feel that much pain, we must be in touch with the life force".

Nines naturally, without thinking about it, make responses to life out of a sense of harmony. They do this because they <u>avoid conflict</u>. Nines don't "think" as much as, they have a "gut sense" of a situation. They don't have to analyze or cogitate.

What can they not stand? Conflict. They won't fight you. They will either shut down and self-narcotize, or they will handle conflict healthily. They will not fight you at all. The diplomat, Henry Kissinger, would probably be a healthy Nine. Nothing seemed to upset him. He could go to any conference table, see everybody's side, and bring the meeting into balance.

Nines have the gift of blending with other people. They can do this because of a non-assuming, almost self-effacing, type of presentation. In fact self-abasement is the trap of the Nine. The more self put-downs they have to make of themselves, the more inner conflict they have. They have a plethora of repressed anger that self-abasement represses. This brings suffering. Self put-downs usually disarm people and reduce tensions, but they destroy self-esteem. Nines, as they integrate, become less lethargic and more action-oriented. They put their skills to work, and begin to know they matter.

Now that you have read general descriptions of each Enneagramatical type, you are ready for the self-assessment in the next chapter. These assessments will provide a starting point for the passageway to consciousness.

Chapter Three
Self Assessment

The Howell Enneagram Profile Questionnaire is one of the several self assessment inventories available to discover one's Enneagramatical type. The Howell Profile Questionnaire is basically a self-screening device that, according to self ratings, indicates the type or types your personality may most resemble. High scores on a particular type may or may not indicate your type because of certain factors:

1. Life situation at time of self assessment
2. Inaccurate self-reporting
3. Denial of one's proclivities and behavior
4. Advanced integration and progress toward consciousness.

The questionnaire is comprised of characteristics associated with a typical person's type and ego fixation. Those who have taken the passageway out of their fixation and are no longer trapped by it, will not score particularly high on any one type. This is because they operate in a more healthy and conscious way. Also, their fixations may be less severe, making such people no longer definable in terms of the characteristics of fixation. Richard Rohr in his book *Falling Upward* provides an excellent insight to this phenomenon. "The task of the first half of life is to create a proper container for one's life and answer the first essential questions: "What makes me significant?" "How can I support myself?" and "Who will go with me?" The task of the second half of life is, quite simply, to find the actual contents that this container was meant to hold and deliver…In other words, the container is not an end in itself, but exists for the sake of your deeper and fullest life, which you largely do not know about yourself. Far too many people just keep doing the repair work on the container itself and never "throw their nets into the deep" to bring in the huge catch that awaits them".(1)

For those persons who the second half of life has enlightened, and those in fewer numbers who are younger and have also shed their ego, this assessment device must be approached in a different way. Answer the questions as if you were younger (between ages eighteen and thirty). This is the peak time of ego fixation before suffering has called life into question. These answers will yield a score which can trace your probable type and its fixation.

Young people who are just now beginning to look at their lives, egos, suffering, and level of consciousness may find the Enneagram and this profile questionnaire useful. They may be able to distill what had been unclear to them about their motives, fears and desires. Finding their type can be a passageway to consciousness.

Any assessment profile device that produces a type number for you is merely producing a set of personality characteristics that define your ego, strengths, weaknesses, and fixations. <u>Knowing your ego type is not knowing the real you.</u> This thought is expressed by Marion Woodman, "If we have lived behind a mask all our lives, sooner or later – if we are lucky – the mask will be smashed. Then we will have to look in our mirror at our own identity". (2)

The real you is your essence, <u>which is the set of spiritual energies and principles that underlie your being.</u> (See Chapter Fifteen, Return to Essence). How you express these energies and principles is your real nature, free from the encumbrances and motivations of the ego fixation which you at one time <u>thought</u> was you. Yes, your personality comes into play in expressing your essence. The wonderful smile you may have, your ability to tell jokes, or the way you hum when you're happy…all these are part of your one-of-a-kind personality. Inborn, they were shaped, then driven by ego fixation earlier in your life, <u>yet now these same characterolog</u>ical <u>traits are expressive of your essence and Holy Ide</u>a which gave birth to them at the beginning of your life. (See Chapter Thirteen, The Enneagram of Holy Ideas). In becoming conscious, your uniqueness remains as does your healthy reconstituted ego which is now also subordinate to and supportive of the expression of your essence.

Before you take the Howell Enneagram Profile Questionnaire, you may want to first assess your own level of expressed essence. This may be accomplished by taking the Howell Level of Essence Indicator which follows.

Howell Level of Essence Indicator

Directions: Mark the following statements as True or False.

	T	F
I live from a sense of trust and security.		
I worry little about how I am perceived by others.		
I know my spiritual purpose and fulfill it.		
I would rather trust the mystery of life as it unfolds rather than force things to be a certain way.		
I see and relate to the deeper, more childlike, nature of others no matter what they say or do.		
I am playful with life because I am free.		
I feel a connection to all life and know that the unseen life force is in all that is alive.		
I accept the limitations of being in a body. My body is not who I am.		
My limitations are opportunities for me to find new ways of spiritually expressing my nature.		
When with another life, I can feel their oneness with me and I am not against their true selves even if I disagree with their words or actions.		

What I own, including position or rank, is not essential to who I am.		
Nature informs me, instructs me, inspires me.		
When I feel angry, I know I have returned to a needless emotion and quickly return to myself.		
Others' shortcomings, and even their terrible crimes are seen by me as unknowing (unconsciousness).		
My shortcomings are forgiven as they come from my unknowing (unconsciousness).		
I have no need to fight people or circumstances; I relinquish my will to force them be a certain way.		
Joy, awe and deep happiness underlie my perceptions, behavior, thoughts, and conversations.		
Most of the time I am poised to see the wonder around me like I did when I was a young child.		
When with another, I have few expectations; I accept others as part of the mystery.		
I am receptively aware and present to each moment.		
Totals		

Joseph Benton Howell, Ph.D.

Scoring the Level of Essence Indicator

To score your Level of Essence Indicator, simply tabulate the number of responses you checked as "True" and the number of responses you checked "False". Your Level of Essence is the score you received by tabulating the number of "True" responses. If as many as five to seven responses were checked as "True", you are likely beginning the return to essence. If as many as eight to ten responses were checked as "True", essence has probably begun to take hold and express itself in very deep and important ways. If there is a "True" score of eleven to fifteen, you have assessed yourself as highly inclined to live in essence as you express yourself and move in the world. A score over fifteen indicates more of a complete oneness between essence and the person.

Scoring Chart for the Howell Level of Essence Indicator

Levels of Essence	Numbers of True Responses
I. Return to Essence	5 - 7
II. Conscious Essence	8 - 10
✓ III. Essence as Way of Life	11- 15
IV. Essence as Person	16 +

This indicator is a self-report measure that varies in scoring totals from person to person. It is a tool only for self-inquiry. It is not to be construed as a standardized assessment device.

The purpose of this self-assessment is to provide people a subjective self measurement of how they perceive their own level of essence. This indicator is not to be administered by teachers of the Enneagram to assess a class or a student. As a tool of self-inquiry, it (as is the Howell Enneagam Profile Questionnaire) is for the eyes of the respondent only, unless that respondent chooses to share it.

The Howell Enneagram
Profile Questionnaire

Directions: On each of the nine following segments each containing fifteen questions, circle or check the number on the Likert Scale which most represents your level of agreement or disagreement with the statements. This is a self-report questionnaire. It is not a standardized psychological test or a statistically validated test of any kind. It is a tool for self-inquiry. Results vary widely among respondents due to the subjective nature of this questionnaire. Results are for the use of the respondent only.

Suggestions: Avoid choosing "neutral" (#3) if possible unless you are truly neutral and have absolutely no other inclination. For example: The statement, "I want to better myself most of the time" was given a score of "4" by the respondent. (See under Agree below).

Strongly Disagree	Disagree	Neutral	Agree	Strongly Agree
1	2	3	4 (X)	5

Scoring: After answering each statement on the following pages, add up your score for each segment and place your nine totals on the lines above each of the nine numbers. Higher scores indicate stronger identification with that type.

Segment Totals

$$\overline{\quad 9 \quad}$$

$$\overline{\quad 8 \quad}\qquad\qquad\qquad\overline{\quad 1 \quad}$$

$$\overline{\quad 7 \quad}\qquad\qquad\qquad\qquad\qquad\overline{\quad 2 \quad}$$

$$\overline{\quad 6 \quad}\qquad\qquad\qquad\overline{\quad 3 \quad}$$

$$\overline{\quad 5 \quad}\qquad\qquad\overline{\quad 4 \quad}$$

SEGMENT 1

1. My judgments are usually accurate.   1 2 3 4 5

2. I work hard for perfection.   1 2 3 4 5

3. When others don't try to do the right
   thing, I get frustrated and exasperated.   1 2 3 4 5

4. I avoid outwardly expressing anger.   1 2 3 4 5

5. Standards, law, and order are far more
   important than relaxation, play
   and enjoyment.   1 2 3 4 5

6. Unfairness bothers me so I work to
   correct it all around me.   1 2 3 4 5

7. Things are either right or wrong, so
   follow the rules and be on time.   1 2 3 4 5

8. Hard work I do not shirk; it satisfies me.   1 2 3 4 5

9. Temptation is lurking to get us off
   track, and I am always on guard about this.   1 2 3 4 5

10. It is more important to be right
    than to be well liked.   1 2 3 4 5

11. I find myself monitoring others'
    behavior, even if I keep it to myself.   1 2 3 4 5

12. Shoulds and should nots about my behavior, and others' frequently play in my mind. 1 2 3 4 5

13. I get down and out when others don't recognize the right choice, even when I point it out to them. 1 2 3 4 5

14. I seem to do better when my heavy sense of keeping things in order is balanced by a light hearted attitude. 1 2 3 4 5

15. Giving people the benefit of the doubt is not a natural inclination, but a freeing experience for me. 1 2 3 4 5

Segment 1 Total _____
Enter this total on the cover sheet above # 1

SEGMENT 2

1. I know very well how to give, and I give often. 1 2 3 4 5

2. I am helpful and am known for it. 1 2 3 4 5

3. I really don't need much at all. 1 2 3 4 5

4. People like to feel they have a strong
   connection to me. 1 2 3 4 5

5. Unmet needs in others stir me to provide
   for them whether I have the energy or not. 1 2 3 4 5

6. I find myself anticipating what others are
   going to need so I can give it to them
   before they even ask. 1 2 3 4 5

7. If someone doesn't have needs for me to
   meet, I'll find someone who does. 1 2 3 4 5

8. When I work hard to meet others' needs,
   I am secretly miffed if my efforts go
   unacknowledged and want to find some
   way to be "not so available" next time. 1 2 3 4 5

9. People need to express gratitude to those
   who give to them. 1 2 3 4 5

10. I feel more loved when I am close to others. 1 2 3 4 5

11. Relationships are very important to me
    and I have many. 1 2 3 4 5

12. Sometimes I give to insure my place
    in the world.   1 2 3 4 5

13. Many times I seem to be of service to so
    many that I am exhausted and over
    burdened.   1 2 3 4 5

14. I tell people nice things about
    themselves frequently.   1 2 3 4 5

15. Whenever I do acknowledge my own needs and
    ask for help, I can give authentically
    out of a fullness inside.   1 2 3 4 5

Segment 2 Total _____
Enter this total on the cover sheet above #2

SEGMENT 3

1. I am usually successful.   1 2 3 4 5

2. I will work tirelessly to avoid failure.   1 2 3 4 5

3. I take short cuts to be more
   efficient in succeeding.   1 2 3 4 5

4. A successful image is very important to me
   because that is what people are
   buying these days.   1 2 3 4 5

5. I can administrate, delegate and get goals
   accomplished well.   1 2 3 4 5

6. I am decisive and a leader.   1 2 3 4 5

7. My getting the job done successfully
   is more important than making sure
   every detail is right.   1 2 3 4 5

8. I pride myself in knowing what people
   want and I have the natural gift to adapt
   to their expectations.   1 2 3 4 5

9. It is second nature to me to "advertise"
   what I'm accomplishing even in
   general conversation.   1 2 3 4 5

10. It doesn't hurt at all to "drop a name" if
    that gets me the identification I need to
    accomplish the goal.   1 2 3 4 5

11. The outward appearances and stated
     beliefs of someone send messages. That's
     why I try to look and talk in ways that
     bring me acceptance by those I am with.   1 2 3 4 5

12. Success is more important to me than
     authenticity.   1 2 3 4 5

13. Failure makes me feel vulnerable to
     rejection and inferiority.   1 2 3 4 5

14. When it's all over, the one with the
     most toys, wins.   1 2 3 4 5

15. Accomplishing for the community and
     its well-being has tempered my passion
     for purely personal accomplishment and
     has given me a solid sense of being
     valued and accepted.   1 2 3 4 5

Segment 3 Total _____
Enter this total on the cover sheet above # 3

SEGMENT 4

1. I like to think of myself as unique.   1 2 3 4 5

2. I secretly weep at the beauty others
   can't even seem to see.   1 2 3 4 5

3. I dress in the understated, but the unusual.   1 2 3 4 5

4. I avoid being thought of as "run of the mill."   1 2 3 4 5

5. I experience deeper emotions than most people. 1 2 3 4 5

6. I am creative in how I live my life.   1 2 3 4 5

7. My past preoccupies my thoughts.   1 2 3 4 5

8. There is a flaw in me, and I am looking for
   the special, perfect person who can
   understand it and help me with it.   1 2 3 4 5

9. I'd rather have one very good piece of furniture
   than a house full of "sticks and stuff."   1 2 3 4 5

10. I have a passion for the arts and the refined,
    well mannered life.   1 2 3 4 5

11. I have been very envious of some people to the
    point it aches.   1 2 3 4 5

12. The plight of abused or neglected people or
    animals haunts me to no end.   1 2 3 4 5

13. I am waiting to live my real life.   1 2 3 4 5

14. Tragedy and heartache are themes which
     captivate me.   1 2 3 4 5

15. Knowing the right cause for me has pulled me
     out of self-absorption into harmony with
     myself and others.   1 2 3 4 5

Segment 4 Total_____
Enter this total on the cover sheet above #4

SEGMENT 5

1. I am wise.   1 2 3 4 5

2. I avoid feeling empty inside.   1 2 3 4 5

3. Knowledge is power for me.   1 2 3 4 5

4. The more I can take in, the less empty and
    vulnerable I feel.   1 2 3 4 5

5. I constantly observe and analyze what I see.   1 2 3 4 5

6. I am useless at a party when I have to
    engage in small talk.   1 2 3 4 5

7. I can fade into the wood work if I feel
    overwhelmed by a situation or a crowd.   1 2 3 4 5

8. My fantasy life is as real and important
    as my conscious life.   1 2 3 4 5

9. I hoard things, usually books, computer
    parts and information.   1 2 3 4 5

10. I need lots of private time to process and
    to sort things out.   1 2 3 4 5

11. It can anger me if someone tries to pry into my
    mind or force information or feelings from
    me.   1 2 3 4 5

12. I do not usually like groups.   1 2 3 4 5

13. Time and resources are not ever to be wasted.   1 2 3 4 5

14. I have a more quiet and non-assertive style
    naturally, yet when pushed, I can be strong
    and even powerful.   1 2 3 4 5

15. Stepping out of my cocoon, to share with
    others and the world scares me at first, but
    assures me that I am not really ever empty.   1 2 3 4 5

Segment 5 Total _____
Enter this total on the cover sheet above # 5

SEGMENT 6

1. I am a loyal person.   1 2 3 4 5

2. I avoid being a renegade or deviant.   1 2 3 4 5

3. Being a team player gives me a feeling
   of family and of security.   1 2 3 4 5

4. I want to be protected by an authority
   figure who values me as part of the team.   1 2 3 4 5

5. Decisions are difficult for me as I want
   to be certain.   1 2 3 4 5

6. I think gaining consensus is the best way
   to keep things going smoothly
   in an organization.   1 2 3 4 5

7. I anticipate the worst case scenario and
   all the dangers it may bring.   1 2 3 4 5

8. I never shirk responsibility and duty
   because I fear the consequences of falling
   short and being blamed.   1 2 3 4 5

9. I second guess myself endlessly.   1 2 3 4 5

10. I am so afraid of what could go wrong,
    that I sometimes think I am cowardly.   1 2 3 4 5

11. I like a tight schedule and clear guidelines.   1 2 3 4 5

12. I am trying to "crack the code" to figure
    out life so I won't be so anxious.   1 2 3 4 5

13. I just know inside myself whether a person
    is on my side or whether they
    would "do me in."   1 2 3 4 5

14. I like to appear harmless, humorous
    and well-meaning.   1 2 3 4 5

15. I surprise myself at how brave I can be
    when push comes to shove.   1 2 3 4 5

Segment 6 Total _____
Enter this total on the cover sheet above # 6

SEGMENT 7

1. I am happy most of the time.   1 2 3 4 5

2. I avoid pain of any kind, physical or mental.   1 2 3 4 5

3. Things could be ideal if people wouldn't
    be so gloomy, heavy, and serious.   1 2 3 4 5

4. I love to take in the tastes, sounds, flavors,
    textures and all the good things of life.   1 2 3 4 5

5. I wish to travel to other places and to delve
    into many interests, hobbies, and activities.   1 2 3 4 5

6. I can be the life of the party.   1 2 3 4 5

7. If some is good, more is better.   1 2 3 4 5

8. I love to be doing something or going
    somewhere all the time.   1 2 3 4 5

9. Being denied or deprived of things I need
    or want, is a nightmare for me.   1 2 3 4 5

10. I do not like to see pain or deprivation in
    movies, art, or in real life.   1 2 3 4 5

11. I am optimistic and lighthearted about the
    future and find myself planning a lot for it.   1 2 3 4 5

12. I like to host gatherings, and go to parties
    and celebrations.   1 2 3 4 5

13. I enjoy making people happy, as do
    entertainers.   1 2 3 4 5

14. I have been accused of having ADD because I
    bounce from one interest or place to another.   1 2 3 4 5

15. I am able to create more depth to my life
    when I let pain come in. It's hard to do, but I
    find that it's worth it.   1 2 3 4 5

Segment 7 Total _____
Enter this total on the cover sheet above #7

SEGMENT 8

1. I am powerful and strong.   1 2 3 4 5

2. I avoid any inner weakness.   1 2 3 4 5

3. Being viewed by others as strong and
   forceful is essential for me.   1 2 3 4 5

4. Only a few persons, like me, can take the
   heat of real leadership.   1 2 3 4 5

5. I have an insatiable lust for life, and all the
   "larger than life" things it brings me.   1 2 3 4 5

6. I appear well-to-do, with plenty of
   resources and backing.   1 2 3 4 5

7. I lose respect for anyone who won't stand
   up to me or fight me back.   1 2 3 4 5

8. I fight for justice, for the underdog or for the
   disenfranchised.   1 2 3 4 5

9. I will not be ordered around by anyone.   1 2 3 4 5

10. Introspection of emotions or sentiment
    does not interest me.   1 2 3 4 5

11. Few persons will ever see my vulnerabilities
    or my tenderness, but I am very aware
    of their presence.   1 2 3 4 5

12. Intimidation is a great way to command
    power in a relationship or organization.   1 2 3 4 5

13. I know where others' underbellies are, and
    I force them to submit or else.   1 2 3 4 5

14. If others don't go along with my program,
    I simply withdraw my support and
    watch them collapse.   1 2 3 4 5

15. When I let my tender, more caring and
    giving side be seen, I feel a greater
    passion for living.   1 2 3 4 5

Segment 8 Total _____
Enter this total on the cover sheet above # 8

SEGMENT 9

1. I am peaceful and OK.   1 2 3 4 5

2. I keep things on an even keel.   1 2 3 4 5

3. I avoid conflict.   1 2 3 4 5

4. I tend to put myself down so people will
   know I'm not a threat.   1 2 3 4 5

5. The world would be a peaceful place
   if people wouldn't get so hot and bothered
   by their "issues." It doesn't matter anyway.   1 2 3 4 5

6. I am thought of as lazy by some, but I just
   don't have the energy level to keep
   up with them.   1 2 3 4 5

7. Harmony is the key.   1 2 3 4 5

8. I can mediate and arbitrate excellently
   because I see all sides all the time.   1 2 3 4 5

9. Give me my routine; sameness is so
   settling to me.   1 2 3 4 5

10. I love being in front of my flat screen.   1 2 3 4 5

11. Detachment from others is my way to stay
    unflappable, calm, and peaceful.   1 2 3 4 5

12. My motto is, "Why stand when I can sit
    and why sit, if I can lie down?"   1 2 3 4 5

13. It causes me high anxiety when outer disasters
    or my procrastination lead to things
    unraveling, and collapsing my sameness.
    That is when I panic.   1 2 3 4 5

14. Underneath my self- abasement, I know I am
    important. Don't discount me, or I'll find a
    passive way to get you back.   1 2 3 4 5

15. I can find an even greater inner balance when
    I set goals and create energy to meet them. 1 2 3 4 5

Segment 9 Total _____
Enter this total on the cover sheet above # 9

Chapter Four
The Ego, Its Fixations and Suffering

There is overwhelming and needless suffering within us. Whether learned or inherited, this suffering is painful to our body, mind, and soul. It is so powerful that it can overtake us and make us an actual embodiment itself. This suffering is found not only within individuals, but in collectives such as families, organizations, and larger segments of the population like ethnic and political groups, and even countries. In collectives, the shared suffering exists due to a common experience or perception, and this has usually arisen due to a common history. Eckhart Tolle addresses the characteristics shared between the personal and collective ego. "A collective ego manifests the same characteristics as the personal ego, such as the need for conflict and enemies, the need for more, the need to be right against others who are wrong, and so on. Sooner or later the collective will come into conflict with other collectives, because it unconsciously seeks conflict and it needs opposition to define its boundary and thus its identity". (1)

Clashes within the individual and conflicts between groups (or collective egos) cause suffering. Leading to the cycle of inner and outer violence, suffering spawns more suffering. A paramount reason people as well as collectives suffer is that their efforts to attain fulfillment clash with the actual facts of reality. This conflict with reality rouses the ego to redouble its force to attain fulfillment. Increased ego force increases unconsciousness and serves to cause more pain. The ego alone, no matter how forceful, cannot transcend the level of consciousness that brought it to its present suffering. Therefore the ego without a deeper awareness continues in its same pattern for the purpose of relieving the suffering. Patterns of ego force called fixations initially seem adaptive, but in the long run they contribute to the dissolution of the individual or collective.

Suffering caused by unconsciousness continues to mount until a critical mass of pain is eventually reached. This critical mass can also be attained quickly by experiencing huge sudden loss. Pain and loss are, at their apex, the person's "wake-up call" to consciousness. Why is it that extremes of loss and pain must occur before we are stirred out of our suffering and unconsciousness? The answer to this question is simply that the critical mass of pain and loss collapses the reason reason to live. The life's frame of reference, its set of givens and its raison d'etre, are no longer there. It is then that the person searches for relief and for a way to continue living. It is then that the person can be receptive to the fact that the ego cannot change the reality of pain and loss. The person must now learn to see things in a new way. This new way is found as the awareness of reality is heightened. This is consciousness. Once the new awareness is experienced, one finds it difficult to return to his previous state of awareness because that brings too much suffering.

The agony of losing what was perceived as vital to one's survival is excruciating and brings on the death of the former self. Losses of this importance can include a person, a job, a reputation, a status, a role, monetary security, a home, health, material possessions, freedom, or even a belief. If a particular loss has caused much suffering, it is most likely that the ego had relied on it for its sense of identity, worth, and meaning. The loss of this "most important thing" cannot be healed by the ego that depended on it.

It is the collapse of the supremacy of the ego that causes the great suffering. Becoming conscious, however, brings to light the precarious dependence on ego. Consciousness also reveals to us that the needless suffering of ego can be diminished and even prevented. This is accomplished by ego's relinquishment of its agenda and openness to other ways of receiving comfort, life and meaning. This is accomplished by forsaking the impermanent and awakening to what is real and permanent. Jesus spoke to this spiritual concept when telling the parable of a man whose house washed away because he had built it on sand. "Therefore everyone who hears these words of mine and puts them into practice is like a wise man who built his house on a rock, the rain came down, the streams rose, and the winds blew and beat against that house; yet it did not fall, because it had its foundation on the rock. But everyone who hears these words of mine and does not put them into practice is like a foolish man who built his house on sand. The rain came down, the streams rose, and the winds blew and beat against that house, and it fell with a great crash (Matthew 7:24-27). (2) Jesus also points to this same spiritual truth when in the desert, he encounters Satan's temptation to change stones into bread. Jesus responded to Satan by quoting Deuteronomy 8:3. (3) "Man shall not live on bread alone but on every word that comes from the mouth of God" (Matthew 4:4). (3)The above are major spiritual truths pointed to by Jesus that lie behind the psychology of ego suffering.

The Ego Identity

It is important to discuss in depth our ego identity. This identity is definitely a required component for living in the world. The ego began its formation in the womb where primitive instincts to survive first began. Without ego there would be no sense of self. One would merely merge with the environment as an amorphous set of impulses. Ego tells us who we are by defining the parameters of self. These definitive parameters are called ego boundaries. The first major ego boundary is the psychic and biological separation between the child's ego and its major care-taker(s).

The ego mediates between the various psychic structures within us, such as the super ego (conscience), the id (more primitive drives), the shadow (inferior side), the anima (feminine aspects), and the animus (masculine aspects). Without a sense of outer boundaries one could not operate in reality. Without ego mediation between the inner psychic structures, the self would fragment, disassociate, or become too confused to operate. Ego therefore is an essential component to healthy living.

As the ego individuates it becomes the child's major force to mediate needs, drives, fears, and desires. Because of its importance in survival and gaining fulfillment, the ego becomes that upon which the child must focus. The personality unfolds around the ego's needs to avoid what it fears and to gain what it desires. In this way the child can develop and individuate. This is necessary in the task of normal development.

The ego can be described more definitively as that protective and mobile structure of personality into which we naturally climb as a vehicle for moving in the world. It provides a buffer between us and other entities. Like an automobile, it provides a certain horsepower or strength, and its make, model, and color provide the image desired. The person so vitally relies on the ego and its personality that the person, in the course of life, comes to believe that the ego and the personality <u>are</u> the person. We can compare this concept of identification with the over-identification some persons have with their automobile, external appearance, or position in life. Such identifications bring about error of identification. People come to believe that the outer image or ego covering is actually who they are. Therefore when the outer image (ego) undergoes a blow, crush, loss, etc, people feel it is actually <u>they</u> who have sustained this loss or diminishment.

The Suffering of Ego Fixation

The ego also suffers because of its propensity to fixate on that which perpetuates its perceived identity, its story and its desires. Called ego compulsions, the perpetuation of this outer identity can become one's mode of operating. Those caught in the unconsciousness of their personality's ego fixation are compelled to repeat behaviors and thoughts that ultimately bring suffering. The ego lacks the objectivity to free itself from the trap of self-perpetuating compulsions. (See Figure 2, Chapter One)The result is suffering.

The nine ego fixations or compulsions and their traps according to Enneagramatical categories are discussed in the following section.

Type One – The fixation is upon perfection, standards, and the rightness of things. The One is compelled to look for all that is wrong in self, others, and the world and to correct it. The trap is perfection.

Case Example: Type One's Ego Fixation

Harold is a restaurant inspector for the health department. He has historically been a good judge of everything. Making his living as an excellent standard keeper, Harold capitalized on this strength. By mid-life, his being the keeper of standards had dominated practically every facet of his life. In the areas of self judgment, and in the measuring of others, Harold had gone beyond merely judging. He had become resentful toward those who did not measure up to his expectations of correctness. To avoid anger and resentment, Harold kept it all inside of him. This resentment was also toward his own performance which he found sorely lacking when he critically compared himself to higher and more rigid standards. He compulsively detected the flaws and mistakes in everything and everyone. This became his mental preoccupation and fed his anger. Harold was trapped in the drive toward perfection. He saw everyone as falling short, and nothing went right. This was the same drive that once had given him a sense of purpose. Now it had put a cloud of depression over his entire life.

Type Two – The fixation is upon what others
need and how to help them. The
Two is compelled to search out
others' needs and desires so they may
fulfill these. The trap is service.

Case Example: Type Two's Ego Fixation

Jennifer was a young wife and mother of three who had just moved into a new neighborhood. In order to form relationships, Jennifer planned a neighborhood party at her house. She sent out invitations to the event. The neighbors came, had a good time, and thanked their hostess as they welcomed her to the neighborhood. Jennifer became hurt and disgusted when she received no reciprocal invitations to any of the neighbors' homes. In order to connect with others, and finding out that the neighbor next door did not drive, Jennifer offered to drive her neighbor to the store as needed. The neighbor was grateful, but did not ever invite Jennifer inside her home. Jennifer wanted to drop her "driving service" because she never felt appreciated by the neighbor. She did finally get out of her driving obligation by saying she no longer had the time. She had found a neighbor who needed assistance with medical problems and who had told Jennifer that she was like a daughter to her. Jennifer was overextended, exhausted, and drained as she became the defacto caretaker for this neighbor. Yet, she kept looking for more people in need in her neighborhood, even though she never received the appreciation she sought.

Type Three – The fixation is on achieving success, and creating an image of accomplishment. The Three is compelled to win, to be on top, and to present an image as a successful person. The trap is efficiency.

Case Example: Type Three's Ego Fixation

Jeff had been a football star who married the head cheerleader. He was seemingly a happy man who in his mid-forties had accumulated all the "right things". He had a perfect family; all his children were attractive, successful, and "upwardly mobile". Jeff had a beautiful home, after many upgrades, and he was awarded the "outstanding salesman of the year" for his company. A competitor at heart, he played golf regularly and coached the bowling team. Jeff had suffered a growing discontent recently, and had never really felt complete. He thought he had reached a mid-life crisis when he told his wife that they just had to get a new home. His wife said, "What do you mean, our house is perfect!" Jeff replied that he did not have any outward sign of his success, his standing, and his accomplishments. He figured that if he worked more efficiently, cut out some of his sports, and increased his sales production they could afford a mortgage nearly twice the one they currently held. He pulled out of his pocket, a picture he had found in a magazine, of the "house of his dreams", and showed it to his wife. He then said, "I would do just about anything to live this dream. It says exactly what I want it to say. It makes a statement. I will then be seen as I ought to be seen, and all my hard work will be worth it". Jeff's wife was not happy, nor would Jeff be happy in his new house.

Type Four – The fixation is upon their need
✳✳✳   to feel authentic, special, and
unique. The Four is compelled
to express sadness. The Four
despairs about not being seen as
authentic. The trap is authenticity.

Case Example: Type Four's Ego Fixation

Jonathan had been highly artistic and intuitive since childhood. He expressed this in his work as a landscape architect. Sought after for his unique ability to sense a person's tastes and how to beautify the land, Jonathan was in demand. He loved the widespread acclaim given him, yet he was never truly happy. He felt something was defective, unrealized. He thought his life would have been better had he not had such a rough past. Admittedly, he did not think his past pain was due to an abusive childhood. He thought it was his unusual sensitivities that caused him immense pain. He said, "I was able to pick up the atmosphere, the tone, and the moods of those around me. The slightest negative feeling from others sent me up the wall. I have been trying to figure this out my whole life. If I could find some answers to this riddle of my life, I would probably feel solid, real, whole". Jonathan tried to find wholeness in one relationship after the other. None seemed to supply the missing feeling. He became disillusioned with life, and thought of ending it all, especially when he saw his peers living their enviable lives. He simply went on creating one spectacular landscape after another, bemoaning his uniquely defective self, and waiting for his real life to begin.

Type Five – The fixation is on taking in
information, observing, and
analyzing. The Five is compelled
to withdraw and collect as much as
possible to fill an inner emptiness.
The trap is knowledge.

Case Example: Type Five's Ego Fixation

Sharon is a worker at a bookstore. She loves putting out new book arrivals. She can be seen handling each book, as if it were a precious baby. She secretly reads when she's on the job. This is done in order to be familiar with as much information as possible "for our customers' benefit" she says. Sharon is a very inward person who feels starved for knowledge. Everything she learns she stores in her head, and for awhile she feels good. But very soon, the feeling wears off, and she's looking in the stacks again for more information. She was passed over for a promotion because she was more interested in learning the merchandise than in selling it. Living alone Sharon is an avid internet user. She compiles data, analyzes it, and feasts on it until bedtime. Sharon has no real friends and is not generous with her time or knowledge. She feels that giving away those valuable commodities would make her feel even emptier than she normally feels. As a result, Sharon is isolated, and spends most of her time reading and fantasizing. She'd rather read a good e-book than have a conversation with neighbors, or even family. Detached from everyone, she had nowhere to turn when she lost her job due to layoffs at her company. In all her information she had no book on how to be in the world, nor was she interested in finding one because living in her head seemed ok, for the time being.

Type Six – The fixation is on being secure and
escaping others' condemnation.
The Six is compelled to find
external support and guidance
because they lack self confidence.
The trap is security.

*

Case Example: Type Six's Ego Fixation

Cecelia had always been a team player. You could count on her to be loyal and devoted to friends, family, and fellow workers at the bread store where she worked. Cecelia was happy with her job as she loved the process of baking bread with her work group, and then interfacing with the public to sell it. Cecelia was vigilant about what was happening on the job and how secure her job was. She lived in fear she would lose her job. She needed the job, and more than that she felt safe with the work team and didn't want to lose that comradeship. She especially counted on her boss to "take care of her", as she was fairly timid when it came to making decisions and trusting herself to handle so many things that came up in working with the public. One day, her boss was fairly cool to her causing panic and anxiety. By the end of the day she was anticipating that he was going to fire her. This went on for weeks, and she couldn't imagine what she had done to cause the boss's personality change toward her. She thought he may have seen her taking some bread home after work one day. She died a thousand deaths over that day old bread snatch. This heightened her fear of being deviant. She began looking for another job, "just in case". Later she found out the boss's moods had to do with his personal life, not her. Cecelia was so scared in her job, but couldn't decide to take a new job or stay.

Type Seven – The fixation is on finding perfect happiness and having no pain. The Seven is compelled to jump from one thrill to the next and to gather as much as possible because "more is better". The trap is idealism.

Case Example: Type Seven's Ego Fixation

Milton was a high school principal. He was always a fun-loving guy who loved activity and was exhilarated with being around people and fun. His teen years were so pleasurable that he chose a profession that would keep him in the same environment that gave him so much excitement and happiness. Part of his passion was to play sports. He particularly loved basketball and could be found shooting baskets with students after school. Life was a cornucopia of fun for Milton. He was viewed by students as their friend and hero, and he actually had fun being a big kid. Things were ideal except that he seemed to need more and more fun and activities with the students to make him happy. One day there was a tragedy at school. One of the students had brought a gun to school, invited another boy to fight after school, and in the fight shot the invited victim to death. Milton could no longer be happy. He was stuck with being a principal at a school in deep pain and terror. He was expected to be totally involved in helping teachers and students get over this trauma. He was not "at home" being this type of principal. He had to be a strict taskmaster now, and being friends with kids the way he had been was out of the question. He looked for another position elsewhere that would be ideal. He moved there, but he still had no fun. He had not faced the pain of the last job because he was so busy looking for an escape. The un-faced pain kept Milton from being happy anywhere.

Type Eight – The fixation is on being strong and
dominating the environment. The
Eight is compelled to take charge
and to avoid their own weakness as
they rule others. The trap is justice.

— Least ID with

Case Example: Type Eight's Ego Fixation

Millie, an outstanding bank president, had exhibited leadership skills since grammar school. A strong personality who lived life large, you knew upon the first encounter that she was a "take charge" person. Many people felt intimidated by her, not because she was mean or unfair, but because she seemed so separate from feelings. Being all business, Millie did not let her guard down to become personal with anyone. She was crisp, direct, and did not hesitate to deliver ultimatums. Her success in banking brought many promotions; her bottom lines were the best in the holding company and made her powerbase very secure. Millie was a crusader who could not sit back and abide things she considered unjust. At the beginning of her career this intolerance worked well for her. As she became more powerful, however, her sense of impartial justice was compromised. Her power fed an almost tyrannical reaction to people or companies that she felt had been unfair. The problem for Millie was she began making her own assumptions of what was just and unjust by acting as judge, jury, and executioner. This autocratic sensibility blinded her to the realities behind actual situations and people. The power she lorded over others became destructive because she was trapped in her own self-made system of justice. She ended up totally alone, and suffered because she didn't know why.

Type Nine – The fixation is on being peaceful and
conflict free. The Nine is compelled
to self soothe, to blend in, and
to "not matter" as a way to avoid
conflict. The trap is self-abasement.

Case Example: Type Nine's Ego Fixation

Hershell was a worker for a lawn maintenance company. He
had been employed by the same business since his early twenties
and was now fifty two. Hershell's job has been the same since he
began, and so has his salary, practically. Spraying chemicals on
customers' lawns was an easy way to make a living according to
Hershell. "I know every house, every customer, and everybody's
do's and don't's...I've got it all down pat...no surprises...no
hassles...I love my job", he says. Barbara, Hershell's wife is not
satisfied with how the company is treating her husband. She says
that his slight salary raises are miniscule compared to the rise in
the cost of living. She tells Hershell that he should demand a salary
commensurate with his experience and seniority. Hershell's reply
is "I don't have a fancy education...I really don't have anywhere
else to work; besides nobody would have me, especially at my
age". Barbara gets mad at Hershell but he responds by clamming
up, getting in his lazy boy and snoozing as she rails against his
passivity. Hershell sleeps more and more as a way to soothe the
bad feelings he has about his employer. One day he had paralysis
in his right side. The doctor at the emergency room asked him if
he had been exposed to any harsh chemicals. Hershell said, "No,
not that I am aware of".

When the Suffering Reaches Critical Mass

When the fixation escalates the suffering to the point the person can take no more, there are three basic choices. The first is to search for relief, the second is to continue in the same compulsive behavior, and the third is to "leave".

Let us deal with the second choice, to continue in the same behavior. What drives an ego to continue harming itself by choosing to continue the ego's compulsion? There are several aspects to this answer. The first is the person's story. Everyone has a life built on something. Those who are run by their egos are preoccupied with making their story full, complete, true, and edifying to the ego's sense of identity called "self". The story is usually about how their desires have been and are fulfilled. For some people, their story is about how their desires are <u>not</u> fulfilled, nevertheless, it is about their ego desires. The personal story is usually reinforced by culture. From birth parents seem to encourage a child's sense of making his or her own story. Most stories include elements of life that the 'owner' of the story feels they deserved or must have to feel a sense of self. This includes family myths, position, titles, desired outcomes, children, people, possessions, status, even moral values, faith, ethics, etc. The unconscious ego passionately drives the person into whatever activity, role, accomplishment, acquisitions, relationship, etc. that will give the outward perception that the person is an identity with an ongoing story. The tragedy is that no one's self-made story works out to the ego's satisfaction. The failure of the story to work out as hoped is the cause of misery and pain. No story works out because no story, no matter how perfectly it is perceived to be, can actually BE the person. The story or personal journey of an individual is not their essence, or their soul. The story can be of service to the soul, only as it is experienced, in the present moment. And it is only in the present moment that we can experience the soul.

Given the fact that loss is built into life, everyone at some point will experience threat of loss or actual loss of an identity built on their ego needs. As life gets more complicated, however with maturation, deaths, absences, or changes of people in the story occur, and as these consequences of life happen, the story is impacted. The story finally meets reality. As surely as Scarlett O'Hara's life's story collapsed even as she held so tightly to it, so will the idealized story of most lives collapse in illusion. The people who choose this second response, continuing the compulsion, would rather suffer than to give up the story even if it's an illusion. Some persons jump however, into a life boat instead of continuing in the suffering. That lifeboat is called "living in surrender" to another story, the story of the One True Source of All Being. That story is real, is conscious, is in the present, and every creature has a part to play in it.

Choice number three is simply to leave. Leaving is done in many ways…all are forms of death, even if the body remains alive. There is a sad resignation on the faces of those who have accepted that they are "checked out" of life. Checking out is terminal resignation, where as surrender is acceptance of reality in order to bring about its inherent goodness and perfection. The people who choose to leave seem absent, dull, and "homeless". Many are given to self-narcotization, which can be drugs, alcohol, food, pornography, or even starving oneself. They lose their will to try and eventually their body and mind follow suit by breaking down. The other way of leaving is suicide, which in a way can ironically be the final triumph of ego itself.

The number one answer to the question "what do we do when the suffering becomes too much", is to search for relief. This search usually begins with the question, "what went wrong…what premise was I building everything upon that betrayed me so?" The answer lies in the self-discovery of who the person thought they were and the ultimate uncovering of the fact they were not actually their ego and its story at all. The search reveals that the ego self (or false self) was the one who betrayed them. It was this self that did not give them a way to reach fulfillment or to endure the pain and losses of life…that the unconscious ego self was not the real person or their true identity after all. So very much, nearly everything was based on a false identity.

Relief from Suffering

The Enneagram's beauty is that in the search for relief of suffering, we are shown who we are in our ego and its unconscious fixation. There is no mistake about it, we in ego unconsciousness, live out of one of nine basic fixations. (See Chapter Four). These fixations were naturally adopted by us as youngsters and were elaborated upon as life continued. The ego and its fixations protected us from the world when we lost touch with our essence and its innocence.

These nine basic personality types are actually life-defining reactions to our having covered over, and lost touch with our truest selves. Sometime in childhood, we learned that being our vulnerable, naked, true self, brought ridicule and pain, so we clothed our nakedness with a false self. It was Adam and Eve who hid from God when they discovered they were naked. When God demanded to Adam to know why he had eaten of the forbidden tree, his reply was the world's first shifting of blame, and the first emotional violence; Adam said to God, "The woman you put here with me – she gave me some fruit from the tree and I ate it" (Genesis 3:12). (4) After their loss of consciousness, Adam and Eve were ashamed of their nakedness (their true self), so they covered themselves. We reflect Adam and Eve's archetypal fall every day when we clothe our nakedness, our essence, with a false self. It is the way it is.

The promptings, guilts, fixations, transgressions, woundings, cruelties, and rejections of childhood forced us to 'flip' our way of moving in the world. We went from being our truest nature to being inside the "automobile" of a false self. Even though we, as children, merely stepped into the vehicle initially for protection and mobility, we gradually forgot our true essence which took refuge there. As time passed we grew so used to the "vehicle", that we assumed we were the "vehicle". We came by this naturally. We and our caretakers had been bringing this about since day one. It was necessary, and it served a purpose. It got us around, protected us, and set up an image around which we would make a story. It seemed as though this was what life was about. In a way it was. It had to be for us to undergo the real purpose of life: remembering, returning to, and growing in our spiritual nature. We could not do this without the soul lessons and wisdom learned in the years of ego prominence. A Sufi saying speaks to this process. "To become that which you were before you were, with the memory and understanding of what you had become". (5)

The following reflection asks for us to understand the false self and the true self. It also shows the importance of the roles of personal discipleship, forgiveness, and transparency to the creator.

My God

In my wondering in my wandering, You are indeed the only One who knows my suffering. You know my trying so hard, my raw emotions, my despair, my anger, my guilt, my frustration that others do not understand. But how could they, Oh God, how could they know the years of life, the places of peace and the places of acceptance I have come to? How could they know how tender and how "in progress" some of the places are? How could they be able to feel the feelings of all these places, for they have not been there, nor have they ever gone exactly where I have been. Nor could I ever walk their very walk. We know only the major sign posts of each other's walks. These are but common places on the trails, but no one knows the particular path of their peers. No one knows the next path they will take which leads to the next fork in the road and sign posts. It is a crazed maze of millions of paths. The loneliness of such singular travel is eased by the understanding from another. The very nearest to true understanding are the words, "I cannot truly understand or know your path, but I can listen to you speak about it. I invite you to speak about it, and I will hear you with the ears of spirit; I will see your essence as you speak. I will speak about my path, with no judgment of you." Judgment from other travelers is not useful. All that's needed is just a nod of acknowledgement that one's experience is beyond the comprehension *fully* of another. "Live and let live" is such a phrase of comfort.

The ultimate comfort for me is the healing voice of God who says, "I know you because My spirit is in your mind, your body, your soul. I truly do travel with you and I know your thoughts, your physical reactions, and your emotions. Indeed, I, your God, experience them with you in every dark twist and turn of your trail. In the middle of the night, when you awaken in a sweat of terror, I am with you knowing the terror and its causes. I am with you to whisper that you are My beloved no matter how terrorized you become with your own thoughts or those of the accuser; no matter how anxious you become, or how overwhelmed you are. I am here with you to experience *all* with you, and to remind you that you are Mine, claimed, understood in detail, and My beloved with whom I am well pleased. I was with you before you were born, before you came to earth. I know your needs, your passageways, your searching, your brokenness, your tears, your self rejections, your projections, your all, your failings, your sins, your inept struggles to live, and your victorious struggles to do so. I, Your God, am the only One who really knows you and in this place of holy sacred authority, I bless you and call you My own, for there is nothing which can separate you from Me. I am with you, you are in Me and, like a shepherd, I gather up My sheep who know My voice for I know each one's whereabouts and habits".

✷ The God of creation is beyond understanding. God's fully experiencing and participating in my life is beyond the intellect. It is a matter of perceiving through simply being.

The Mother-Father God's hands rest upon my head and bless me more than any human can bless me. It is a true blessing, a blessing of my entire life.... a blessing that will not disappear, ever.

When this is bestowed, the blessings of others are mere gifts. The blessing of God, however, is a complete affirmation by the One who knows me totally. Thanks be to God for such anointing. This blessing has reciprocity, which is discipleship, for without discipleship, one cannot comprehend one's blessing to its fullest extent. Without discipleship one cannot feel the full co-creation between God and oneself, therefore the fellowship is not to its fullest reciprocity or involvement.

The cost of discipleship is the abandoning of those distractions which provide us our false self. Our false self is the accumulation of masks which hide our true nature. Covering our broken selves are the masks which were shaped by what the world may expect of us. These masks become our armor as they become thicker and thicker. The masks beckon us to come to the "costume ball of life"…to dance among the other masked identities. The masks are so alluring, so glittering.

As long as we promote and develop our false identity, we are ever so far from our true self - the beloved and co-creator with God. This false self is a fanciful lure, like fishing lures of many colors, feathers, bobbles, shimmering reflective surfaces, fancy and attractive gyrations, spinning, darting back and forth in their promise of a beautiful feast, if it can be caught.

The false self, however, with all its "promise" cannot be caught, ingested, or lived out with any authenticity because it is what it is, a facsimile of life glorious, mere paint, glue, and shiny tin made to resemble the inborn. The sublime glory of the false self is not what it seems to promise. We swim to the lure for we are duped into believing something so outwardly dazzling must have something of substance behind such a prize! But when we settle for the lure, we are hooked into living in costume. Authenticity, the true self, is the way of the cross because it embraces living out of the beautiful and attractive, as well as out of the ugly and broken. The union of these two different sides of ourselves and God's blessing of them in wholeness makes the truly glorious available to us. True glory, true salvation, is in the bringing of our total self to the cross. We then do not even have to make excuses for our dark side, our sins, and our inner terrors. Nor do we seek the accolades of this world, for now our reference point is in our companionship with God.

God's whispers, God's word, God's guidance, God's invitation to continuous wholeness are the ways of the true self, which when grasped are so utterly sublime and glorious! Now that the false self is seen as but an empty shell, once able to be lived in, but now totally uninhabitable, it is no longer our home. Our true self, our naked essence, our authentic beautiful and broken self is our new identity.

Our new home is a place of new references, new sights, new goals, and new steps to climb. It is home because we can live here in our own skin, without fear of rejection, without fear of being misunderstood.

To their sneers, their efforts to disenfranchise, to shame, to mock, to shun, to judge as inferior and non-includable, we each can now say, "I move in the world in different currents of energy. You would not readily understand but you can if you wish. Bless you, and now I make my way through this world with being captivated by the voice of love. I repeat its words to you. I see with new eyes, a different land I now point out to you. It's a land upon this land but you can see it only with soft, fresh eyes. I'm moving, living, and loving in it. Won't you see it with me? Won't you hear the voice of love with me? Can't you see how beautiful you are? This is far better than your calling another unworthy only to bolster yourself up as worthy. You set yourself up as judge of worthiness. Give up that position to enter the new country before you. Listen ...... can you hear it? The new voice is far better. Its love lets you drop your weapons and the armor of your false self to dwell in what you thought your fight could win you: favor, love, acceptability, redemption, and life victorious. These come not through battle, but through surrender."

Chapter Five
The Three Levels of Functioning and Consciousness within Each Type

Impairment of ego functioning has long been associated with maladaptive or mentally unhealthy living. The type of mentally unhealthy living I am speaking of is not necessarily the range of classic mental illnesses described in diagnostic manuals. I am speaking of the person who may be free from a psychiatric diagnosis yet is impaired in self-awareness and in being conscious of others and the world. To some degree, this describes all of us at a certain point in life. It is a subtle "disease" of the ego. When the ego fixates on a compulsion, however, the "disease" becomes serious. The level of severity of the ego fixation correlates positively with the level of impairment and maladaptive behavior of the "disease". Likewise, those who are freer from the ego fixation, are those whose lives are lived more consciously and on different terms.

These terms have to do with cultivating a deeper understanding of their true nature, and the 'bigger picture' of reality, including others and their context.

Therefore it is clear that the less ego fixation, the more conscious the person can become. The most understandable explanation for this is that the severity of the person's ego fixation increases the distortion of reality; the more that reality is distorted, the less chance there is for them to become conscious. In a way, the more distortion of reality, the thicker is the veil between the person and consciousness. This is where the fundamental principle of Holy Perfection comes into play. (See Chapter Thirteen, The Enneagram of Holy Ideas). Reality is underpinned by an ultimate perfection of all things. Even the ego's distortion of reality as it grows in intensity and suffering can lead to a positive search for relief and finally to becoming conscious. Indeed, the long human journey to enlightenment begins with the search for relief from the suffering.

The Levels of Consciousness and Mental States

How are we to understand consciousness in relationship to mental illness and various other mental states? Whether neurobiological or "conditioned", mental illness is not necessarily caused by the ego fixation. If that were true, it would be possible for many sufferers of mental illness to "snap out of their illnesses" by ridding themselves of their ego fixation. This is not entirely possible. In some, the ego fixation can intensify a mental illness; the lack of ego fixation can also de-intensify a mental illness. In fact many persons with mental illness, mental impairment, and mental retardation have become conscious and operate healthily. People with mental illnesses have actually used their illness as their portal out of ego fixation into consciousness. Indeed, mentally ill persons can have a better self-awareness than can non-mentally ill persons who are completely deluded by their ego and its fixation. It all depends on what is one's definition of sanity and insanity. Who would you consider the most healthy functioning to be: a self-aware person who is diagnosed and presents as mentally ill and who is conscious, or a person deemed sane by our culture who is unconsciously trapped in a serious ego delusion? As Ken Wilber states, "You can be at a relatively high level of spiritual development and still be at a relatively low level in other lines (e.g., the deeper psychic can be progressing while the frontal is quite retarded). We all know people who are spiritually developed but still rather immature in sexual relations, emotional intimacy, physical health, and so on". (1)

We must remember that physical and/or mental diseases are not necessarily the causes of unconsciousness. They are impediments to living "normally", according to society. Those very impediments can be the opening or portal to consciousness. And it is conscious persons who are sometimes seen by society as marching to a different drummer, weird, odd, or maladaptive. Like Saint Francis of Assisi, these persons may just not "fit in" any longer. Consciousness exists with unconsciousness like oil does with water.

The following is an excerpt from an interview with Juan, a mentally ill man, age twenty-eight. Juan is diagnosed with paranoid schizophrenia. The father of two, he maintains employment at a cabinet-making factory. Though he has a serious mental illness he has an accelerated level of consciousness especially for his age.

"I am the only one who can support my wife and family. They deserve all the good things life can give, even if I have this mental illness. When I notice people at work are talking about me, I calm myself down because I know that's the sign my medicine needs tweaking, or that I'm stressed. I used to just go up to someone I thought was talking about me and confront them or worse. I know better now. It's my problem not theirs even though some days it seems like I can even hear what they are saying about me. Some days, the voices are so bad in my head, that if it weren't for my family, I'd quit. I used to want to blow my head off, but I realize that I am part of my children and my little community. I would take part of them away if I were to kill myself. I don't want to take anything from them. I just want to give to and protect them. I keep on my medicines and stay in counseling even though there's a stigma, and it makes me feel weird to be so different. When I get too big for my britches and want to stop either one of those, and I have, my wife "strongly reminds" me of what is at stake. I will never let my desire to stop the medicine, come before family. That's just selfish of me".

In this interview, we can observe several themes of consciousness and lack of ego fixation. It was the mental illness itself that brought about Juan's awareness of the subtle but deadly power of his ego. He knew that left unchecked, his ego fixation would bring about his demise. When his ego was in control, he refused to see his mental illness as a problem for himself or for others. He lived a life of rage, paranoia and confrontation. When he'd reached as much suffering as he could stand, he relinquished ego control of his illness, searched for and got outside help. He now has a healthy self-awareness that is older than his years. Juan sees reality in an accurate way, he has controls for any possible relapses, he has a deep sense of love that outweighs selfishness and he sees how his soul is inextricably linked to the souls of others. He lives in an expanding consciousness, and he is schizophrenic.

Mentally retarded persons are not of the group classified as mentally ill. Persons in this group have long been victims to the notion that they are unable to perceive the world accurately because of their intellectual incapacities. On standardized Intellectual Quotient examinations, mentally retarded persons score in well below average ranges. Their fund of general information is usually low, their ability to calculate numbers, to comprehend written material, and to analyze data, is severely limited compared to those of normal IQ scores. My work with the mentally retarded has revealed to me that consciousness is not necessarily affected by intellectual impairment. In fact, the veil of the ego is so thin for many mentally retarded persons, that they are completely transparent to the Divine, and in some cases show advanced consciousness. (See Chapter Eighteen, The Flowering of Consciousness). Please review this excerpt of an interview with Jean, age forty with an IQ of 58, living in a group home.

Jean: I am happy here. I get good food (laughs).
That makes me fat, but I don't care none. It's
my fat and ain't nobody gonna take it from
me, unless they really want it (laughs).

Interviewer: What are we here in the world to do, Jean?

Jean: (Puts arm around Jimmy sitting next to her...)
For this stuff (hugs Jimmy and laughs).

Interviewer: What about God and heaven?

Jean: You better watch out what you say about
God...there's a watcher and a looker right over
there (points to another part of the room).

Interviewer: What's there, Jean?

Jean: It's…(looks at Jimmy)…it's the watchers
          and lookers. Jimmy sees them too.

Interviewer: What do the watchers and lookers do?

Jean: (laughs and sips on a soft drink) They look at us;
          they watch us (pokes Jimmy who laughs with her).

Interviewer: Why do they watch and look?

Jean: Ain't you ever heard of angels? (laughs).

Interviewer: You mean angels are watching and looking?

Jean: (looks deeply into interviewer's eyes) Do it all
          day long…talk to us…love us…tell us what's
          what. Tell us 'bout God.Don't tell nobody.…

Interviewer: Don't tell who?

Jean: The bosses here. They don't see 'um (laughs
          and sips on straw). They don't know. Can't
          you see 'um? Jimmy sees 'um. Don't you
          Jimmy? (Jimmy points to them and nods
          'yes'). Several other residents who have
          heard the conversation say, "I see 'um".

This interview was similar to many other interviews with mentally handicapped persons who, though intellectually impaired, have matter-of-fact, routine interactions with and openness to the unseen, the transcendent, and the Divine.

In the interview with Jean, there is not an ego barrier. The ego fixation is not there. Jean is playful, as is someone of essence, and is not inhibited in expression of affection, or in expressing her ideas. It is of note that in this interview and in others similar, the mentally handicapped persons were all noticeably hesitant to speak of the "unseen" things. This is a function of the self-protective ego which does not want to be misunderstood. When a certain trust level occurs, however, those interviewed were eager to speak of the angels, and more. Theologian and writer, Henri Nouwen, had very close interactions with mentally handicapped persons. He writes about these special people's complete openness to the Divine. In fact, Henri Nouwen chose to be associated with the mentally handicapped to learn from them a level of faith and consciousness he could not find so readily in the world. (2)

On the other hand is Phillip, a thirty year old medical doctor, also married and the father of two. He has no diagnosed mental illness or personality disorder. This is an excerpt of an interview that illustrates how an ostensibly mentally healthy individual can be unhealthy and unconscious, simply because of his ego fixation.
"The ideal thing for me would be to use my plane to fly to different places on weekends. My only problem is I have extra work in the office since I extended my hours. Just can't fit it all in. I golf with the guys; I pull night call; I work extra. I take the kids roller skating and camping. There's hardly any time for Carla and me, but we manage a night out once in a while. I am going so fast that I was stopped for speeding last week. Glad I hadn't been drinking. I was headed for beer. It (beer) helps slow me down and not think so much. Life is so good; I wish I had time to love it; I just don't have enough time to do all I want to do. I just go from one thing to the next. I thought being a doctor, having a family and a nice house would be a perfect life. Why am I so restless? Why have I not got that happiness? Maybe it can happen if I reduce my schedule and

actually use that airplane to get away for some weekends. That's what I'm gonna do".

At first glance, this is the talk of an overworked physician, caught up in a busy life. Upon closer inspection, however, we note an ego fixation of the type that relentlessly keeps its bearer on a quest for perfect happiness. All else must submit to this quest. There is little mention of others except in the context of happy activities. There is no mention of quietude, intimate exchanges, contemplation, self-inquiry or how he fits into the bigger context of medicine or others' lives. Self-absorbed, Phillip seeks more activity as a way out of unhappiness. He describes himself as a separate entity in full control of everything. He therefore sees his dilemma as solvable by his own reasoning. He views himself as the source for his own help. Phillip is in a closed system of self-delusion. He erroneously thinks that merely manipulating his hours at work, and flying away on weekends will be the answer to his lack of perfect happiness. He is driven by a fixation of his ego and is unconscious of it. Meanwhile he is missing his life, his marriage, his children, and his purpose in the world. If unchecked, this delusion is quite dangerous, and will worsen causing great suffering before consciousness and sanity can be reached.

Three Levels of Functioning within Each Type

At the end of this chapter is a list of all nine personality types of the Enneagram. Each type is divided into three levels of functioning: 1) healthy and conscious, 2) average, and 3) unhealthy and unconscious. The levels are derived by the level of freedom that the type has from its ego fixation. The level of healthy/conscious functioning, for example, is the level with most freedom from the fixation and, therefore, the level of most consciousness. Level two is average or "semi-conscious" functioning. This covers the huge population of persons who are still influenced by the ego and its fixation. There is enough awareness, however, about reality at this level that the person moves through the world, for the most part, effectively. Average or semi-conscious persons cannot be described as healthy or conscious because their ego fixation is still that with which they most primarily identify. Average is the level through which persons may travel on their integrative journey from unhealthy unconsciousness to healthy consciousness. Average is also the level from which one may start one's disintegrative journey to the level of unhealthy unconsciousness. The average or semi-conscious level can be the holding tank for persons to live out their entire life, because society "oks" this level of functioning. It is this overwhelming large group that does little thinking on their own, and who is easily manipulated by media, cultural 'norms', and achieving a self satisfied existence. A person who reaches level one or level two does not return permanently to lower levels of functioning. The transformative process to consciousness is so life changing that one can never perceive life the same way again.

Notice that the personality characteristics of each level describe personality. Remember that personality is not who we really are. We are essence. The personality characteristics listed for each of the types at levels two and three are characteristics that broadly demonstrate the type's ego fixation. At level three the severity of the ego fixation is the most intense. At this level the ego fixation is so prominent that essence is fully blocked. At level two it is partially blocked. The ego fixation is so prominent that essence remains fully blocked at level three and only partially in awareness at level two.

Conscious healthy people are living life from the energy of their essence. The characteristics of people at level one are personality characteristics of those who are conscious of their true nature and who live it. Fully describing the characteristics of essence for level one would entail an explanation of each type's Holy Idea. For a more in depth explanation of level one's characteristics, see Chapter Thirteen on The Holy Ideas and the descriptions therein.

Mention has been made in the literature about the role of stress and its effect on the levels of functioning. Yes, under stress, there can be relapses into unconsciousness with its unhealthy behaviors and thinking. This is because of the many years of habitually operating in the ego fixation, its traps and avoidances. When there is a relapse for the conscious, healthy functioning person, it is usually of short duration. The shock of sudden stress, or the weight of prolonged stress temporarily alter the perception of reality. The relapse is usually short in duration because of the complete soul transformation into a new awareness that had occurred when reaching consciousness.

There is another reason for the recovery from relapse: there is the emergence at consciousness of an observing alter ego. This silent friend is the observer who alerts the person to the fact that his thoughts or behaviors are merely relics of the past which can be easily shed. In unconsciousness the observer was "asleep". Now, the awakened alter ego observer empowers the person through shear awareness, to return to his own thoughts that fit his <u>true</u> nature. The person then returns to his real place of consciousness.

For further elucidation of character traits of the levels, please see the chapter on the instinctual subtypes. (Chapter Eight) See in this chapter how the ego fixation affects the conscious, average, and unconscious levels among the instinctual subtypes of each main Enneagramical type.

In reviewing the three major levels within each type, it is important to understand that there are gradations of each level's intensity that blend each level with those adjacent to it. The discovery of the levels within types is attributed to Don Riso, whose link between the Enneagram and psychological classification is ground-breaking. (3) (4)

THE TYPES

✳ ONE
LEVEL 1 - HEALTHY / CONSCIOUS
Serene Discerner of the Right Way
Diligent Standard Bearer
Good-Natured, Up-Standing Teacher, Guide, Mentor

LEVEL 2 - AVERAGE
Idealistic World-Corrector
Judgmental Monitor
Hard-Working Perfectionist

LEVEL 3 - UNHEALTHY / UNCONSCIOUS
✳ Irritable, Condemning Purist
✳ Depressive Fatalist
✳ Out-of-Control Resenter

✳ TWO
LEVEL 1 - HEALTHY / CONSCIOUS
Self-aware, Empathetic Server
Humble, Actively-Giving Altruist
Grace-Filled, Relational Nurturer

LEVEL 2 - AVERAGE
Helping, Caring Friend
Smothering Do-Gooder
Flattering Giver

LEVEL 3 - <u>UNHEALTHY / UNCONSCIOUS</u>
Maker of Dependencies
Coercive Controller, Prideful, Domineering
Self-Proclaimed Saint

THREE
LEVEL 1 - <u>HEALTHY / CONSCIOUS</u>
Honest, Successful Achiever
Inclusive, Responsive Leader
Fair-minded, Proficient Administrator

LEVEL 2 - <u>AVERAGE</u>
Success-Seeker
Image-Dominated Competitor
Efficient, Goal-Setting Winner

LEVEL 3 - <u>UNHEALTHY / UNCONSCIOUS</u>
Narcissistic Go-Getter
Deceitful, Self-Serving "Con" Artist
Sociopathic Aggressor

✭ **FOUR**
LEVEL 1 - <u>HEALTHY / CONSCIOUS</u>
Self-Understanding, Unique Creator
Exquisitely Inspired, Artist
Passionate Advocate of the Neglected

LEVEL 2 - <u>AVERAGE</u>
Imaginative Sophisticate
Searcher for the Illusive & Unique
Self-Absorbed Crusader

LEVEL 3 - UNHEALTHY / UNCONSCIOUS
"Misunderstood", Lamenting Depressive
Envy-Ridden Odd Ball
Tragic, Pining, Self-Destructive

✳ **FIVE**

LEVEL 1 - HEALTHY / CONSCIOUS
Fulfilled, Knowledgeable Observer
Grounded, Reflective, Influential
Perceptive, Involved, Wise Authority

LEVEL 2 - AVERAGE
Analytic Theorist
✳ Introverted, Insatiable Absorber
✳ Avid Collector, Gatherer

LEVEL 3 - UNHEALTHY / UNCONSCIOUS
✳ Isolated Hoarder
✳ Delusional Hermit
✳ Empty Dweller in Fantasy

SIX - *Birth, for ? Tem*

LEVEL 1 - HEALTHY / CONSCIOUS
Integrity-Based, Self-Confident Affirmer
Consensus-Building Leader
Centered, Committed Faithful

LEVEL 2 - AVERAGE
Team Player
✳ Undecided Chameleon
"Can Do" Over-Accomplisher/Over the Top Strong One

LEVEL 3 - UNHEALTHY / UNCONSCIOUS
Anxious, Security Addict
Overreacting, Dependent Alarmist
Fear-Ridden, Counter-phobic, Phobic

SEVEN
LEVEL 1 - HEALTHY / CONSCIOUS
Hopeful, Realistic Inspirer
Grateful, Enthusiastic Optimist
Happy, Grounded Visionary

LEVEL 2 - AVERAGE
Happy, Fantasy-Driven Celebrator
Scattered Multi-Interested Generalist
Insatiable Acquirer, Traveler

LEVEL 3 - UNHEALTHY / UNCONSCIOUS
Impulsive, Hyperactive Darter
Distracted, Frenzied Over-Perfectionist
Depressed Denier of Reality

EIGHT
LEVEL 1 - HEALTHY / CONSCIOUS
Action-Oriented, Compassionate Hero
Involved, Altruistic Commander
Powerful, Servant Leader

LEVEL 2 - AVERAGE
Enterprising, Intimidating CEO
Justice-Seeking Dominator
Strong, Confrontational Adversary

LEVEL 3 - UNHEALTHY / UNCONSCIOUS
Tyrannical Ruler
Isolated Ego Maniac
Cruel Oppressor

✱ NINE
LEVEL 1 - HEALTHY / CONSCIOUS

O.K., Harmonious Achiever
Grounded, Receptive Supporter
Energized, Effective Peacemaker

LEVEL 2 - AVERAGE
✱ Balanced Mediator
✱ Calm, Unruffled Neutralizer
✱ Conflict-Avoidant Passivist

LEVEL 3 - UNHEALTHY / UNCONSCIOUS
✱ Self-Neglectful, Passive-Aggressor
✱ Narcotized Disassociator, Slothful Detachment

Chapter Six
The Secret Passageways of the Arrows

How The Arrows Point the Way to Disintegration or Integration of Consciousness

In Figure 6 you will notice that each number on the Enneagram's circle has two arrows, one pointing toward it and one pointing away from it. For example, originating at number three and pointing away from it, is an arrow that leads to number 9. Pointing directly to number three is a second arrow which originates at number 6. These two arrows point to each type's direction toward integration or disintegration.

As was stated in Chapter One, each type is caught in a trap and must find its way out of it. The arrows are the passageways out of the traps. The use of the arrows is done through counter intuition rather than apparent logic. Our first impulse in moving away from our traps is to move toward what appears attractive or beneficial.

This would be to follow the arrow that leads away from our type number and points toward another type. Becoming more like the type at the tip of the arrow's head is seemingly the easiest route; it is the path of least resistance. It may take decades before we discover that the direction of going **with the arrow** leads to a type that is not helpful, but actually fraught with suffering. Though this type seems to be our answer in completing our sense of self, it handily seduces us to become a manifestation of its unhealthy and unconscious aspects. It does not pull us out of the problems, traps and sufferings inherent in our type. It only worsens them, and leads to deeper suffering.

If, however, we use counter intuitiveness and go to an energy not so readily familiar to us, (indicated by going **against our arrow**), we find another energy. In its healthy or most conscious manifestations it is the antidote to our suffering. This type's number, found by going against the arrow, contains our specific energy for consciousness, integration, and redemption. By using the positive, conscious, healthy aspects of the type found by going against our arrow, we can find relief from our suffering.

Disintegration

These are the steps to finding the type which, in its unhealthy form, causes suffering and disintegration for you.

1. Find your type's number on the Enneagram.
2. Look at the <u>arrow that begins</u> at your number and shoots or points away from your number toward another number.
3. Follow that arrow until you get to this arrow's head. This is called "going with the arrow" or with the flow, the path of least resistance.
4. What type is the number to which the arrow head is directly pointing?

99

5. Look this type up in your list of Types
   and Levels of Integration. (See Chapter Five.)
6. This type's strong points and its panaceas seem to
   be what would help you. But they do not. This
   type's disintegrative aspects actually seduce your
   type into unhealthy states of mind. The average
   and unhealthy characteristics of this seemingly
   beneficial type are painful or even deadly to you.

Integration

These are the steps to finding the number of integration for your type.

1. Find your type's number on the Enneagram symbol.
2. Find the <u>arrow head</u> that is nearest
   to your number and points to it.
3. Beginning at the arrow head, follow the line
   of the arrow to its end. This is called "going
   against one's arrow" or going against the flow.
4. What is the number of the type at the arrow's end?
5. Look this number up in your material
   on Types and Levels of Functioning
   and Consciousness (Chapter Five).
6. This type in its most healthy or conscious level
   is the antidote to the suffering of your type.
   When the healthy and conscious attributes
   are integrated with your type wholeness is achieved.

The Continuing Cycle Of
Disintegration And Integration

Using the arrows for spiritual development does not stop here. Advanced teaching allows us to see that the pathways of disintegration or integration continue by going to (becoming more like) the number found by going either with or against the arrow flow. For example: Type One disintegrates (or becomes unconscious) when she **flows with her arrow** (the path of least resistance) to the unconscious unhealthy aspects of type 4. She continues to go with the arrow from type 4 to the unhealthy aspects of type 2, following the arrow from type 2 picking up the unhealthy aspects of type 8. From type 8, if she continues into disintegration, she will follow the arrow to the unhealthy aspects of type 5. From the unhealthy aspects of type 5, the 1 will follow its arrow to the unhealthy 7. This completes the disintegrated pathway of type 1. This journey, when repeated, takes her each time to a lower realm of awareness and spiritual disintegration.

Type One will integrate by **going against her arrow** (like swimming upstream) to the healthy aspects of type 7. She will continue the process of integration, or consciousness, by going against the arrow from 7 to the healthy aspects of type 5. From here she will go against the arrow at type 5 to the healthy aspects of type 8. One ventures into more consciousness by going against the arrow from point 8 to the healthy 2. This process continues from point 2 going against the arrow to the healthy 4. This completes the consciousness process of type 1. This "journey" can be repeated over and over for integration of the person, spiritually taking him/her to new realms of spiritual understanding as they spiral upward in consciousness.

Figure Six
The Arrows

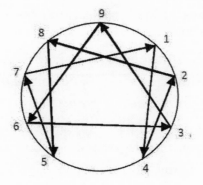

All points that are not on the primary triangle of 3, 6 and 9, will go through the above process passing through the six numbers which are not on that triangle. These numbers are 1, 2, 4, 5, 7 and 8. The route these numbers take follows the outline of the hexad. The 3, 6 and 9 of the primary triangle stay on that triangle to integrate (attain consciousness) or disintegrate (become unconsciousness).

These figures indicate the arrow flow on the two separate pathways of the Enneagram.

Figure Seven
The Primary Triangle and the Hexad

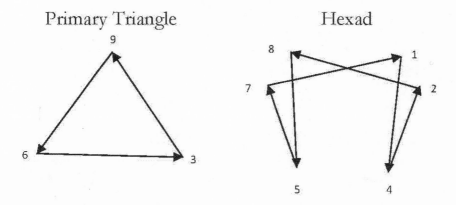

Primary Triangle   Hexad

Examples of How Each Type Goes Against Its Arrows Toward Consciousness and Integration

Type One and Passageways to Consciousness

The One has the amazing gift of discernment. Her knowing the right way to go, serves her well as she grows in consciousness and integrates her being. <u>The virtue of type One is serenity</u>. This is the key to her moving in the world without ego resentment toward all who in her judgment do wrong (or who are not right). The healthy One preserves her gift of discernment and becomes whole by <u>moving against</u> her arrow to the healthy aspects of type Seven, the birthplace of her soul child. The realistic optimism and hopefulness of type Seven, when integrated into type One, turns her in the direction of consciousness. Not bogged down or preoccupied with judgment, monitoring, or criticality, type One can be the standard bearer while moving in the world with serenity. The One's <u>Holy Idea of Holy Perfection – Holy Growth</u> helps her go through the portal to consciousness. Now she is conscious of others and herself as being works in progress, who don't have to be "perfect" or "right" to be acceptable. The one now can continue consciousness by moving to the healthy Five, Eight, Two, and Four by going against her arrows, integrating and receiving blessings for her soul. She can rejoice and be glad!

Type Two and Passageways to Consciousness

Type Two is the giver and the helper. His <u>virtue is humility</u> whose meekness is evidenced by his lack of pride in giving. Instead of controlling and flattering others, as he would if he went with his arrow, he is more interested in helping without taking credit and without spotlighting himself. He became this kind of person by going <u>against his arrow</u>, to the type that in its healthy form, is the antidote to his suffering. Brought on by trying to gain power over others by "giving", the Two's suffering is particularly painful because he never secures the love for which he's trying to "bribe" others. The Two has gone against his arrow to the healthy Four for his integration; here he embodies the self-understanding and insight necessary to get himself out of "self" and into the world as an altruistic contributor. The healthy Four never denies his own needs; he knows them well, and as the integrated Two becomes more like a healthy Four he owns his overriding need for love. He gets it, not by "giving" as a means to an end, but by accepting freely given love as a natural by-product of selfless giving. The Two returns to his own soul's birthplace by going to healthy Four. This is unfamiliar territory at first but meekness together with the <u>Holy Idea of Holy Grace – Holy Will – Holy Freedom</u>, allow the Two to jump through the portal of essence to a greater awareness of his true nature. A receiver as well as a giver, he can now be out of the trap of service while living in reciprocity.

Type Three and Passageways to Consciousness

Type Three is the achiever. By setting goals, by competing, and by being successful, many things are accomplished by the Three. Three's love of achievement lets many people benefit from her activities. She embodies the <u>virtue of truthfulness</u>. This virtue, when paired with her <u>Holy Idea of Holy Hope, Law, Harmony and Will</u>, allows the Three to turn away from suffering and move in the world with accomplishment and integrity. When going with her arrow, however, the Three suffers; ego vanity takes over and she relaxes into taking the easy way to accomplishment through image making and deceit. The world finally rejects the unconscious Three, who lacks the substance she promised. Rejection is one of the worst agonies she can suffer because she equates this with not being loved. <u>By going against</u> her arrow, the Three turns from the pathway of suffering to discover her true essence at point

Six's healthy state. Here she finds her soul child's birthplace and remembers her real self. Now she acts with a spirit poor in self and rich in concern for others, and the community. Success and efficiency are still evident yet they now operate in a new kingdom – the Kingdom of heaven.

Type Four and Passageways to Consciousness

Type Four says to the world, "I am unique". He is called the "creator" by many because this artist's one-of-a-kind "take" on the world, leads to special abilities and productions. The unhealthy Four suffers frequently with ego melancholy. He wants someone to save him from his unauthentic life and thereby falls into the trap of authenticity. He is on a search for his real life. His passion of envy causes more suffering as he can never find a "savior", and is jealous of those whose lives seem to have found happiness and authenticity. By going against his arrow, the Four turns away from self-absorption and the depression it brings by going to the healthy type One where his soul child lives. The healthy One who has the gift of discernment knows the right thing to do with life. This right thing contains the very direction, the right cause or occupation that lifts the Four to conscious being. It takes him out of the trap and passion of his ego compulsion and into his virtue of equanimity (composure). By finding and going through the portal of his Holy Idea of Holy Union with the Divine – Holy Origin, the Four can pass into consciousness and continue going against the arrows of his hexad "for righteousness" (type One) sake".

Type Five and Passageways to Consciousness

The Five says to the world "I am wise" and contributes to the world by absorbing, collecting, and storing knowledge. This can be her trap causing her to hoard knowledge. Her suffering begins when her passion of stinginess separates her from people and focuses her on filling the endless emptiness with knowledge, "stuff", or food. The Five is so empty she detaches from others, and fantasizes a self made world. She does not want to be intruded upon by those of the real world, and decompensates mentality to stop this suffering. The healthy Five turns and goes <u>against her arrow</u> to the healthy Eight of her soul child whose strength empowers her to combine her wisdom with powerful movement in the world. Knowledge used for the welfare of others, combined with Eight's strong guardianship of the underdog, the Five is now anything but a recluse. Five's <u>virtue of detachment</u> is her <u>dis-identification</u> with knowledge as being her true self. She is now fully receptive to a new way to be filled, and is now involved in the world. When remembering her essence, the Five can begin to live out of a new confidence as she moves against the arrows to the other types' healthy aspects going from Eight to Two, to Four, to One and then to Seven. By doing this the Five is coming strongly into her own and has a message for the world. The Five's <u>Holy Idea of Holy Providence – Holy Transparency – Holy Omniscience</u>, gives the Five a constant way to satisfy her hunger and thirst.

Type Six and Passageways to Consciousness *Key Piece*

The Six is a person of loyalty, a wonderful team player and group participant. Family, community, and all kinds of affiliations are championed by this loyalist. The Six however, is fear-ridden and scared of alienation by the group. He wants unity, consensus, and to be included. His suffering comes by the growing fear of being discovered as non-acceptable, deviant or below standard. He seeks protection from this fear by an authority figure to which he pays homage and "obeys". Uncertain of his future or his true place, decisions are hard for him; he wants to please everyone, and prevent his becoming a scapegoat. By using <u>his virtue of courage</u>, and his <u>Holy Idea of Holy Trust – Holy Strength – Holy Faith</u>, the Six can enter the state of consciousness and wholeness. This results in his <u>going against his arrow to the healthy Nine</u> who is full of peace, a sense of place, and ok-ness. Six then goes to the conscious level of point three to accomplish peacefully without fear or frenzy. This place, when remembered by Six, is familiar to his soul child. This is the place where essence is combined with what life has taught him. This is his portal to being a new creature with a pure courageous heart, and an inner authority that can "see God" for himself.

Type Seven and Passageways to Consciousness

The Seven says "I am happy". The joy and excitement of such a person is contagious. Celebration, hope, and optimism are essential to life's fire because who are we without rejoicing except dull and boring? Type Seven suffers when she avoids pain and seeks constant pleasure. This leads to the <u>passion of overindulgence</u>. The suffering of the Seven intensifies as she cannot tolerate anything but happiness and pleasure and becomes trapped by a compulsion to achieve the ideal, or perfection. This cannot be achieved in the real world, so the Seven suffers as her hopes for continual happiness are dashed. By going against her arrow, however, the Seven goes to the quiet, reflective healthy Five. The conscious and healthy Five who embodies wisdom and is detached from ego identification centers the Seven by providing thoughtful deliberation and study. This place of her Soul Child activates her <u>virtue of sobriety</u>, which is the antidote to the unhealthy Seven's overindulgence. By returning to her essence (the healthy Five), she becomes conscious and can now face the pain and grief she avoided. In doing this she receives the blessing of comfort, and embraces her <u>Holy Idea of Holy Co-Creation – Holy Plan – Holy Work</u>, which is a portal for further integration and growth. She then travels the hexad against the arrows to incorporate more consciousness at each point. No longer is her pain denied: it is comforted.

Type Eight and Passageways to Consciousness

Type Eight is the consummate leader. He says to the world, "I am strong", and is willing to tackle the most ominous threats to his command. His sense of justice becomes more than a mission. It can become his trap and ego compulsion. Willing to take a stand and conquer others who challenge him, makes the Eight a formidable figure with an ever growing power structure. He disintegrates by following his arrow with arrogance (his passion) to the unhealthy Five. He suffers there from abject isolation as his lustful strength disintegrates into raging power over others. In creating his own kingdom, he withdraws his powerful support (ego vengeance) as his ultimate manipulation of others. The isolation to which he is relegated sucks the life out of him, for there is no one left in his kingdom over whom to exert his strength. Going to his healthy Two, by taking the passageway against his arrows, turns the Eight's life around. At point Two, he returns to his essence, and the place where he began his journey. It is a place of vulnerable giving and involved caring. This is the energy of a healthy conscious Two, who when combined with Eight's <u>Holy Idea of Holy Compassion – Holy Truth</u> creates a conscious humanitarian leader. The lust for all the ego trappings of his power structure disappears as it becomes clear to the Eight that his rage can be healed with compassion. This clarity simplifies his purpose. <u>Simplicity becomes his virtue</u>. He becomes merciful instead of wrathful and thereby receives that mercy himself.

Type Nine and Passageways to Consciousness

Type Nine is known for being peaceful. She is a natural mediator because she sees all sides of every situation, and maintains an even disposition with nothing seeming to ruffle her. She is, at her best, the quintessential arbitrator. She can represent everyone's view and help reach peaceful compromise. She avoids conflict, however, and when she disintegrates, she falls into the trap of self abasement, which diminishes her importance in the eyes of others. Her passion of laziness relegates her to the emotionally paralyzed and ineffectual. To integrate and become conscious, the Nine must go against her arrow to the healthy Three. At this point she meets her Soul Child again, and lives out of the space of action directed for the good of all. Then she continues going against her arrows to the healthy conscious Six. Success is focused at this place on the well being of others not a self image of being successful. Laziness and self narcotization are burned away as the healthy Nine grasps her Holy Idea of Holy Love – Holy Unconditional Love. In her essence she has the inner confidence to take action to manage conflict, and to move out in the world as a peacemaker and an unconditionally loved child of God.

Examples Of How Each Type Follows Its Arrows Toward Unconsciousness and Disintegration

Type One and Passageways to Unconsciousness

Type One is caught in the trap of perfection. He compulsively guides others while pointing out the right way to go. He becomes a standard bearer who assesses and judges others in an effort to keep things "right". As he decompensates into unconsciousness, his guidance is seen by others as critical, even as chiding. Because he knows the right path, he is dismayed by others who don't seem to know it, or who don't follow it. When confronted with people like this, the One who is unhealthy becomes self-righteous and indignant saying, "How dare they not do what is right?"; "they should know they are deliberately breaking the rules"; "I'll see they won't get away with this". These are the remarks of an out of control One who is a self appointed judge. The overriding <u>passion of the One is anger</u>, which he avoids because it isn't, in his mind, "right" to express anger. He represses this emotion and follows his arrow, to the unhealthy Four. In the Four's self-absorbed despair, he becomes depressed and even self-destructive. In the implosion of the unhealthy One, he sinks further into lamenting being misunderstood and in resenting those who misunderstand him. Sometimes he explodes with uncontrolled angry outbursts, bringing on the very thing he has always tried to avoid. He follows the arrows to incorporate the unhealthy aspects of points Two, Eight, Five, Seven, then back to himself as fully unconscious.

Type Two and Passageways to Unconsciousness

Type Two is <u>trapped in the compulsion of service</u>. To do for and to help others are the ways her ego has found some sense of mastery over a world she is not sure will love her. She is so giving that she tries to insure her place by becoming irreplaceable. Her passion of pride takes over as she looses her sense of motive. Self-understanding, and the acknowledgment of her own needs. When under stress, she moves with her arrow into the unhealthy space of the Eight and thus becomes unconscious. She lords her power over others as does an unhealthy arrogant Eight by saying, "I will withdraw my supply, my giving, and my helpfulness from you if you do not do or act as I say". She then may groom others to be dependent upon her. This gets her "love" by strong-arming others. The unconscious Two is rejected by others in the end, as her manipulations are seen for what they are. As a way to get back at those who don't go along with her "program", unhealthy Twos act like the unconscious Eight by seeking revenge. The Two then follows the route to the unhealthy Five, then Seven, then One, then Four, then back to a self full of suffering and pain.

Type Three and Passageways to Unconsciousness

The Three is <u>trapped in the compulsion of efficiency</u>. Being successful is his way to make the world a place in which to survive and thrive. But if the Three under stress begins to disintegrate, and becomes unconscious, his <u>passion of deceit</u> completely takes over. The once outstanding achiever is now so desperate to feel "on top of his game" that he follows his arrow to the space of the unhealthy Nine. At unhealthy Nine's self-narcotization and paralysis of spirit, the disintegrating Type Three succumbs to numbness. Gone now are Three's efficient action and responsibility to others. He "goes to sleep" on his own sense of community, responsibility to others, and his acumen for expert administration. He becomes lackadaisical taking the easy way to success by deceiving others with image, schemes, or chameleon like personas. In his ego compulsion, the unconscious Three's empty image and promises are exposed. He disintegrates further by following his arrows from the unhealthy Nine to the anxiety-ridden unhealthy Six. Then he returns to himself as a failure, who is completely unconscious of how he "made it" there.

Type Four and Passageways to Unconsciousness

The Four is bound up in the compulsion to be different. This is her way to satisfy her yearning for admiration and love. She is caught in the <u>trap of authenticity</u> which becomes a never-ending search for her true self. She is creative and masterful in making herself and her world unique. Yet when she disintegrates under stress, she flows with her arrow to the seduction of the unhealthy Two. Here she takes on the characteristics of obsessing about relationships, and of being preoccupied with getting others to attend to her needs. She seeks a special someone to rescue her from her fears of abandonment and to finally understand her. She meanwhile is caught in the <u>passion of envy</u> which, when activated, sees others as having the authentic existence for which she pines. She sinks into even more suffering when becoming like an unhealthy Two because self-absorption is heightened with the search for a codependent relationship. She obsesses about finding the person she imagines will save her, yet is discontented with everyone she uses to fill that bill. She says "everyone has a life, but I am still waiting to live mine". This suffering continues as she descends into the cycle of disintegration from the unhealthy Two, to the unhealthy unconscious Eight, Five, Seven, One, then back to herself.

Type Five and Passageways to Unconsciousness

The Five finds himself <u>trapped by the thirst for knowledge</u>. At the basis of this is the avoidance of inner emptiness. He tries to fill himself with observations, information and even "food". The Five loses himself when he becomes so locked into gaining information that he lives solely in his head. Detached from others, he constructs a life around thinking, categorizing and collecting information. When this goes to an extreme, he goes with his arrow to the unhealthy unconscious Seven who has lost the anchor of reality and has let the fantasy life become where they "live". The <u>passion of the Five is stinginess</u> which is the result of the increasing need to fill an empty hole in himself. This stinginess is manifested by withholding and withdrawing from others. When gone to the unhealthy Seven, Type Five is given to an unrealistic world of make-believe and fantasy. Living in his own world of stingy hoarding, this Five leaves the mainstream. This causes a further deterioration and the Five continues to follow the arrows to the unconsciousness of points One, Four, Two, Eight, returning to himself as having collected bountifully, extreme unconsciousness.

Type Six and Passageways to Unconsciousness

Seeking <u>security</u> is what traps the Six in a quest for what can never be attained. He doesn't trust his own sense of inner judgment or authority. He wants security, safety, and protection by an authority figure to which he pays homage. His passion is <u>fear</u>. He is afraid of being deviant, and avoids this in every way. He devises a way to be seen as a team player, a "regular guy", the authority's "right-hand person", etc. Hiding behind the authority figure, the Six tries to please that authority continuously. Afraid of displeasing the authority figure or losing his position, he follows his arrows to the unhealthy Three. At this point he gets in a frenzy of accomplishment to secure the authority figure's approval of him. Image now becomes everything as he is totally dependent on the perception others have of him. Doing and achieving wears the Six out because he is acting out of fear and desperation. The base fear is annihilation and scapegoating which he finally brings on himself. He finds that he is being ousted by the authority figure and scapegoated by peers. By being so dutiful, and by embracing a false image, the Six loose all confidence in himself at the chaos point of the unconscious Three. In continued disintegration, he follows his arrow to the unhealthy Nine. Here, the Six experiences overwhelming anxiety with self narcotization. When he returns back to Six, he is as a scared "drunk in the alley", too unconscious to escape the approaching muggers.

Type Seven and Passageways to Unconsciousness

Caught in the <u>trap of idealism</u> Sevens seek to achieve perfect happiness. This search is witnessed in the Seven's grasping for the cornucopia of hope and pleasure. In avoiding the pain of life, she lives in the future, and does not want to face loss, grief, brokenness, or imperfection. The Seven tries to cover up any discontent by planning for and seeking one pleasure after the other. When fun experiences wear off others are sought to replace them. There is a manic flurry of activity around the Seven whose passion is overindulgence. The Seven who disintegrates begins the process by taking on the unhealthy characteristics of the unhealthy One reached by following her arrow. The unhealthy One wants perfection in the sense of rightness; the disintegrating Seven wants perfection in terms of perfect happiness. To the Seven this seems right because pain is seen as bad. The quest for perfect happiness in this broken world is impossible to attain. The Seven's adage "if some is good, more is better", proves to be highly frustrating for her because everything and everybody cannot conform to what always feels happy and fun-filled. By following her arrows from the unhealthy One to the unhealthy Four she then asks "why are my hopes always dashed? This is unfair." Unconsciousness intensifies as the Seven continues to go with the arrows. Mania and depression cycle the Seven downward away from hope and optimism to unconsciousness.

Type Eight and Passageways to Unconsciousness

Seeking justice is the trap of the Eight. This trap springs from Eight's inherent ego compulsion to avoid her weakness. In a covering of strength and ability, the Eight marshals others to action by leading and by using her power to take care of the underdog and the weak. In disintegration, unconsciousness takes over and the compulsion to flex her muscles dominates the Eight's presence. Her passion of arrogance blinds her to the negative effects of her power over others. In setting up her power base she rules her domain not so much as a benevolent justice seeker, but as a dictator who intimidates. "Here I am deal with me" is the stance taken by her, whether quietly or by brute force. Power is her game. Because the Eight has a huge appetite or lust for the good things in life, she "rewards" those who follow and obey her. By following her arrow to the unhealthy Five, the Eight disintegrates. At this point she uses the Five's strategy of <u>withdrawal</u> to make a strong power play and punish those who are seen as insubordinate. She withdraws her support, her blessings, and her power from those who don't pay homage and become her subjects. She ends up commanding the drawbridge of her castle, but in the spiral of unconsciousness ends up alone sealed off from others in her fortress tomb.

Type Nine and Passageways to Unconsciousness

Nines avoid conflict. <u>This traps them in self-abasement</u>. Putting himself down diminishes his visibility and his stance, thereby making him unconscious. Having no strong opinions or preferences removes the Nine from being a source of conflict or controversy. Being generally non-committal puts the Nine in a "no-man's land" of being on everyone's side. Even though he has strong opinions and even very controlled rage, no one would know because of his peaceful demeanor. The Nine who becomes unconscious denies his feelings and opinions at all costs, to keep peace and to prevent conflict. His <u>passion of laziness</u> is manifested in nursing an "I don't care attitude" or an attitude of "it's not important." By following his arrow to the unhealthy Six, the unhealthy Nine takes on the Six's palpable fear. This fear is shown in uncontrolled anxiety as the unhealthy Nine cannot be conflict- free inside his own mind or in relationships. Living in a shutdown conflict- free world, others begin to shake him into taking a stance. From the unhealthy Six he follows his arrows to the unhealthy Three and loses his spirit to truly accomplish anything. Self- narcotization now is the only way to remain "conflict- free". He enters unconsciousness and anxiety–ridden paralysis.

What is in backpack

Chapter Seven
The Wings of Each Enneagram Type

Each of the nine types on the Enneagram "wheel" is flanked by another type. For example, the Enneagram Type One is preceded by the Type Nine, and is followed by the Type Two. The two flanking numbers are called "the wings". The wing is not the type itself but is supplemental to the person's type, and adds characteristics and leanings to the type. Though many people find a close affinity between their type and <u>both</u> of their wings, on the Enneagram, most persons have a stronger identification and understanding of just <u>one</u> of the two wings. This strong wing is auxiliary to the major type it stands beside. Below is a list of the Nine Enneagramatical Types described with each of their wings. The person chooses which of the two wings flanking their number is the one with which they have the strongest identification. Many couples report the sharing of a wing

ONE

The One with a strong Nine wing combines the perfectionism of the One with the peacemaking of the Nine. Fairness and reaching the right solution are all-important. Emphasis is placed on using discernment in creating harmony in their relationships, by knowing the right path for those involved, and by providing guidance in creating solution-making in which all views are taken into account.

The One with a predominant Two wing has the major gifts of discernment and sense of standards expressed as being of service to others. Here the major emphasis is upon the One's need to see things done rightly supported by the empathy of the Two for the needs of others.

TWO

The Two with a dominating One wing is primarily and foremost a helper who has a well-developed sense of right and wrong. Preoccupied with how to meet the needs of those around him, the Two with a strong One wing moves in the world meeting needs while being secondarily and complementarily interested in doing this with their sense of perfection, order and correctness.

The Two with a strong Three wing is compelled to be of service while a Three's attribute of success underpins this. Therefore this personality is preoccupied with empathic need-meeting while being a recognized success at performing their service. Competition for the place of being the best is embedded in caretaking and responsiveness to others' needs, or wants.

THREE

The Three with an emphasized Two wing is primarily focused on achievement and success with a well-developed sense of what people need or want. Successful endeavors are built upon the understanding of the motivations and needs of others, and a sense of achieving success while employing service oriented endeavors as the way to accomplishment.

The Three with a strong Four wing is driven by achievement/ success and image, while wanting to achieve unconventionally or extraordinarily. This person, fueled by efficient achievement, expresses the Four's sense of uniqueness and being set apart from the crowd in the choice and manner of endeavor.

FOUR

The Four with a dominant Three wing is empowered by the passion to champion a cause which, without his, would have gone un-potentiated, unnoticed or neglected. Inherent creativity and artfulness are paired with their achieving forward movement in setting and meeting goals, expertly and efficiently.

The Four with a Five wing emphasis sees life from the inner perspective. His "uncommon wisdom" is animated by a unique 'take' on his purpose or meaning in life. His singular search for clarity and meaning, leads him to the Five wing's value of observation, learning and synthesis of information so that a unique contribution to the body of knowledge can be made.

FIVE

The Five whose strongest wing is the Four is also given to the introverted way of life. Filling an inner emptiness is a huge motivation as the Five lives in the world with authority and expertise around his knowledge. This Five has a bent toward his wing's unique creativity as this trait supports the overriding archetype of "the wise person".

The Five with a prominent Six wing is primarily a collector and repository of valued knowledge. This person, while continually seeking more information, is loyally focused on the betterment and security of those whose welfare is that with which he is most associated.

119

SIX

The Six with a strong Five wing is a bastion of warmth, integrity and protection. Creating safe spaces for compatriots, this Six uses the Five wing's wisdom and observational strengths as ways to caringly knit people together with common ideals, beliefs and commitments.

The Six with a pronounced Seven wing is an idealist who works for the group's welfare and prosperity. With the Seven wing's sense of hope, optimism and future-oriented planning, the Six will work untiringly to bring her affiliates, family or organization to its ideal, with a personal sense of fidelity and vision.

SEVEN

The Seven with dominant Six wing functions is propelled by a sense of hope and abundance. Her levity and buoyancy are major characteristics as she involves others in her Six wing's sense of dutiful accomplishment for "the clan". The toil and "dirty work" of providing security for the group is empowered by the Seven's compelling ability to generously provide cheer, good will, and a cornucopia of visions for the future.

The Seven with a strong Eight wing is a lightening rod of energy and strength. Having an insatiable appetite for the good things of life, this person has a positive disposition, is future oriented, and is unflinchingly optimistic. She uses her Eight wing's sense of strength and justice to push forward in the world, and to influence others in mighty ways.

EIGHT

The Eight who has a predominant Seven wing is a commanding personality who displays a lust for life in a fun-loving way. The Seven wing complements the Eight's sense of power and authority by providing an insatiable desire for the bounty of life. This Eight balances strength with his Seven wing's engaging ever-expanding love of the range of what gifts life has to offer.

The Eight whose emphasis is on the Nine wing is a relaxed bastion of strength. This Eight's power nature has more subtle overtones of peaceful unruffled authority and inner resolve. This Eight's decisions and leadership are conducted with his Nine wing's sense of fair mediation, because all sides of the situation can be seen, and judged without hesitation.

NINE

The Nine with an expressive Eight wing is a settled person who presents a calm inner strength. Though slow to come to decisions of action, once the activity is finally begun, this Nine uses her auxiliary Eight wing to be grounded, solid and unshakable in her decisions and follow through.

With a strong One wing, this Nine combines her settled fair-mindedness with the One's desire to "go by the book". This Nine, whose overriding desire is for harmony, good will and comfortable environments, seeks to accomplish these (albeit slowly at times) by using well-worked-out beliefs, morals and standards, and by pointing to these as the safe and equal guidance which can bring peace to all concerned.

Chapter Eight
The Instinctual Subtypes of the Enneagram

The instinctual subtype is a sub-layer of personality within each of the nine major types. A person's subtype is an underlying perspective of reality that pervades his/her entire being. This subtype is the all-important lens through which the person instinctively perceives, interprets, and moves in the world.

The three subtypes are:
1. Self-Preservation
2. Social-Affiliation
3. Sexual-Syntony

Each person's subtype is only one of these three and is the arena in which the issues and compulsions of their personality type are played out. The two remaining subtypes are significant areas of attention and are addressed in daily living; these are called the non-dominant subtypes. The non-dominant subtypes are <u>not</u> the primary set of concerns, interests, and perceptions that forms the person's dominant subtype.

Called the instinctual subtype, this set of concerns is primary because it is linked to the person's sense of survival. Stemming from early psychic damage in childhood, the subtype becomes a central focus for the child because the wounding occurred in the subtype's particular area of concern and carries psychic pain and shame. For example Self-Preservation subtypes, having been wounded or traumatized in the areas of security, safety, or supply, view the world out of these still-present vulnerabilities. Likewise, the Social-Affiliation subtype was traumatized early in life in the area of "fitting in", social rank, and finding his place among others. Therefore this vulnerability and woundedness remain of primary concern and shape his world view, behavior, and mental preoccupations, etc. The Sexual-Syntony subtype experienced wounds or trauma in the area of intimacy, gender, physical attraction, and psycho-sexual relationships. These areas remain vulnerable and therefore are protected by the vigilant attention given to them. Syntony is a word that emphasizes the sexual sub-type's desire to find fullness of life within a relationship to a romantic partner or partners. Syntony can be compared to the dance of partners.

In summary, the subtype can be compared to a vulnerable traumatized child inside us whom we protect from the world. We are their "go betweens", who care for and take this child with us wherever we go. In so doing we deal with the world through the ever-present task of nurturing, protecting, and interpreting reality in terms of this wounded child of ours.

Most people know exactly the type of wounding they sustained which "broke" them. There are some persons who do not remember being traumatized, wounded, or even slighted in any area of their early life. In this case, the person can give thought as to how one of the three subtypes became a prominent preoccupation.

Some possibilities are:

1. The wound is repressed and remains unconscious;
2. The trauma associated with the subtype area is denied due to its potentially overwhelming psychological and spiritual impact;
3. There was no direct wound as such, but only the <u>fear</u> of being wounded in this area which led to its becoming a central concern anyway;
4. One's parents were wounded or traumatized in the subtype area, and passed on their shame, fears, concerns, subtype focus, etc. onto the child who transferred these subtype concerns to themselves.

When the compulsion of the ego began to form, it did so as a response to the pain, shame, and hurt the world caused this vulnerable innocent being. The subtype is the area this compulsion was developed to protect. It may take time and spiritual work to remember the pain or hurt, but recalling it is not necessary to heal the wound.

Of note is that Maslow's Hierarchy of Needs states that unless our physiological, safety, and security needs are first met, other higher order needs including the social and sexual cannot be met adequately.(1) This would suggest that everyone's preoccupation (or subtype) would naturally be self-preservation. The wisdom of the Enneagram's energy flow also integrates the truths of Maslow's Hierarchy of Needs and is consistent with them in helping people become conscious. The subtype therefore, is congruent with the truths of Maslow's Hierarchy of Needs, because the social subtype and/or sexual subtype are viewed by the persons holding these preoccupations, as <u>survival</u> needs. They do not feel safe to advance in meeting higher order needs, unless their subtype areas feel safe.

In rare crisis situations the area in crisis necessarily becomes the central focus temporarily. Therefore, in medical emergencies, self-preservation has to become the focus. In a social-affiliation crisis such as not being selected by the club for membership, this becomes the focus. And in the area of sexual relationships, when a lover rejects us, this is the central concern. After the crisis, however, the subtype issues surface again to preoccupy the person as her central concern. Even in crisis, however, the issue of the crisis is filtered, processed and understood through the perspective of one's instinctual subtype.

What about the importance of the non-dominant subtypes? They are, of course, very important, yet they are not the central focus. They are as layers beneath the first and thickest layer of subtype. The other two non-dominant layers would be of lesser thickness than the dominant subtype layer.

Figure Eight shows examples of how two different Enneagramical personality types can have differing dominant sub-types and differing non dominant sub-type layers beneath them.

Figure Eight
Examples of Dominate and Non Dominate Sub Types

Type 2   Type 8

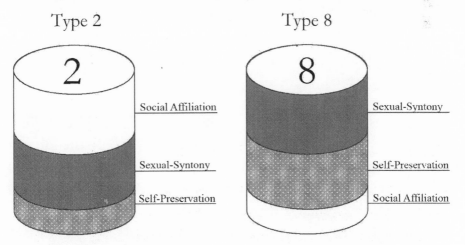

Social Affiliation

Sexual-Syntony

Self-Preservation

Sexual-Syntony

Self-Preservation

Social Affiliation

The instinctual subtype's pain is healed as the person becomes conscious and integrates toward a healthy pattern of living. This means that as the person moves against her arrow (see Chapter Six) to her point of integration, the wounding of the subtype is healed. Conversely, if the person goes with her arrow to her point of unconsciousness and disintegration, her subtype's wound becomes even more severe, and healthy functioning is impaired.

The following subtype descriptions define each type's preoccupation, how it is expressed and addressed by the personality of the type. The subtype is then described in terms of how it is healed as the person reaches consciousness. It is then shown how matters worsen in the area of subtype if the personality disintegrates.

It is important to mention that unless one has found a way to live in consciousness at all times, she is apt to move up the scale toward healthy adaptation of her subtype issues only in periods of consciousness. Likewise, in periods of unconsciousness, the least healthy adaptations of subtype issues are expressed. Movement downward is usually brought on by stress and the reappearance of the type's compulsion. Movement upward toward healthy consciousness is usually brought on by spiritual transformation (see Emergence of Consciousness - Chapter Ten).

The Instinctual Subtypes of Each Enneagramical Type

Type One: Self-Preservation

This instinctual type is a combination of upholding right standards with preserving one's family and one's self. The gift of discernment is focused on keeping things secure in all areas of life. Anger is avoided not only because it is "wrong", but because the expression of such a negatively perceived emotion may also jeopardize his sense of safety and wellbeing.

At his most conscious, Type One has a great self-acceptance and self-awareness of his preoccupation with maintaining security and stability. Though this is his focus, he does not does he overly magnify his preoccupation. Nor does he lord over others with judgments, criticisms, and pronouncements of right or wrong-doing in service of self-security. His optimism and hope soften his preoccupation and reduces it as a block to happiness. He sees life as an unfolding <u>Growth</u> (Holy Idea), process, not as a fail-safe system of security.

At his least conscious, self-preservation Type One is serious, judgmental, hyper-vigilant, and fears he is not worthy to be protected. His discernment skills focus on a despairing anticipation of what may put him in danger, or in an insecure position. These dangerous factors and persons bring on the compulsion of ego resentment toward an imperfect world. Unable to contain anger at this situation he disintegrate by becoming hyper-vigilantly paranoid as he distorts his perception of the world as dangerous and "gone wrong".

Type One: Social-Affiliation

The Ennea-type One who is preoccupied with social-affiliation issues is someone who combines the gift of discernment with the issues of her standing in society – this standing can be her place in the small realm of the family, or in the largest affiliations in the neighborhood, in political parties, in churches, professional groups, etc. She uses her gifts as a standard bearer to solidify her place in and amongst her affiliations as she senses she is <u>valued</u> for this ability.

At her most conscious, she has developed a good-natured acceptance of this dynamic. She is less rigid and more adaptable because she knows that being the stickler for judging right and wrong can topple her social position if taken too far. Her happy disposition found at her point of integration (Seven) helps her to be a likable discerner who finds her true place with others and is valued in it. She sees life as a <u>Growth</u> process (Holy Idea), not as a perfect final product.

Ones of this instinctual type who are unconscious are taken over by ego resentment of others when they feel they or their standards are wrongly perceived. They disintegrate to a rigid socially isolated stance as they disintegrate to the maladaptive type Four. Their anger seeps out as alienation and outrage with contempt for those who they think cause them to be left out.

Type One: Sexual-Syntony

This instinctual subtype, when predominant in Type One, is a blend of the standards of right and wrong with the issues of intimacy. The gift of discernment is used by this instinctual subtype, to know such things as who is "coupled" with whom, who is a right or a wrong match, and most important, how to keep his own intimate relationships (especially their own partnership) on the right track.

At the most healthy conscious level this personality has shed the ego compulsion of keeping score, judging, and finding fault with everything. The Holy Idea of <u>Growth</u> frees him to be tolerant of others. He no longer quests for perfection in relationships (intimate or casual), but he strives for the right fit between him and his partner. Discernment helps in reading his partner's moods, wants, needs, and desires which enhances syntony.

Unconscious, unhealthy sexual-syntonic type One, can be either over-possessive of a partner or he can be isolated from intimacy due to an over-critical aptitude. He can pick up the least bit of imperfection, betrayal, wrongdoing etc., in a partner. At his very worst he "imprisons" his partner and become paranoid that the beloved will escape into the arms of another more perfect person.

Type Two: Self-Preservation

In this instinctual subtype the giving/helping nature of Type Two is wedded to issues of self-preservation. This may seem like two opposites who have found union, but it is not. In fact the self-preservation Two knows instinctively that to help others is a means of creating security. Given to avoiding her own needs, the self-preservative Two must either accept her need for security and all the "self-ness" that involves, or repress this need so forcefully that she lives as an unconscious being.

The conscious self-preservation Type Two, is not run by her ego, and therefore she not ashamed to strive for security. She knows that taking care of number one is not necessarily "bad" when viewed as a way to ultimately be in a position to serve honestly. The concept is illustrated by a parent and child on an airplane losing cabin pressure. The parents must place the oxygen mask on themselves first before they can consciously aid their child. The conscious self-preservative Two does not get caught in the trap of service because she knows and openly attends to her own needs as well as others. Through Grace (Holy Idea), her needs are, ultimately, met by God.

The unconscious self-preservation Two who, caught in the trap of service, denies her self-preservative instinct and represses any needs she has. This type of Two is oblivious to her "me first" attitude that unwittingly slips out of her self-sacrificing persona. She meets her self-preservation needs "clandestinely" by manipulating others to meet her needs. Many of these types find glory and control by being of "service" to an "important" person. Thus, this unconscious self-preservation Two operates as the power behind the throne.

Type Two: Social-Affiliation

Type Two's social-affiliation instinctual subtype is a blend of the helping nature with the sense of identity in "belongingness".

This Type Two loves to give and to be loved for his loveableness. He orients his life's energies around these. As a natural helper and giver the Two of this subtype is preoccupied with his place among others. He needs the self-value gained by being appreciated for that place. This preoccupation becomes a major way the Two focuses on others' needs instead of his own.

A Two who has become conscious by going to his healthy soul point at type Four will have great insight into the pitfalls of his social neediness. In knowing how his ego can take over and run his life into a chaotic clamoring for adoration, the conscious Two turns to his Holy Idea of <u>Grace.</u> This idea in whatever form it manifests in his psyche provides the type Two with a solid sense of place in the world. No longer dependent upon the acclaim of others for validation, this instinctual subtype can work with and enjoy people in humility without elevating himself to the status of being "god" like.

Unconscious persons of this Two instinctual subtype are ambitiously making the social climb in whatever context or arena of significance his ego has chosen: church, "society", clubs, sports, academics, professional organizations, politics, etc. By giving and helping he seeks a place of significance and adoration to soothe his insatiable need to be loved. In getting "blessed" by the other "stars" of his chosen arena, he gets a foothold into a life of social significance. He suffers as this glittery life proves empty in the end.

Type Two: Sexual-Syntony

Type Two in this instinctual subtype blends her gift of giving with the issue of interpersonal attraction. Seeing life through the lens of sexuality, couple love, and intimacy, this Type Two finds her self-worth in being deeply involved with partnership. At the bottom of this involvement is the need to be loved by another for what she can give in intimacy and in interpersonal attraction. For many this takes on the aura of sexual attraction and romantic love.

For the conscious person of this instinctual subtype life is focused on interpersonal attraction, yet she has insight into this vulnerable area of their wounding. Not falling into traps of service for partnership, this person builds honest relationships with her conscious needs being put on the table up front. She has knowledge of her own inner attractiveness and is a recipient of her Holy Idea of Grace. This idea relieves her of seeking value through achievement of an ideal romantic relationship and/or intimate partnership. Her supreme value is spiritual attractiveness – a by-product of her living a life of grace.

The unconscious unhealthy person of this subtype is taken over by the externals of intimacy and sexuality. Life can become a game of seduction and being seduced. Self value can be gained through unhealthy "bribery". This type's bottomless pit of neediness is worked out in the arena of attraction to and by others. Suffering occurs as this "game" can never always be won.

Type Three: Self-Preservation

The Type Three's self-preservation instinctual subtype is a mixture of the quest for success with the drive for permanent security. In whatever realm this type chooses to be successful, (position, money, acclaim, material possessions, etc.) he cannot do enough to secure its permanence. Success is equated with status, wealth, fame, etc., therefore all "proof" of success must be preserved and increased, or else he would feel as a failure (his avoidance).

Conscious and healthy types of the genre are alert to the illusion of permanence, and have gone to the spiritual instead of the material to find security. He has placed God's Will (Holy

Idea) above his ego and has turned his need for security into an inner sense of trust in the enduring, unchangeable spirit which underlies all things.

The unconscious Type Three of the persuasion at its worst is trapped in efficiency to continuously provide material and ego security. His frenzied behavior is fueled by the passion of deceit. Life becomes one effort after another to increase and secure the chosen area of "security" (wealth, celebrity, role, possessions, etc.), even if this involves lies, self-deception, or even sociopathic behavior. Much suffering occurs as the perpetual requirement to increase success meets inevitable failure.

Type Three: Social-Affiliation

This Type Three is preoccupied with attaining success and maintaining that image. This Three is continually taking stock of her image. She searches for ways to know how she may be viewed, for she tends to measure success or failure by what she think others' opinions of her are. She is driven to avoid the image of failure and uses the talking style of propaganda as well as affiliations to give the impression she has prestige.

The conscious Three of this instinctual subtype is enlightened about status, and the opinions of others. She has found out how fickle the opinions of others are, and how empty it is to depend on social standing and to rely on ego importance. She has developed ways to transform her preoccupation with people's assessment of her, into an interest in honest self appraisal. Knowing who she is and being a solid person gives her "spiritual success" in achieving God's will, God's work,(Holy Idea).

The unhealthy unconscious Three of this subtype is in the dark about her motives. She thinks the court of public opinion is where she will find success or suffer failure. She is trapped in efficiently arranging image by being with the "right" people and by affiliating with the "politically correct" groups. No real satisfaction is gained, however, because people and opinions are constantly changing. No amount of propaganda or advertising can continuously shape image to cover up the truth: all people have periods of success and failure. She cannot "socially" change truth.

Type Three: Sexual-Syntony

Type Three's instinctual subtype of sexual-syntony is a combination of the drive for success with the focus on sexual prowess and the "dance of partnerships". The main thrust of this type's striving for success is the "win" in areas such as attractiveness, attraction, ideal gender characteristics, desirability as a partner, achievement in intimacy, dating conquests, and other issues of sexuality and partnering. Success or failure is judged through the lens of sexual-syntony.

The conscious Three of this type and subtype is a healthy adjusted person with a healthy sense of his sexuality and desirability. Though he views life through the preoccupation of issues such as partnering, courtship, romance, and finding and building the right syntonic relationship, he has broken the compulsion to achieve in these areas. No longer does his ego require conquests and successes in these issues in order to be successful. He has placed sexuality, physical image, and romantic intimacy in a realistic perspective of sub sets of spiritual attraction, (God's will,God's work, Holy Idea) This transformation elevates the issues of sexual attraction to the essence of attraction between people on the spiritual level.

With the unconscious unhealthy type of sexual-syntony Three, there is a preoccupation with physical attractiveness in its gender and sexual connotation. There is an agenda to shape himself physically and mentally with his idea anima or animus. His success as a person is determined by his achievement of the image of sexual desirability and syntony even if deceit must be used.

Type Four: Self-Preservation

The Four who is a self-preservation instinctual subtype is a blending of the need to be unique with the need for security. This special blend is created like an artist mixing two paints to create a unique "color". The passion of envy is added to this mix as the Four's ego compulsion takes over. Fours envy those who have their safety, physical, and emotional needs nicely and permanently secured. In the quest for authenticity (their trap) self-preservation Fours seek relentlessly to be unique while working to get all security needs locked down. This "impossible" dream drives her either deeper into her compulsion or into consciousness.

For the Four of this subtype who has reached consciousness, there is a healthy view of her blend of uniqueness and security. She knows that she cannot find real security in this place of existence, except in the dimension of consciousness. With this illumination, her compulsion vaporizes into experiencing a security by creating with God through Union with God (Holy Idea). This union brings to her the authenticity so longed for. She is also released from envy.

The Four of this persuasion, is suffering from reckless self-absorption. Her envy is in full swing as she stops at practically nothing in grabbing what she wants and needs. She is unconscious of her compulsion to play the unique victim. She has a ruthless sense of entitlement in procuring self-preservation. She deteriorates in functioning as ego-centricity blinds her to her downward spiral.

Type Four: Social-Affiliation

The instinctual subtype of social-affiliation for type Four is a mixture of being unique with fitting in with others. The Four in this mode is letting his "specialness" be emphasized, even exaggerated, in the social arena. The Four whose trap is in finding authenticity looks to others to bestow this honor upon him. He uses peer affiliations or groups to be the backdrop to highlight and acknowledge his unique authenticity. The person of envy rears his ugly head when others, instead of the Four, seem to gain the reference groups' blessing.

The conscious Four of this instinctual subtype is fully aware of an unhealthy dependence upon others or a special someone to authenticate his uniqueness and therefore validate his "lovableness". As an aware person, he transcends the trap of envy by jumping into <u>Union with God</u>, (Holy Idea), Who then gives the ultimate authentication (blessing). This frees the Four from the suffering of self-absorption and dependence upon a social group for a way to fit in uniquely. He finds the right way to move in the world.

The unconscious Four of this subtype feels defective and is so preoccupied with self and how others perceive him, that he is ashamed that he cannot fit in. He can feel so dejected that this tragic motif begins to take center stage, and he falls into despair. He is given to self-inflected wounds, vegetative melancholia, and thoughts of death.

Type Four: Sexual-Syntony

Type Four's sexual-syntony instinctual subtype is a combination of the unique person and the preoccupation with passionate intimate relationships. This creative individual puts an artistic spin onto love relationships. The Four's trap of authenticity is couched in the sexual-syntony arena as she asks the following question: How may I find that one unique beloved who can know me, partner with me, and perfectly match my special desires and needs?

The conscious Four of this subtype is drawn toward the passionate, sexual games of the art of loving. Her preoccupation with finding complete syntony with another has been exposed to her as an absurd wish. Acceptance of reality and divesting of the ego compulsion, have shown the conscious Four that no one person or small set of intimate friends will ever give her the authenticity for which she yearns. <u>Union with God</u> (Holy Idea) is a portal through which she passes in developing a new consciousness that puts romantic or intimate relationships in a realistic perspective.

The unconscious sexual/syntony Four is suffering with an overactive compulsion to find the consummate lover and savior. This is termed by her as the quest for a rare or quintessential love. This involves drama, exhilarating chases, sexually laced emotional duals for the beloved, and at its worst, a sociopathic pull toward elimination of rivals. This Four hates anyone who would spoil her love life.

Type Five: Self-Preservation

The self-preservation type Five is an amalgamation of Five's being wise, with his penchant for protection of his wisdom. His love and accumulation of information give the Fives a large inventory of this commodity. Yet the self-preservative Five is afraid something or someone will hack into their stockpile. As a result, an entire lifestyle is built upon his strength of knowledge, but he becomes trapped by it as well because there is no way to healthily move in the world without sharing his wisdom.

The conscious Five of this subtype has not given up securing his knowledge; he is just not preoccupied by the threat of losing it. This happens when this Five becomes aware of <u>Divine Providence</u> (Holy Idea), which removes his fear that all his valued knowledge could be "stolen". Knowing that God will continue to provide new knowledge, he can go to his healthy Eight, and speak or write his truth without fear.

The unconscious Five of this subtype is given to obsessing about securing his reclusive mode of living and remaining withdrawn and camouflaged. This guarded vigilance insulates him from the world and reduces him to self stimulation through continuously reviewing his information. He also is reduced to fantasizing as a way to find "interaction". This self-preservative Five deteriorates as he hoards rare things or knowledge. These once made him feel full or sought- after, but now he has no room for others or himself.

Type Five: Social-Affiliation

The social-affiliation type Five is a pairing of type Five's wisdom with her preoccupation with her place in her social group. At first it would seem that only a healthy Five could need people. Yet this type of Five is given to using people to accentuate her domain of knowledge. These Fives are given to becoming experts in certain areas and guardians of esoteric knowledge. For her to cultivate this specialty, she must have people in her life to validate her knowledge. She is drawn to "useful" societies, clubs, publishers, clans, news reporting, literary and library organizations, orders, lodges, etc.

The conscious type of this category is willing to let down her defenses to others, out of the confidence that her contributions of knowledge will always be replenished by God's Providence (Holy Idea). As a result she can embody the healthy Eight and interact with people empathically, not seeing them as objects to secure her standing as a wise expert, but as feeling individuals with whom she may also get personally involved.

The unconscious Five of the social-affiliation type has avarice for social standing centered on what she knows. She is caught in the trap of knowledge because she hoards it, but must share it in order to still have a social place in which to be acknowledged as an expert. By finding such a rare body of knowledge over which she is an expert, her life follows along with the process of withdrawing from real personal involvement with others. She will end up losing the esteem from others she so covets.

Type Five: Sexual-Syntony

This type of Five is looking for someone with whom his intense thirst for knowledge can be shared. His preoccupation with mating, pairing off, and the romantic dance, brings a life of pursuing. Possessing the partner will provide the Five with a person to share knowledge and to fill his emptiness. There is a strong sexual intensity to this relationship, as the Five is generally monogamous and clingy to one person who understands his knowledge base, talking and thinking style.

The conscious Five of this classification is not inhibited but is free flowing in interactions with potential partners, lovers, etc. He has confidence that the best person will come along eventually and he is not a "loser" if things don't work out. He shares his knowledge and is not possessive of his partner because he has found a spiritual source of fulfillment that does not depend exclusively on another person. He relaxes and lets God's Providence (Holy Idea), replenish his knowledge and his relationship.

The unconscious instinctual subtype of this genre is either over-confident with potential lovers, or is very inhibited. At his worst he feels undesirable except to those who can "get into his head" where he feels his real treasure lies. Repressed sexual feelings can be unleashed on a person who he can dominate and own. As he deteriorates, this Five drives away the person he possess because he hoards his partner as he would a piece of knowledge.

Type Six: Self-Preservation

Six at this instinctual subtype is both loyal and hyper-vigilant. These two combine well for the family and friends of a Six, because her loyal watchdog stance includes those in her inner circle. Avoidance of deviance makes the Six extra cautious of being overrun by others who may find out her defects, and "do her in". Therefore the self-preservation Six is ever watchful of the traitor, betrayer, or disloyal person. Fear of not being "preserved" for the Six has more to do with the fear of what people can do to her rather than what creature comforts she may not have.

The conscious Six of this subtype is alert and aware of her fear-based proclivities. Because of this, she turns to God for help in moving through the uncertain world. Trusting in God (Holy Idea) and living in that trust is the way the Six escapes her trap of security. She hopes for everything and expects anything, and that's ok.

The unconscious Six of the self-preservation genre is paralyzed with fear. She thinks others will take her security whether it is a job, a possession, a role, a status, money, etc. She becomes a coward as she, in a paranoid fashion, sees everyone as a potential betrayer. This takes her natural warmth away and reduces her to an anxiety-ridden "Chicken Little" waiting for the sky to fall.

Type Six: Social-Affiliation

Type Six of this persuasion is a fusion of the Sixes' loyalty to group affiliation. Fraternal orders, societies, social clubs, churches, synagogues, mosques, sports clubs, etc. are given to Six affiliate types. Here he is at home because his loyalty can be put into action. His place in the crowd is secured, he loves the feeling of camaraderie and trust, and he can embody a group spirit.

The conscious Six of this subtype is caught in the trap of security, but he knows he cannot look to a group for this. The group mind or its authority figure may be fickle; the most trusted leader may end up as untrustworthy, or the entire group may disappoint him in some way. Therefore, the conscious Six of the social-affiliation type Trusts God (Holy Idea) to be his confidence in relationships and in life. When friends or family betray this Six, he remains courageous and strong. He knows that well-trusted groups are just as vulnerable to emotional and physical violence as are well-trusted people. He does not live in fear.

The unconscious Six, of this subtype, is frightened of being thrown out of the group to whom he has attached. He imagines that some deviance or defect will be used against him and he will be thrown out as a scapegoat into the desert. As a result he attaches to the group's authority figure for protection. He works in a frenzy to please this person and secure his position. He is blindly loyal. In the end he is shunned.

Type Six: Sexual-Syntony

This type of Six weds the following two concepts: loyalty and partnering. The Six is seeking syntony with everyone because of her group mindedness. And for the special person with whom she wants to partner she wants almost total syntony or emotional synchronicity. She is not comfortable if her partner doesn't express acceptance. Fear of her own deviance makes her paranoid. She is scared her partner will see the deviance, hate it, and kick her out. She tends to do everything she can to solidify the relationship and see approval of her in her partner's eyes.

The conscious Six of this subtype is very comfortable with her partner. She is aware of her deviance and defects, yet she also is conscious that this is human. She is loyal and kind to her partner but has learned to courageously "take it" when she perceives she is not desirable. Trust in God (Holy Idea) trumps trust in others.

The unconscious Six, of this subtype, is full of doubt regarding his attractiveness. He may spend lots of time and money on becoming strong and beautiful for he feels he is unattractive. He may over compensate by fixating on image, by being preoccupied with performance and by his own seduction of others. He deteriorates when his efforts prove false and his self image crumbles. He is reluctant to begin again as cowardice and fear take hold.

Type Seven: Self-Preservation

Type Seven combines her love of happiness with her subtype of self-preservation by blending hope, optimism, and happiness with the attainment of comfort and safety. Here, the happy, pain-avoiding Seven translates comfort and safety into forming close bonds with family and in procuring as many creature comforts as she can. This Seven is a glutton for all that keeps herself fat, happy, and secure from loss.

The conscious person of this subtype is aware of her predisposition to plan for the future, to anticipate fun as well as to avoid a rainy day. The Holy Idea, however, breaks the spell of the Seven's ego compulsion to acquire more and more. By going to the contemplative and observant healthy Five, this Seven can relax and join with divine energy in <u>Co-creating with God</u> (Holy Idea). This activity replaces the preoccupation of searching for comfort and safety, because pain no longer incapacitates her.

The unconscious Seven, of this subtype, is driven to secure her space, her relationships, and her safety. She feels she can never be happy without these things preserved. As the world in its many changes, disposes of her comforts and security she has to build it all up again. She becomes manic and unconsciously amasses more comfort and more security only to have it all go away again. She can never attain perfect safety or comfort. This forces her to ask: "Is there anywhere I can live happily"?

Type Seven: Social-Affiliation

This Seven's subtype is a blend of Seven's avoidance of pain with her preoccupation with status and social rank. Her passion of gluttony is manifested in the subtype by her insatiable desire for acceptance by and well regard from others. As a result, she does not flit from place to place, but clings to others who she feels has the position or status she desires. She obligates herself to them as a way to ascend the ladder. She perceives that her highly regarded status will bring freedom from pain. She views social rejection as a highly painful experience. She feels that her social standing and the right friends will bring this. She is willing to sacrifice mobility for syntony with the perfect friend or friends.

The conscious Seven of this social subtype is no longer working for the approval of others. Life has taught her that even being highly regarded, having social rank and sacrificing her wonder lust will not save her from pain. As losses accrue in life she becomes conscious of her soul child, and her Holy Idea of <u>Co-Creation</u>. This divine intimacy transcends all human esteem given by rank and social "acquisitions". She can now travel in a relaxed way, and no longer have to climb.

The unconscious, unhealthy Seven of the social subtype lives in constant disappointment. She is always dissatisfied with the rank or standing she has among her reference crowd. She tries to reach a perfected status, but can never get complete satisfaction. She disintegrates with desperate clinginess.

Type Seven: Sexual-Syntony

Paired with this Seven's avoidance of pain through attaining happiness is the gaining of an ideal romantic life. This Seven does this by planning, traveling, and indulging in extreme fantasy. He is the consummate cosmic traveler whose odyssey is a distraction from the pain inherent in the world of stability. He longs for the perfect partner, but this person is illusive. Distractions inherent in jumping from "one pond to another", keep him from forming deep bonds. He is easily swayed because he lives in the unrealistic expectation that his fantasies will come true. His life is in constant motion swimming along without noticing the tidal wave lurking behind him.

The conscious Seven of this subtype is grounded. Though he loves the ideal, he is claiming his virtue of sobriety by not being gullible or naïve about fantasy. He can find a partner if he goes to his healthy reflective Five and settles down. In settling and Co-creating with God (Holy Idea) he is totally aware of himself, and reality. He can face pain, and get out of the wild goose chase.

The unconscious Seven at this subtype is fragmented, and jumps from one person and situation to another. He is totally alone, with only superficial relationships. Thought of as a drifter, he has no anchor and doesn't even know his fantasies are false.

Type Eight: Self-Preservation

The need to be independent, self sufficient, non-deprived, and safe combines with Eight's strength in this subtype. Because the Eight avoids her own weakness, she in the expression of this subtype, builds a rugged life that seems as a bastion of security and power. Safety is synonymous with the image of the fortress which she personifies by her lust for life within its strong, impenetrable walls. She suffers from the trap of justice – she helps the underdog but vengefully punishes the disloyal wrong-doers. Her reign of terror, meant to do justice and preserve herself, comes to an end when she has driven even her loved ones away.

The conscious person of this subtype has awakened to her misused strength. She has gone to her soul child and has embraced empathy and Compassion (Holy Idea) which she vaguely remembers as once having had. She moves in the world without arrogance, but with the real need to blend strength with giving. She finds real security in living this way instead of by the sword.

The unconscious Eight of the self-preservation subtype is preoccupied with her fortress and her turf. She is a tough individual who doesn't use interpersonal niceties, but tries to get needs met through intimidation and a crusty, even rough, barnacle-covered exterior. She controls others to survive and prides herself on being Spartan. She withdraws her support to punish when others do not comply. This unhealthy Eight is totally alone without receiving the compassion or mercy she is at her barnacle-covered core.

Type Eight: Social-Affiliation

The social-affiliation subtype Eight brings together power and friendship. At the point of strength, the Eight of social-affiliation makes allegiances a natural way to expand his power base. His power usually alienates others, but his buddies give him a feeling of belonging. He wants to have buddies who are strong, but not as strong as he, because he must avoid inner weakness. He will, in the trap of justice, keep these friendships in line with revenge if they betray the fraternal agreement.

The conscious Eight of this subtype allows <u>Compassion</u> (Holy Idea) to enter into his affiliation and social preoccupations, and relationships. No longer is this Eight intimidating his buddies, holding them hostages, or punishing them. There is a live and let live brotherhood, or club in which this Eight can be vulnerable and loved.

The unhealthy Eight of this subtype is lost in the power plays he designed. Brotherhood has turned into a mafia and he is the Godfather. Fear and terror reign as those who were once buddies are marshaled into a battalion around this Eight. All is lost when those enlisted desert their commander. This Eight loses.

Type Eight: Sexual-Syntony

This Eight marries strength and conquest to win the beloved. She desires possession of the body, mind, and soul of the person she loves. She feels she is vulnerable to the deepest of rejections if she loses control over this person. She will be trapped by her sense of justice by going for the jugular of any threat to her beloved. The partner's well-being is just as important as her own. This Eight covers up her weakness by parading her strength and by showing off her adoring partner.

Consciousness is attained when this Eight realizes how self has deteriorated into its own weaknesses. She wakes up to the knowledge that her partner has sacred needs and is a person in his or her own right. Through Compassion (Holy Idea) and giving toward her mate, she finds healthy ways to connect without intimidation.

The unconscious Eight of this subtype dominates her mate, possess and monitors all comings, goings, and even thoughts. She has transferred all her inner sense of power to the romantic relationship because this is where she has felt the weakest. To break the partner psychologically is a typical act of this Eight who'd rather have an obedient zombie on her arm, than a real person. The worst scenario is that she consumes her beloved so much that both are destroyed.

Type Nine: Self-Preservation

This Nine's subtype is a merging of Nine's yearning for peace with satisfying his appetite. This conflict avoidant Nine is hungry and is in need of satisfying that hunger in order to feel peaceful. He associates fullness with being anesthetized. His preoccupations conjure up the image of the pig asleep in the sunshine. The Nine of this persuasion chooses the material over the spiritual because his laziness makes him opt for immediate and tangible gratification. The problem is that this way works for a little while, then wears off, giving rise to the real world that contains the conflict he had hoped to avoid.

The conscious Nine of this subtype has become diligent in forming action plans to find peace. He sees in his Holy Idea of

<u>Unconditional Love,</u> that he is able to face conflict creatively. This empowers him to turn down the self-narcotization of food and goods. He embraces his virtue of active peacemaking to find peace for himself.

The unconscious Nine of this subtype is overindulging. He uses and abuses food and drink to narcotize against conflict. He is deluded that "going to sleep" will bring safety, security and peace. The fat pig in the sunshine ends up on the breakfast table.

Type Nine: Social-Affiliation

This Nine wants to belong but feels awkward and unworthy of the group. Through self-abasement she tries to dismiss the importance of belonging but this doesn't seem to work. This subtype joins the Nine sense of peacefulness with the longing for social-affiliation. She tries to appeal to others through stories, by self-effacing attitudes, and in her harmonious accepting attitudes. This draws people in, yet the Nine of this type has a continuous inferiority complex which makes her so angry at those who would exclude her. The anger is expressed passively and this can alienate the very ones whose acceptance she desires.

The conscious Nine of this subtype wants peace and loving relationships. She knows she cannot have loving harmonious relationships without being able to deal with conflict inherent in all human contact. Being in touch with her <u>Unconditional Love</u> (Holy Idea) from God, gives her the confidence to embrace others without anxiety. She is conscious of this dynamic.

The unconscious Nine of this genre is asleep to life. Through narcotization, detachment, or lethargy, she lacks energy to relate to the others she so needs. Laziness and the feelings of inferiority make her want to sit in her chair alone. Even going through the motions of being with others lacks life and authenticity. Her lazy-boy recliner is her home.

Type Nine: Sexual-Syntony

This Nine finds a union between peacefulness and romantic love. He wants the life and action seen in his beloved. To get this, he detaches and actually merges with the personality of the beloved. He thinks this will bring balance without any conflict, but it can't. When the partner realizes that the Nine has been so lazy that he is living through him or her, a real conflict occurs. This is what this Nine had hoped to avoid by merging. Now he must work through conflict for the couple to survive.

The conscious Nine of this subtype simply goes to his soul child and becomes industrious with action. Loved Unconditionally by God (Holy Idea), he sees himself as separate loving entity too precious to lose his identity in someone else. He maintains his personhood, asserts preferences, makes peace, and enjoys the interchange in his relationship.

The unconscious Nine of this instinctual subtype is in his own world by proxy. He has relinquished his identity in order to hide in someone else who he thinks he can love from his own private world. The beloved soon realizes he or she is merely a fascination for the anxiety ridden Nine. Ouch.

147

Chapter Nine
The Ennea-Types in Cinema

When learning the Enneagram personality types, it is beneficial to observe the flavors of each type and how they express their consciousness and unconsciousness. In this chapter are eighteen type descriptions of characters in various films. Because we so readily resonate with famous character roles and other "iconic" personas, these are helpful in learning type distinction. For example, it is said by some that President Ronald Reagan's style was that of a type Seven in that he was known for his joyfulness and optimism. Some say that Mother Theresa is a good prototype for the healthy type Two in her selfless giving and nurturing of the dying on the streets of Calcutta.

I have found that movie portrayals are very illustrative of personality types in all aspects of their healthy and unhealthy expressions. In the following section, the first set of the nine

Enneagram types are presented. These are the nine personality types depicted in their healthy and conscious level of functioning.

In the second set of nine movie vignettes, the characters depict the unhealthy and unconscious level of the type's functioning.

Though only short vignettes of each movie are described in these reviews, to supplement the learning process you could see each of these movies in their entirety. This way, you may pick up the energy and style of each type in even more particular nuances and details. You may also, by viewing the entire movie, look for complications, inconsistencies, or other "idiopathic" dimensions such as relapses in consciousness, movement with and against arrows, and "the wings" of each portrayal. It may also be interesting to type conscious and unconscious characters according to their instinctual subtypes.

Many of the characters chosen in these movie clips are so well-known that their personas are embedded in the collective psyche of our culture. These famous movie characters embody the archetypal characterological panoplay of the entire global village. These characters and their roles access our own internal familiarity with personality archetypes. A Mrs. Doubtfire, a Scarlett O'Hara, or a General Patton can teach more about their type in one pivotal line of the script, than we can learn in a seminar.

These movies as type selections were first reviewed by a committee of persons well-versed in the psychological and spiritual issues within plays and movies. It is quite possible that you would disagree with some of the typing in this presentation. That is a positive thing, because different perceptions of type create productive conversation in the learning process.

The Conscious Type One
The Sound of Music
Captain Von Trapp maintains a life of order and discipline. He even parents his children in a military like fashion. Once his life is influenced by the hopeful and happy Maria, however, the Captain becomes a healthier Type One. Instead of focusing on flaws, micromanaging and judging others, Captain Von Trapp opens his heart to music, playfulness and romance. Maintaining his gift of discernment the Captain who loved his native Austria does not feel it best that his country joins Nazi Germany. By holding fast to his sense of right versus wrong, Von Trapp makes the hard choice to secretly leave his homeland with his family. He would rather leave his status, possessions and home than live under a regime that he feels is wrong. By going to his soul point, the healthy Type Seven, this character combines his sense of right and wrong with hope, optimism and lightness of heart for the future.

The Conscious Type Two
The Miracle Worker
Annie Sullivan, a healthy, conscious Type Two, is the dedicated teacher of the blind and deaf Helen Keller. Even upon her arrival she lets it be known how eager she is to begin her work with her new student. Her healthy Two character immediately portrays her giving nature by blending teaching with giving the gift of a doll she had brought for Helen. Having a deep understanding of her own makeup and needs, Annie has great insight into her innate will to serve. The film shows how Annie does not let ego overtake her humility; this movie shows how Annie is willing to stop her teaching of Helen, if that is the family's choice. In the scene with Jimmy, Helen's brother, at the cottage window, she recounts the pain of her past and the

zeal she has now for helping others come out of darkness. At the bottom of her motives is the will to never give up. She says, giving up is her idea of what the original sin was. Annie was honest with her hope that Helen would one day love her, not as a mother replacement, but as the special teacher she was to her. In the end Annie receives love and respect from Helen. By going to her soul point at the healthy Type Four, Annie exemplifies being conscious of her own needs. While meeting these needs she is able to unselfishly help Helen, even if it meant that she might not receive the love she had hoped for. The excitement in Annie's face at the well depicts beautifully the holy empathy of the conscious Type Two.

The Conscious Type Three
Erin Brockovitch

This film typifies a Type Three's talking style called propaganda. Near the beginning of the movie Erin is "selling herself" to a would-be employer. Notice how Erin uses attractiveness, image and her assets to land the job she seeks. Being a conscious Type Three, she maintains honesty, as she promotes her talent. She is truthful, even about her weaknesses (but she puts a positive spin on those so she "looks" even better). The second scene clip shows Erin's heart for people and her ability to feel their pain. This is a hallmark of the conscious Type Three who escapes narcissism and ego centricity by reaching for a higher mind and a higher will. The movie depicts healthy Type Three's competitive nature and how it can be used for the good of others. The reference Erin makes to David and Goliath reframes competition as a "righteous battle." The Three's aggressive nature is also portrayed. Notice how she leverages her achievements by using efficient strategies. The story line shows Erin with her boyfriend and illustrates the healthy Three's satisfaction is securing a win for herself and the community. Being admired for a true win far exceeds false admiration for winning through deceit. Erin has gone to her point of integration at the healthy Type Six by assuming the characteristics of loyalty, integrity and family/community mindedness. In the final scenes the reward of Type Three's goal accomplishment is shown as she accepts her bonus without clamoring for the ego's lime light.

The Conscious Type Four
Miss Potter

Miss Potter is a natural born artist. A writer as well as a watercolorist, one of her most endearing features is her colorful and vivid imagination. This film beautifully shows how her illustrations "come to life" on the paper and how her writings are playful, interesting and full of joy and wonder. As a Type Four, with a propensity for sadness and withdrawal, Miss Potter did have the signature tragic motif appearing in her life. When actual tragedy does occur, Miss Potter is first given to being an unhealthy Type Four. With the help of a friend she goes to her soul point of the healthy Type One and takes the right course of action. She conquers grief and melancholy by swinging into the right causes of publishing for children as well as preserving the environment with the proceeds from her success.

The Conscious Type Five
Yentle

In the beginning scenes, Yentle is portrayed as having an insatiable love of books, learning, observing and collecting knowledge. Her passion for these is so great she goes into camouflage and assumes the identity of a man. Her need for wisdom and knowledge caused her to forsake her own gender to become a student of Rabbinic Law. As this Type Five grows in a healthy sense of self, she integrates at the healthy Type Eight. The power of the healthy Eight combined with her wisdom brings her out of hiding strongly into the real world around her. Yentle is a healthy conscious Type Five speaks her truth and embodies it. As she travels to a new life among new people she rises above the compulsion to merely fill her inner emptiness and yearns to be aloft with wisdom and strength. "Papa watch me fly."

The Conscious Type Six
It's a Wonderful Life
In this movie a man is filled with the anxiety and fear of a Type Six. A family man, he displays average Six behavior in his loyalty to others and his concern for his village. When things get tough, his anxiety is overwhelming. He fears his own defectiveness and deviance. On the bridge he thinks of jumping in the freezing river to end his misery. Instead, he becomes conscious by seeing the realities of his own inborn courage and worth which no one can take from him. In the end, his knowing what means the most to him overrides any fear. George finally finds that he is loved in his own right and goes to his soul point of the healthy Type Nine by living out an inner confidence and sense of ok-ness. No longer is he feverishly pleasing others to ensure his place. He is a living embodiment of the courage he had once lost.

The Conscious Type Seven
The Big Chill
In the movie's beginning, friends have come to mourn the passing of their dear friend Alex. Notice their frank, soulful

discussion including tears, intimate disclosures, pain, anger, remorse and humor. These people, though good friends, are joined in observing sadness. They do this in a healthy way. They have combined levity and joy with pain and grief. The Type Seven energy of this group is conscious and healthy because they have gone collectively to the soul point of the healthy Type Five who can observe, process and be with whatever is. Watch for how these friends celebrate consciously and even in loss are hopeful and optimistic. Watch them dance, eat, sing, play, and mourn.

The Conscious Type Eight
Patton

In the first scene General Patton is instructing his troops. The aura of the powerful Type Eight is palpable. This commander is bold, direct and highly decorated. His language is powerful and exudes the gutsy passion of vengeance. This leader, who uses strength and graphic descriptions, is a leader who seeks justice while protecting those under his care. His speech engenders bravery and a crusading spirit in his troops. In the scene in which he visits wounded troops, he has gone to his integration point of the healthy Type Two. Here he is demonstrating empathy, humility and the sanctity of relationship. Note his compassion.....note he kneels before the wounded soldier.....note he whispers in the dying soldier's ear.....note his tears. This man is an embodiment of power and compassion.

The Conscious Type Nine
The Secret Life of Bees

The mother figure in this film is August Boatwright, who delights in nature. She is at one with the mysteries of the natural world including the secrets of the lives of bees. August speaks in ways that bring harmony and balance. For example, she makes statements throughout the performance, that bring peace instead of conflict such as, "the color of the house doesn't make any difference." "I loved him enough to marry him but not enough to lose my freedom." In the movie, the child's daddy returns angrily to retrieve his daughter from August's house, where she has taken refuge. August does not react to the father's aggression. Watch her as she consciously responds. August goes to her point of integration to the healthy Type Three by setting the goal of accomplishing peacemaking. She harmoniously diffuses the explosive enmity between father and daughter. When the father said he was taking his daughter, Lilly home with him, August did not confront, resist or counter his argument. Instead she responded by respectfully referring to him as "Mr. Owens" and by announcing to those present that he was Lilly's father. She then calmly spoke of how well Lilly is loved at their home and if she stayed she would be taken care of and sent to school. Her disarming statements were as swift and powerful as Solomon's sword. Her natural peacemaking worked.

Ennea-Types In Cinema The Unconscious/Unhealthy Types

The Unconscious Type One
Doubt
Possessed by judgmental criticism, control of others and hyper-vigilance, this scene depicts a Type One at its point of disintegration. This nun, unconscious of her motives and compulsions, engineered the removal of Father Flynn from his post as priest of the school. When she accused him of child molestation she had already condemned him in the court

of her own mind. Believing in the infallibility of her own judgment, she had no doubt, about the guilt of this priest. She became judge, jury and executioner simply through her over-vigilant and over-active radar for wrong-doing. Innuendo, gave her probable cause for a rush to judgment. Becoming so trapped in seeking perfect righteousness she stepped away unconsciously from her own sense of morality. This scene shows the nun in the despair, unhappiness, self doubt and alienation of the unhealthy Type Four. Even with her self-doubting, her tears and lies for the sake of goodness, she remains rigid in living out her self-made interpretation of right and wrong-doing.

The Unconscious Type Two
Jolene

In this film, the extremely unconscious Type Two is depicted by Brad as he manipulates his way into the life of Jolene. Using the powerful techniques of feeding, charming, flattering and showering with gifts, this unhealthy Two completely seduces this woman to fall into dependence upon him. He gains total control. The pride of an unhealthy Two is portrayed by Brad's assumption that he knows what she wants and that he can provide it. He does not take no for an answer and lavishes Jolene with false admiration and a premature proposal of marriage. Also of note, is Brad's precocious intrusion into the religious beliefs of Jolene framed in a manner of "great concern" for her spiritual welfare. His Type Two control energy can be seen in how he treats the hired musical ensemble at his contrived roof top dinner. Pulling the carpet out from under the musicians is an unhealthy Two's typical response of withdrawing support from those who are no longer needed. This means that Brad has gone to his point of chaos by assuming the characteristics of an unhealthy Type Eight. In the end, Brad's wooing of Jolene had nothing to do with empathic or altruistic love, but everything to do with being trapped in unhealthy service for selfish gain.

The Unconscious Type Three
Gone With the Wind

Scarlet is the quintessential efficient goal achiever. Even if she has to become as someone else other than herself, to get what she wants, she will play the role expertly. Coming across with a certain image is so paramount for Scarlet that she will even use deceit to accomplish her goals. Scarlet's chameleon-like aptitude is portrayed beautifully in the scenes she pretends to be well-to-do after she has lost her fortune and status. Throughout her dialogue she propagandizes what she has to "sell" to others. Her hot pursuit of what she wants, including another woman's man, is accomplished with precision. Her passion to avoid failure at all costs is encapsulated with her words, "I'll never go hungry again." The overriding need to avoid failure and to win over everything is featured in the scene on the steps after being rejected by her husband, Rhett Butler. Unconscious that she has lost the most important things of all, her integrity and her family, she continues seeking success and new challenges. Scarlet has reached her point of disintegration by going to the unhealthy Type Nine. She has become slothful, detached and asleep to her own efficiency and sense of loyalty.

The Unconscious Type Four
Vincent

This movie is of the life of Vincent Van Gogh. It is done in a verbal monologue of his letters to his brother. The vivid words scream of the preoccupation of Vincent with the defective, with the inconsolable suffering, and the depression of an unhealthy Type Four. He says of this depression, "I must forget myself in my work or it will crush me." Such an observation made by this artist depicts the acute self absorption of a Four who has gone to the neediness and self gratification of an unhealthy Type Two. Vincent's letters to his brother are also indicative of the disintegrating Four who goes to the unhealthy Two's search for someone who will truly understand him. At its most unhealthy form that Four will envelope this person in a symbiotic union. The dismal language of Vincent drones the melancholia of the disintegrating Four. Also portrayed are the unhealthy Four's feelings of superiority, specialness and uniqueness as he alludes to ordinariness as being "inferior." Vincent's references to suicide toy with this notion almost as an escape. He says, "My pictures are a cry of anguish." His writing about profound resignation to suffering and death is a constant theme. The four hands of his Pieta are representative of the hands of an unhealthy Type Four reaching, however frustratingly, for their authentic life never to find it. Finally, Vincent recounts in some of the last lines of this segment. "Nothing could have pleased me more than never to awake again ...... too overwhelmed with grief.....too hard a life to die for...surroundings weigh on me more than I can say." These statements are illustrative of the disintegrating Four who, in the path of least resistance, can no longer stay out of despair.

The Unconscious Type Five
A Christmas Carol

Ebenezer Scrooge is an unhealthy Type Five who has retreated as a recluse into a false security of his own self made world. He shuts out the real world by doors and locks while the emptiness he fears abounds within his soul. While lapping up his soup as if to fill his inner void, the look on Scrooge's face reveals his bottomless inner black hole. Note the scene in which Scrooge sees the painting of the Last Supper on the tiles of the fireplace above him. This image highlights the irony of Scrooge's abject emptiness underneath the painting of a holy supper that does fill its partakers. The disintegrating Five's lack of attention to outer appearances is well represented by the cob webs hanging in his home. The ringing of the bell announces the intrusion of the real outside world upon his self-made world of fantasy. Scrooge never invites intrusion because he will be overwhelmed by it demands. Living in his mind, not his body, his head is filled with fantasy which has now begun to turn against him. Scrooge mutters to himself, even dialoguing, with his own imagined world. This disintegration to the unhealthy Type Seven is depicted by his living in fantasy. Scrooge depicts the miserly, stingy Five who saves and hoards in hopes of filling that emptiness. He fears giving anything to anyone because if he does, there will be even more emptiness inside.

The Unconscious Type Six
Joyeaux Noel

In this World War I theater of battle in France the conscious healthy chaplain wants to stay with his troops he accompanied from his parish in Scotland. The visiting Scottish Bishop thinks that the chaplain is a traitor by having performed a religious Mass for the German and French troops on Christmas Eve. Representing the religious establishment, the blindly loyal Bishop is an unconscious Type Six who views the world as a "we versus they". By going to an unhealthy Type Three, this Bishop has disintegrated into the frantic efficiency and frenzied "accomplishing" of an anxiety ridden Type Six. He states that to protect our clan we must kill and that killing should be done with the greatest of enthusiasm. His myopic view of goal accomplishment to please authority, forgets the broader consciousness of peacefulness. The Bishop is trapped in a world of group egos who challenge other group egos for superiority. He is so frightened of "the others" that his paranoia and fear bring him to preach that killing is what you do to enemies.

The Unconscious Type Seven
Mrs. Doubtfire

The father in this movie suffers from a strained marriage. The pain of this problem is denied instead of faced by this man. Denial is his manner for all unpleasantries of life. For example; he vaporizes the fact he has just lost his job by denying it to his children and happily changing the subject. Consumed with the spirit of "let the good times roll", he lavishes a birthday party upon his son who knows he doesn't deserve it because his grades are bad. Making his own fantasies come true, the father plans an over the top party for his son. This party occurs in mom's absence, under the guise of "While the cat's away, the mice will play." By going toward disintegration this father takes on the characteristics of the unhealthy Type One who seeks perfection. In this case, perfection is translated as perfect denial, perfect happiness and perfect ego gratification. When caught by his wife the father says he was planning to clean it all up before she got home. Planning is the ego state of a Seven given to disintegration. As Mrs. Doubtfire, the father, in the unhealthy state of denial, portrays the unhealthy Sevens' gluttony and over-indulgence.

The Unconscious Type Eight
The Devil Wears Prada

Miranda's outrageous demands purposefully belittle others. Ruling through intimidation, this central character does not consider others as much as her own vision and arrogant control. Person's names do not matter for people are simply pawns to be used in the strategic game of the fashion world. The unhealthy Eights incite fear into their kingdom's servants. Dismissing others quickly shows how easily this powerful, unhealthy Type Eight can withdraw support from anyone who bucks them. The scene in which Miranda speaks of her girls' piano concert shows how she would fire her loyal secretary Andi "if things didn't go as she wished". Miranda could not bear to see others' weaknesses. Seeing Andi's weaknesses enraged Miranda. Unhealthy Eights cannot face weakness in them or in others. Notice the scene in which Andi overhears her powerful boss being reprimanded by her own husband. Andi was treated with vengeance for having heard this conversation.

The Unconscious Type Nine
The Color Purple

We witness in this film the excessive passivity of an unhealthy Type Nine portrayed by Albert. He was expecting his girlfriend Shug, but instead, Shug arrives with a new handsome husband. Even in this dramatic change of circumstances we can observe the unhealthy detachment and emotional paralysis of the unhealthy Nine. He stands passively on the porch while his girlfriend and her new love flaunt their relationship in front of him. Further deterioration of the Nine is shown when Albert is overwhelmed with anxiety at the mail box when he notices the bullet holes. See the paranoia and fear take over. To deal with anxiety there is a major shut down in his functioning. His fields are overgrown, animals are unattended, his house is a wreck and he is self narcotized with alcohol. Refusing advice to take action he says, "There ain't no life here, just me." Albert has gone to the unhealthy Type Six who is overwhelmed with fear. The destruction of the unhealthy Type Nine is brought about though detachment from reality along with is self narcotization. These dimensions are depicted when Albert under the umbrella is drunk and unaware. Indeed, he is in his own world.

Chapter Ten
The Emergence of Consciousness

When do we become aware.... fully aware? We never become fully aware of everything because we do not have infinite capacities. However we have the power to awaken from a type of anesthesia that has caused us to go to sleep to our real life and to reality. Becoming aware of our purpose, to the blockage to living out our purpose, and to the divine connection of all things, are awarenesses that come from enlightenment or consciousness. There are various stages of becoming consciously aware.

The following stages are those that we follow in becoming aware. These stages are experienced differently by everyone, yet no stage can be transposed with another, for each is a layer of experience which gives birth to the next. The archetypal image of the tree tells the story of the emergence of consciousness. Like the proverbial tree, consciousness begins at the roots of being and proceeds up the trunk until the branches appear. The branches give structure for the flowering of consciousness. The stages symbolized on the trunk must come before consciousness can flower.

The ego is necessary for the person to develop. This tree diagram (Figure 9) illustrates how the ego identifies with its compulsion before it goes through the suffering and search for relief of the ego pain. The search yields the discovery of the all important portal or opening through which the person must pass in order to reach the realm of consciousness. This is discussed by Anthony Stevens in his book, *On Jung.* "For most men and women the midlife transition is marked by various kinds of upheaval, and, disagreeable though these disturbances are, they do have the psychological advantage of providing stimuli sharp enough to wake one up, (for one has to wake up if one is to individuate). This is particularly true when crisis hits dramatically – as for example when one loses one's spouse or one's job". (1)

For most, the process of suffering is what motivates the search for relief. There are some exceptions to this. Some persons have been given the gift of enlightenment spontaneously without a suffering preceding it. These instances seem very rare. Another exception is consciousness coming to children or younger persons before the ego suffering has begun. In these instances, there is a premature onset of the sense of mortality imposed by life-threatening circumstances such as war, imprisonment, illness, or abuse, etc.

Most persons have to wrestle with their ego, its fixation, and the results of egoic based living. Egoic thought traps people into a false identification out of which many have lived their entire lives. For these people, the suffering never got unbearable, or if the suffering was great, it may not have been enough to cause the person to search for relief. This tree diagram shows the path of spiritual transformation of people whose suffering has indeed given them the "good fortune" of searching for the portal to consciousness.

Figure Nine
Stages of Consciousness Emergence

THE FLOWERING OF
CONSCIOUSNESS

RETURN TO
ESSENCE:
CONCIOUSNESS

THE PORTAL
OF SELF
REMEMBERING

SEARCH FOR
RELIEF

CRITICAL
MASS OF
EGO SUFFERING

EGO
SUFFERING

EGO FIXATION
AS
WAY OF LIFE

EMERGENCE OF
EGO-FORCE

FIRST WOUNDINGS
AND
PERSONAL SHAPING

ESSENCE IS SOURCE
OF IDENTITY

SOUL BORN INTO BODY

Stages of Consciousness Emergence
Stage 1 – Soul Is Born into Body
Soul, the essence of our being, enters the world with us to embody and emanate divine intelligence, over flowing love and immortal spirit. In its innocence, the little child uniquely expresses these soul dimensions as one of nine broad ways to "be" in its new world.

Stage 2 – Essence Is Source of First Identity
As a small child, our essence, rooted in soul, springs forth our unique personality. There are nine basic soul energies that express our essence. Of these nine, only one is "the match" that best expresses each person's individual essence. This one particular soul energy gives us a way to express our essence identity and begins to move us in the world. The nine soul energies are: 1. Growth, 2. Grace, 3.God's Will, 4.Union With God, 5. Divine Providence, 6. Trust In God, 7. Co-creation With God, 8. Compassion, and 9. Unconditional Love. (2) Please see Chapter Thirteen on The Holy Ideas for a more in-depth explanation.

Stage 3 – First Woundings and Personality Shaping
Essence is slowly covered by defense mechanisms that protect it from soul wounding. Wounding, whether it is gradual or sudden, comes in the form of rejection, abuse, reward, punishment, abandonment, negativity, misunderstanding, etc. Parents, peers, schools and culture consciously and unconsciously influence and shape the child to abandon his or her essence. A thought-based personality adapts most readily to the demands of the world, protects its vulnerable self, and gradually becomes the child's central focus. It becomes the command center for negotiating with a world that has lost the value of essence and relies upon thought.

Stage 4 – Emergence of Ego Force

The new "central command" or the thought- based personality, replaces essence as the way to move in the world. The soul based life force is "forgotten" as the child now believes his or her ego IS their central command. The world reinforces his/her adaptation to the new command and the child uses it to avoid being further wounded. The central command continues to preserve self and evolves as an ego that administrates self preservation and self gratification. This ego is identified as the self.

Stage 5- Ego Fixation as Way of Life

Ego becomes the primary mode of self preservation and self fulfillment. Thoughts and material forms are used to create more ego identity. An ego based story is conceived and the ego force exerts itself to build its own universe. Others are seen as characters or ego attachments which have "scripts" in the ego story. That which is owned or sought, such as people, possessions, status, roles, positions, etc. is representative of the ego identity with which one now identifies. One of nine basic ego identities captivates us. It becomes a false identity that is a reaction to the loss of essence and is fixated upon the completion of ego's aspirations. The hope is that the ego will come to fulfillment and realize its full identity in its self made story. People and things are forced to become what the ego fixation needs them to be. Life's energy and thought go into satisfying the ego fixation. Successes and failures occur. Successes in defending the ego and in materializing its story gratify the ego. Failures to do so cause pain. The nine Enneagram types and their basic ego fixations are: 1. Ego-Resentment, 2. Ego-Flattery, 3. Ego-Vanity, 4. Ego-Melancholy, 5. Ego-Stinginess, 6.Ego-Cowardice 7. Ego-Planning, 8. Ego-Vengeance, and 9.Ego-Indolence. (3)

Stage 6 – Ego Suffering

The ego fixation takes a deeper hold as one becomes more fully identified with it. In early adulthood the ego fixation's successes seem to help confirm that it is working for the person and that indeed he is composed of his ego. The failures of ego are easily dismissed because he knows of no viable way to be other than that to which he has already identified and begun to build a life. As the failures mount, the fixation's inherent trap sabotages him and causes him to fight the disintegration of his identity. This tension causes suffering in relationships, faith, behavior, self concept, one's story, etc.

Stage 7 – Critical Mass of Suffering

As life progresses, the impermanence of all ego supports, (people, things, power, wealth, status, position, etc.) becomes more obvious. The realizations that she has no ego safety and that there will be mounting losses as life continues, puts her on shaky ground. Add a crisis on top of this and she is convinced for sure that she is not a ruler of her own universe. Having an ego support that is indestructible is found to be an illusion. By now the ego's original story is shown to be unlike what reality has spun and even the achievements of the ego have not brought us the consummate fulfillment they promised. Ego and its false identity cannot alone heal the suffering of mounting losses. A religious faith or spiritual path which had been subsumed as an employee of ego doesn't work because their real boss (ego) is now incapacitated. Ego can deny its own collapse and the suffering that causes it, the person can leave, or she can search for relief.

Stage 8 – Search for Relief

One needs another way to move in the world. One can no longer take the pain and disillusionment of the ego. The search may remove faith and spirituality from the dictatorship of ego and let them "speak" for themselves. Now there is openness to spirit's message in whatever way it chooses to manifest because there is an ultimate receptivity to trans-ego help, even to the Divine.

Stage 9 – *The Portal of Self- Remembering*

The receptivity one now has to the Divine message attracts him to the very opening or portal he must go through to escape the imprisonment of the self-made "me". The portal is an opening that is actually made of his suffering, but transformed in some way, to create a new way to live. When he remembers his essence, his true self, he can live out of <u>that</u> being instead of ego fixation. The essence is what provides the receptivity to the transformation of suffering into a new way of life. This is his passageway to his freedom. The soul revitalizes as one's nature is once again expressed in its truest form.

Stage 10 – *Return to Essence: Consciousness*

The life that had been lived up to this point, has passed through the portal of self-remembering of its essence. This life has its own wisdom learned from the gathering of its ego force all the way to its being demolished. This wisdom is alchemically united with the essence. The result is the emergence of a new consciousness. This new alive awareness of life spirit, purpose and the divine source is no longer veiled by ego. This new consciousness brings awareness of the divine connection of all beings as well as life's relationship to this living planet. This consciousness replaces the pre-occupation with self, with thought and with material form as the bases of reality and embraces the <u>source</u> of all being as the ultimate reality. One is alive with the knowledge that living in the present, not the past or the future is the way of living consciously. As one grows, one flowers in consciousness.

Chapter Eleven
Christ, Children and Consciousness

The Zen Buddhists have a question that helps us understand that we are spirits before we inhabit the body. To this end the Zen Master asks, "What did your face look like before your parents were born?"(1) Somehow we are able to understand that question and until "rational" thought takes over, we indulge ourselves in imagining that spiritual picture of ourselves. What is it that allows us to accept, even for a moment, the idea that we are primarily spiritual beings who temporarily occupy a body? Could it be because we once lived exclusively out of spirit in our first years of life?

To gain a glimpse of our own spiritual picture, all we have to do is look into the eyes of a very young child. The deep connection to the divine can be readily noticed if you have the eyes to see it. There is an implied trust reflected in these eyes, as well as a presence of overflowing love. The future, the past and the ego mean nothing to this child – all is about expressing in the present moment, the needs to love and be loved. There is also a divine intelligence in this young child's presence; not the measurable intellectual quotient, but because of innate trust, there is a transcendent knowing that all life is spiritually one.

Along with the child's soul dimensions of overflowing love and divine intelligence, is the transcendent dimension of immortal spirit. Exuding from this little child is the undying spirit of its very own soul. The soul does not depend on ego, on words, antics or even on personality traits. The characteristics of the soul transcend personality. The soul is the silent, yet expressive presence of the child and is her only way to "be" when she first enters the world. One has only to hold a little baby in order to "listen" and "see" its soul. As they grow, words may become part of their expression, but the words too come from soul, not ego-thought. Their honesty, simplicity and innocence are but a channeling of the divine energy through their presence.

The child's soul dimensions of over flowing love, divine intelligence and immortal being express themselves in the soul through one of nine holy truths. These three dimensions correspond to the three basic centers of the Enneagram described in Chapter Two and displayed in Figure Five. Overflowing Love is the pure soul dimension of the Heart Center; Divine Intelligence is the pure soul dimension of the Head Center; and Immortal Being is the pure soul dimension of the Gut Center. The nine holy truths, called the Holy Ideas, are also described by Peter Hannan as the nine faces of God.(2) Jesus Christ spoke of these same nine truths in the Beatitudes.(3) The Apostle Paul describes nine corresponding fruits of the spirit. (4)

The nine basic personalities of the Enneagram, in their truest sense, are formed as reactions to the forgetting of our essence and its Holy Idea. This essence remains at the core of each person for their lifetime even though it is slowly veiled by the layers of ego personality (the false self.) This essence is said to be on "our face" even before our parents were born. It is also this essence to which we must return if full consciousness is to be reached. William Law, professor of theology at Cambridge in the early 1700s, strongly influenced the theology of his day. He spoke of the phenomenon of the soul's existence before it enters the body. "The essences of our soul were a breath in God before they became a living soul, they lived in God before they lived in the created soul, and therefore the soul is a partaker of the eternity of God and can never cease." (5)

Most people have lost touch with their essence (also called the soul child). Jungian analyst Marie-Louise von Franz summarizes this aspect of returning to childhood in the following, "The child is an inner possibility of renewal. But how does that get into the actual life of an adult? ...whatever else from which the child may suffer, it does not suffer from remoteness...it is fully alive". (6) At critical points in life, or at times when suffering is overwhelming, a spiritual search for that aliveness referred to by von Franz, can replace the ego's compulsions. Yearning for fulfillment and peace increases as the sense of mortality becomes more real. This is when people many times yearn for and search for their essence, even if they have not used the word 'essence'. The phenomenon of returning to childhood is wonderfully portrayed in the modern screen play and film, "The Trip to Bountiful." (7)

Inherent in the ego's effort to make the person's life "work out", are the dangerous traps found in each of the nine ego compulsions. Why must we ever "leave" our inborn essence (soul child) and cover him or her over with an ego and the inherent traps of egoic living? The answer to this lies in the early wounding of our soul and psyche. As a young child, there is a life changing trauma or a series of psychic wounds that occur. The pain of this wounding is so great that the child naturally compensates by protecting its vulnerable self. Depending upon what type of energy (of the nine basic energies) one is born with, a corresponding ego defense emerges to cover up and protect the vulnerabilities of the essence. Each of the nine pure expressions of God in the soul child (Unconditional Love, Growth, Grace, God's Will, Union with God, God's Providence, Trust in God, Co-creation with God and Compassion) is covered by its corresponding ego defense that replaces essence with a false personality. (see Chapter Thirteen, The Enneagram of Holy Ideas) The ego defense seems to protect the person so well that she identifies with it and loses her essence, or soul child. The defense develops over the years into an entity all of its own.

As the soul child is forgotten, the identification with the ego expands. As the person clings to the defense and diversifies it, there is a fixation upon the ego defense. This is called the ego compulsion. One of the nine ego compulsions each person shifts toward, and identifies with, finally covers up the soul child. The transitions from essence (soul child) to ego fixation are as follows; From a pure expression of Unconditional Love to Ego Indolence; From a pure expression of Growth to Ego Resentment; From a pure expression of Grace to Ego Flattery; From a pure expression of Living out of the Will of God to Ego Vanity; From a pure expression of union with God to Ego Melancholy, From a pure expression of God's Providence to Ego Stinginess; From a pure expression of Trusting in God to Ego Cowardice; From a pure expression of Co-Creation with God to Ego Planning; From a pure expression of Compassion to Ego Vengeance.(8)

Each of these ego fixations is a thought form and is a natural defense of the wounded and hurting soul child. Each replaces the soul child's pure consciousness with ego and its unconsciousness. As the ego compulsion is embraced it envelops the person and differentiates within him. Eventually each compulsion also differentiates its wings (auxiliary functions) its instinctual subtype and its level of integration vs. disintegration. (See Chapter Seven)

The fully engaged ego compulsion is said to be unconscious because ego has assumed such a blinding self serving place of prominence that the divine is at best an "employee" of ego. A collapse results as the losses and stresses of life eventually prove to be too much for the ego compulsion. The traps of each ego compulsion compound its great suffering. The suffering rebounds as the ego uses its same familiar defenses to assuage and reduce it yet the suffering only compounds and intensifies. When a critical level of pain is sustained the person begins searching for relief and longs for a peaceful life without suffering. Deep within is, at best, a vague remembrance of how life once was and how living was once not about ego. For some the remembrance is very vivid. For the searcher, there is a yearning for living an unburdened life once more and he or she is wants to return to "live there" again.

The Essence and Ego in Christianity

Jesus Christ spoke about suffering and what must be done to prevent it. He offers the kingdom of Heaven as the solution. Jesus knew that most people would eventually get to this place. He was describing the answer to suffering in terms of returning to one's essence when he spoke of childhood.

Matthew 18: 2-6

And calling to him a child, he put him in the midst of them and said, "Truly I say to you, unless you turn and become like children, you will never enter the Kingdom of Heaven". (9)

According to this passage, children are what we must become like (again) or we will never enter the Kingdom of Heaven. How much more explicit can Christ be? The kingdom, which is the spirit-filled conscious life, can be gained only by becoming the child we once were.

Matthew 18: 10

"See that you do not despise one of these little ones, for I tell you that in heaven their angels always see the face of my Father who is in heaven". (10)

Here we see Christ referring to the soul in terms of immortal spirit. He speaks of the close relationship children have with heaven's messengers (angels) as they always see what humans cannot: the face of God.

Mark 10: 13-16

And they were bringing children to him that he might touch them, and his disciples rebuked them. But when Jesus saw it, he was indignant and said to them, "Let the children come to me, do not hinder them, for to such belongs the kingdom of God. Truly I say to you, whoever does not receive the kingdom of God like a child shall not enter it." And he took them in his arms and blessed them, laying hands on them. (11)

In the Gospel of Mark we find Christ emphasizing the mind of the child as belonging to the Kingdom of God. The importance of children (and the qualities they represent) was made clear as Christ was indignant that the disciples were dismissing what was actually essential. Again it is written that in receiving the kingdom of God, like a child, is the way to enter it. How do children receive things? They receive with an innocent and pure reflection of God within them. Christ did not say the way to enter the kingdom is through perfection, self-glorification, adult ingenuity, ego defenses or intellect.

Paul wrote the following reference to the child in First Corinthians 13: 11-12.

When I was a child, I spoke as a child. I understood as a child: but when I became a man, I put away childish things.
For now we see through a glass darkly; but <u>then</u> face to face; now I know in part, but then shall I know even as also I am known. (12)

In this passage Paul could be transmuting the phenomenon of childhood essence being replaced with adult egoic thought. If decoded to explain a return to essence, the passage may be understood in the following way:

"When I was a child, I spoke as a child. I perceived life as a child out of a close, unbroken connection to God. But when I became an adult, I put away childish things in favor of adult defenses and aspirations. As adults we see things unclearly but then (when we were children) we saw things <u>consciously</u> without the blinding ego. As an adult, I know only partially the truth but then (when as a child again) I will be fully aware and conscious even as God is fully aware of and conscious of me."

If the portal, or gateway, to return to our essence is, in fact, our own childhood, the birthplace of our soul child, we can go through that holy opening to live in a new consciousness (the kingdom of heaven). Christ tells us that this kingdom is <u>within us</u>, and is not a physical place, but a state of consciousness. The soul child can help create this consciousness if we can <u>re-member</u> him or her.

The process of re-membering is aided by the Enneagram which tells us who our essence is by showing us our Holy Idea. How our essence was expressed pre-verbally will be expressed somewhat differently from its verbal expression. Both are essentially the same because they stem from the same Holy Idea and the virtue of the ego type. For example: Type Sixes find their essence at the healing Type Nine by using their Holy Idea of Trust in God.(See Chapter Thirteen) By using their virtue of <u>Courage</u>, they can make the trip against their arrows to re-incorporate their "lost" divine characteristics (found in their soul child) into their total being. These divine characteristics are called The Virtues. (See Figure Three-The Enneagram of Virtues) All this is done by the person who now has wisdom learned through the life and the suffering endured in the ego compulsion. In summary, the person alchemically re-integrates his soul child into the wisdom he has learned in life. A new unique creature is formed. (See Chapter Fifteen – Return to Essence)

By reading the descriptions of our Soul Child (in the next chapter) and by remembering our first selves, we can begin to reconstruct our essence. A photograph of ourselves as a baby or young child will reveal this spiritual presence within us. By looking into the eyes, we may be able to see the reflection of God.

Chapter Twelve
The Soul Child

Deep within us there is a little child. The spiritual teacher A.H. Almaas is the originator of a widely used term for this concept: the soul child.(1) This child is our first self.…. our real self and forms the essential makeup of our soul. Everyone's soul child is unique, just as each flower, snowflake, tree or animal is different from all the others of its kind. Uniquely expressing God, this inner child is fully transparent to the Divine.

When we came to life on earth we entered as our child. Being fresh from heaven, we were so linked to the Divine that we did not even know of a separation between us and God. Living only in the present moment, our soul child was undistracted from pure conscious being. Without being immersed in thought, our soul child simply expressed three divine aspects of God: overflowing love, divine intelligence and immortal being. The soul child knew no other way to live except by being an embodiment of these three properties. They are natural and require no work or thinking. He or she not only embodies but expresses these properties by allowing God to shine through them.

There are nine basic categories of soul children based on the nine pure expressions of God. The soul child is not primarily driven by ego; he or she radiates life by expressing purely divine properties. In babies and very young children divine innocence and purity are evident. Just look into the eyes of children to see the soul child shinning fully and freely. The light of pure consciousness can readily be seen in the very young who have not yet been "introduced" to the darkness of the world.

Year by year, as the child experiences the world, wounding and pain occur. An emerging ego becomes a protective covering for his vulnerable soul child. The ego becomes so well developed that the soul child gets completely covered over and is sealed inside the protective covering of the false self. Eventually the covering becomes stronger and the major focus of the developing child. As essence of the person (their soul child), becomes obscured it can rarely shine through. One is so identified with his/her covering (the ego) that they think they <u>are</u> the covering. Identification shifts to the protective covering rather than staying with the soul child. With increased identification with the ego, the soul child goes to sleep and is forgotten.

In actuality, the person has forgotten their true self (essence) and has identified with a false self. This false self, unconsciously, becomes fixated on repetitive behaviors to satisfy the ego's fears and desires. These repetitive behaviors are called ego compulsions. Just as there are nine types of soul children, there are nine corresponding types of ego compulsions, (protective coverings). The ego's compulsions bring about an accumulation of negative consequences as life unfolds. These eventually present unavoidable personal disintegration and pain which form the basis of the emerging life dilemmas: How can I continue to be as I am, and also continue to bear this repetitive pain? What can I do now to get fulfillment? I know that I cannot bear this suffering anymore; how can I find relief? How can I reverse the disintegration I have been experiencing? The ego's compulsions are found to be useless in achieving the ego's desires, so now these new and pivotall questions arise.

Self-Remembering

An awakening must occur to stop the painful cycle of suffering. Old ways of finding comfort are abandoned in searching for relief. The person wants peace and a passageway to wholeness. Many in this phase feel that they long for the days when things seemed uncomplicated, and when they lived with joy and contentment. This signifies a longing to return to essence, to their truest nature, when they felt the bliss of being one with creation. This longing for re-connection to our essence gives us new eyes and new ears with which to experience our world. It's the longing to return to our soul child. The ego longs for contentment which it has confused with satisfying the desires of its compulsions. Only when the compulsions are abandoned can the soul child be awakened. This is called self-remembering.

To find our soul child we look to the point of integration of our type by going against the arrow pointing to our type's number on the Enneagram. The healthy aspects of the soul point or point of integration are our essence, or soul child. Reintegrating the soul child into our conscious psyche becomes our spiritual practice and is a portal to consciousness.

Jesus referred to this portal of consciousness when he said, "Truly I say unto you, unless you change and become like little children, you will never enter the kingdom of heaven." (Matthew 18:3) (2) The person re-members their soul child again as they change to become as a little child: one's own soul child. However, reuniting with the soul child makes a new creation, which is a combination of one's pure essence with the wisdom gained from the suffering of one's ego. Living out of this new creation brings consciousness or the kingdom of heaven. The kingdom of heaven is now where we live, move and have our being.

The following are nine descriptive narratives of each soul child. Of course, not every child exactly fits the examples presented. The descriptions can, however, offer broad illustrations of how each of the nine soul child energies can be expressed in an individual.

Type One's Soul Child

You will find the soul child of type One being a free spirit. He can be found most often having fun which most children are apt to do. For this soul child however, the fascination with fantasy, imagination and joy runs very deep. This soul child enjoys life to the fullest, resisting sleep and wanting to stay up so that he misses nothing.

She will want new and exciting toys, colorful things, and will have a hopeful and joyous attitude. She is not preoccupied with the mundane or routine. She loves breaks with the routine, and loves people. She is ever so extroverted, making friends easily and reaching out to others not so much for relationships as for the doubling of enjoyment because it is shared. She values special occasions and delights in any celebration. Indeed all of life is to be savored and here for her enjoyment.

He can rarely be discouraged. He has many interests and wants to learn new games, hobbies and pass-times. He can be seen giggling and laughing uproariously as his zest for life is his passion. He cannot get enough of it. He looks to the morrow with optimism and hope. Somewhere over the rainbow is an appropriate theme, for bed is welcomed only as a doorway to the activities of tomorrow. He is easily distracted from the negative. The colors and the activities of living are like Christmas morning awaiting him each day. Adventure, exploration, and planning are his passions. This soul child seems to shine as he makes things, like God is "helping" him.

When the inevitable wounding attacks the soul child, he clings to the compulsion of Type One: to be right; to be hard working, and to avoid the inherent anger of having his passion cancelled out by his environment, his authorities. Now it is not acceptable to be frivolous, fun-loving, and optimistic. In fact, to be so invites disdain from the world which he now experiences as survivable only by the strength and power of being precise, correct, and within proper standards. Rightness must now supersede hope and fun. The tenants of right versus wrong now take center stage as the need for perfection replaces the fun-loving nature. Only through the tiring of his/her stilted compulsion, will the One finally rediscover that fun-loving and hope-filled child. Embracing the essence of the soul child is the only way for the One to discover the highest form of perfection, which is the expression of optimism and hopefulness. The remembering that no one is perfect, that we can relax and enjoy the process of life because it is really about growing, and that happiness and hope are essentials for life, are the keys to the One's integration of soul.

The One's soul child is not ashamed to laugh, play or have fun. Judgment of self and others are replaced with a childlike quality of acceptance of others as players in the great party taking place.

The One is now freed from having his nose to the grind stone all the time. Thanks to his soul child, who was suppressed all his life, the One now sees the future as full of promise, hope and growth.

Type Two's Soul Child

You can see the soul child of type two as a budding unique self with a passion to follow his own drummer. Not given to any pre-existing norms, this child makes his own way apart from any cookie cutter pattern. He is artful, passionate and longing for self-expression. You can watch him be the one to choose the toy no other child chooses. You can see him playing alone in his imagination or with others thinking up some different way to play. He knows just what he needs and wants, and he is not ashamed to get these.

She will not fit the mold in temperament or behavior. She may want to wear different clothes, or none. She may want to bathe in bubble bath and request her special music to bathe by. She may be given to eating "odd" foods on her own schedule. She may want her bed placed at an angle to see the morning sun come through the curtains in a particular way. You can find her arranging the dollhouse and picking out the décor for each room just as she pleases. She will be interested in the forlorn, the animals, the un- wanted in the shelter, or the whales whom she hears are endangered. She is particular, knows she is special, and spends much of her time reassuring herself that this is true.

He longs for someone to truly understand him, but does not want to be pigeonholed. He has a lust for life in his own unique fashion and doesn't like others to outdo him in this department. When they seem to outdo him, he gets even more creative in ways to be unique among the crowd. His want for others' uniqueness or for their unique things, is not yet envy. He doesn't know envy as yet, however he feels "funny" when out done in his own arena of "specialness". When asked where he comes from he says, "From heaven" and seems to remember it.

She focuses on the creativity along with the emerging gift of helpfulness, which is but a seedling of what it shall be once the wounding is finished. Knowing what is needed and the how she can be of service she still chooses creativity as her over-riding passion. Once the wound occurs, (the wound here is the message that uniqueness is not valued) the Two's soul child defends herself with the compulsion of the Two: to be a giver, to be of service, to avoid her own needs. Somehow she has gotten the message that her creative passion is wrong, an unacceptable way to be. She takes up helpfulness as a way to move in the world. This soul child senses she must never again experience unleashed, uncontrollable creativity. This soul child goes dormant only until the type Two rediscovers her, and allows her the supreme gift of unique self-expression while claiming her own needs openly, unashamedly.

The Two's soul child, if the Two can finally accept it, gives the Two the ability to focus on his own life, and his own needs. This develops the personality as a person who dares to give with boundaries and with limitations, and without giving out of desperate neediness. Now, thanks to his soul child, the Two can accept his own needs as valid, and his own life, not the lives of others, as his main project.

Type Three's Soul Child

Type Three is the person of success. She is the prototype winner, the best of the best. The Three, however, is at its core a child of duty and loyalty to the pack. She is more interested in the family and community than in self-promotion. What does the Three's soul child look like?

She is a person on the playground who always wants to be chosen to be a part of the team or the game. She does not want to be the star or to bring attention to herself as much as she wants her friends to value her and include her as a member of the gang. She will not pick friends to get her anywhere, or to be "seen with";

she wants her friends to always be there for her and to be invited for a sleepover.

She is aware of the importance of keeping herself safe. She does not want to risk life or limb. Going down a high sliding board is approached with caution. She would much rather have groups over for games and food. When one of her friends is hurt she will want to kiss the hurt. When parents are not well she will want to "cook" breakfast for them even if it is cereal and juice. She wants to please her authorities, because she needs them to approve of her and to protect her from the unknown. She will not often stray from parental authority; she will be obedient and carry out the parental or teacher requests. She planted seeds one day and afterwards said, "I know these will grow into big watermelons."

He is given to being "cute". This attribute gives him a harmless aura, that is no threat to anyone; he is loved by all. Emerging is the Three's need to accomplish and the giftedness of multiple personas, but this is to gain favor more than to deceive. At the point of wounding, the soul child goes away. No longer are the pack and the authority crucial issues. These are replaced by the quest for success. Others are not seen as benign brothers and sisters of a pack, but are seen now as competitors for the prize. The need to win and to be best, sets the Three apart from the crowd, and removes him/her from the need to appease authorities. The soul child's need to see himself as part of the family, the community, etc., is now replaced by the Three's drive for accomplishment and the avoidance of failure. Only when the Three sees the damage he has done to himself and others in using any means to succeed, will he re-discover that true happiness and fulfillment lie in the return to integrity and the core consideration of the people around them.

When life shows the Three that a breakdown of accomplishment is at hand due to the immense stress it places on the psyche, the soul child is able to be remembered. This little soul child with her loyalty to the family, the pack and the community, reminds the Three of what is real (truthful). Real is the need to be accepted as one's true self, not as one who is accepted for one's successes. Remembering one's allegiance to those out of whose context she comes, puts the Three into contact with her first truths and her belonging to something greater than she. Now the drive to succeed can be fueled by the storehouse of energy supplied by the loyal interconnection of persons and their systems. True success can now be accomplished.

Type Four's Soul Child

Before the Four forgot her essence, she was a rather precise little person. She knew so very much and seemed to go with an inner knowing. She was beyond her years in the ability to see the essentials of things. So many times after she would speak, adults would say: "Out of the mouths of babes come words of wisdom". She was particular with needing things to be "just right". She would, for example, want her sheets to be smooth and unwrinkled, her stuffed animals to be in a certain order, and her bath water to be at a certain temperature - no hotter, no cooler, with just the "right" amount of bubbles. She had a concern that things be done by others in a particular fashion. Like a sheep dog, she could be witnessed herding people into the room for a birthday party or into the car to go somewhere. She could be hard on herself when she didn't do things by her own criteria, like crying at the "wrong time". Yet she could always change her attitude toward happiness and not dwell upon the critical.

She was the one who even as a baby seemed to know the appropriate expression to place on her face at any given time. And she would, as she grew, be able to bring confusion to a halt by naming the source of the problem and by saying how it could be "mended". The light of discernment flowed freely from her face, and the fire of her inner knowing burned brightly within. In all her innocence, she never turned her gift of knowing into bossing or ordering others; she merely spoke her truth never doubting that others would value it as much as she, for truth and order seemed so natural to her and so valuable. She just knew everything was just the way it should be even if temporarily, it didn't seem to be.

He was wounded by those in his life who were opposed to his way of moving in the world. They poured water on his bright fire. When they came cracking down upon him in his wisdom, he learned that his way was not valued, that it was even chided, so he "forgot" his wise ways, his sense of discerning the right path from the wrong path. Instead he found a way he could not be squelched - a way no "pot shots" against his sensibilities could take him down. He became, therefore, not so perfect, less exact, almost "odd". He could not be categorized easily and he sought to be special. This way, his freeform artfulness gave him expression. His wound became his personal tragedy that no one could question. If they did question him, they were amongst those who just "couldn't understand" such unique suffering, such special ways of moving in the world. Along with this defense, the emerging Four, lost his fire, lost his essence of connectedness, and longed for an ideal relationship with someone who would understand him

By remembering his brilliance and gift of discernment, and by acknowledging his own wholeness (not perfection), this type can find purpose and connectedness within rather than from without.

Type Five's Soul Child

This child came here with a sense of power and strength. He knew he was strong because he had an unbendable will. He tried very hard to be the leader, and was fearless in learning new things and conquering new territories. He saw others struggling to be leaders, to take control, yet he knew ways to eclipse their efforts; with one natural move or proclamation, he could be ahead of everyone. He knew how to care for those weaker than he, whether it was a younger sibling or even a bird with a broken wing. He had a great desire to seek new domains. Even on the play-ground he could be the master of the monkey bars or the leader of the team. He could even feel the power attributed to the bully. He wanted much, and could hardly do enough or own enough. His strong self was tempered by his knowing his own terrors, his own weaknesses. He was very compassionate to those who were hurt or weak.

In his innocence, he made judgments of how things should be carried out in his own domain, in his family, and on his teams. His strategy was to make judgments based on compassion and to be the strong little Eight who took responsibility to see that those plans were carried out. Identifying with the adult power person or leader in a group, he aligned with them in order to operate from the established power base. The older he got, the less he needed to identify with an adult, because he now had his own power base. At first he identified with the coach and echoed him…then he became the powerful team leader in his own right. Emerging with loss of innocence was a distinct understanding of his own weakness but he covered these with his strengths.

These weaknesses, together with her strengths were not acceptable to those in power over her. She then developed a way to protect herself, by withdrawing and detaching. This way, she could still have power, but it was over her own inner life, which she as a Five developed with mental and fantasy gymnastics. Emptiness was now the inner void, which comes as the Five's detachment and withdrawal as an observer, steal the soul child's lust for life, and the strong involvement with the external world.

With the remembering of the soul child's passionate involvement in life and the power once championed naturally, the Five can use the wisdom gained, by moving strongly in the world. This movement into the external - this sharing of self is the fulfillment of the void which plagued the Five for his/her lifetime.

Now the Five can move powerfully into the world and become involved with her brothers' and sisters' lives. Books and wisdom, observation and saving, are building blocks for a stronger way to give, to bond and to share with others in a strong influential way.

Type Six's Soul Child

The Six's soul child has an essence of calm and peacefulness. Anxiety is not part of the picture, for the soul child is beset with wonder and adventure. She lies lazily with her back on the soft grass making clover chains, whilst the bees buzz around her. Knowing she is safe and secure, she gives her handiwork to her friends and even to her dog and cat. Crowns, necklaces and bracelets are for all. This soul child sees the dark clouds in the distance, yet she focuses upon the white puffy clouds billowing in front of her; she sees elephants, faces, clowns, and knights with armor. As the thunder gets louder, she sinks deeper into the clover, which shields her from the quickening breezes. Nearer the padded ground she feels the safety of mother earth enveloping, grounding, strengthening her. She doesn't flinch when the sprinkling rain begins to fall. She sees the rainbow which she acknowledges would never have appeared if she were not on the edge of the looming storm. Rainbow, storm, darkness, light; she sees the value of them all and relaxes into the great and wonderful mystery. She knows she is loved, unconditionally.

She always feels the mystery. It makes her happy, and full and free, and it makes her want others to feel this. She has known this for a long time, forever, and she wants to tell you this face to face, away from any doubt, fear, or worry, away from anticipation of disaster. Into that heavenly country she goes, where the ground of being is safe enough, where the trust in God is so apparent, that anxiety is not known, only the peace that this soul child was born in and lives in. There is no fear of the inner indolence, in fact, it is embraced, and out of it comes calm accomplishment rather than laziness. This soul child is so grounded in peace in her strength and trust, that she knows these are part of her. These qualities blossom in use for creativity not for defense. She can be a beacon of peace to her pack, leading out of trust in God, versus banding the pack together out of fear. She is loyal, not out of duty, but out of sheer respect for the others' true essence, their expression of their own connection to God, however they conceive God to be. She is playful; not to escape condemnation or annihilation, but playful out of relaxed love's longing for itself. She is able to build industrious groups because the peaceful nature attracts others into systems of creativity and building which require much cooperation. She never needed an authority figure to hide behind, or to rebel against, for she never let fear into her soul. She therefore let the ground of being be her authority, and she never pulled her ear away from the heart beat of the earth upon which she laid. She let her connection with nature be so strong that God was her authority and so she led others and herself deeper into the mystery.

When her wound occurred, she lost memory of peacefulness. To survive, she replaced peace with vigilance and clinging to others' protection or she became a dare devil to defeat her fears.

Once her soul child is rediscovered, the Six can relax. Fears and doubts of the world are replaced with the soul child's inner connectedness to the ground of being. This confirms to the Six that she is an indispensable part of creation to be held by it and in it, not as an alien, but as part of the entire realm of being. This soul child's essence gives the Six the courage to become her unshakable self. She is now peaceful and whole.

Type Seven's Soul Child

The soul child of the Seven is the keen observer, the quiet reflective collector of knowledge and wisdom. This child is gifted with deep inner knowledge and has a thirst for exploring the inner world of the mind and spirit. The Seven's soul child is born into the space of wisdom and yearning for knowledge. She is seen at the ocean's edge, reading books, which feed her spirit and explore the spiritual dimensions of her inner space. She is able to move in and out of her reflections and meet others; she is even able to share with them her wisdom. She gives selectively, for she has the innate need to save. She doesn't yet know the pain of fear or of deprivation. She is so enamored of the wonder of God's wisdom that she makes life an adventure into this world. Emerging is an essence not tainted with avoidance of the sameness, the repetitive rhythms of the universe, or of human pain involved in the death and resurrection in life. Rather, her wise and creative essence is used to provide wonder and fantasy.

The inner wellspring of divine knowledge and revelation from heaven would never have been unless this soul child had been so meditative. Contemplation let her delve into her inner being, that dark mossy place where in the damp and dark, new life is spawned. This soul child knows this secret and does not avoid the dark, damp and painful. She knows the value of new life and the all-pervading deepest happiness of co-creation. She gives birth, he gives birth, even in pain and does not want to escape life by "lily pad hopping" when the labor is seemingly too great. She sits with pain until the new life emerges. The solution is not found in the bottle, the needle or in getting "more and more." It is the <u>knowing</u>

which keeps her truly happy. She is completely transparent to God, and awaits God's bounty expectantly.

And so, the Seven is, at her deepest core, the little Five who is not yet compelled to avoid pain and to seek distraction through gluttony, the novel, or constant movement. This child is wise, reflective and creative. When she was wounded her reflective, observing, and powerful mentality, were forgotten. She began to grasp movement and superficial fun as ways to protect her, and to avoid pain.

The Seven finds healing in remembering her soul child, and incorporating her aspects of reflection, and studied wisdom into the personality. This soul child seems so foreign to the Seven, because of its seemingly boring exterior. But if the Seven can remember in the now the days of quiet, the fear of pain and deprivation will evaporate. As the world opens up the cornucopia of rich spirituality, far superior to constant hyperactivity of mind and body, the Seven becomes whole.

Type Eight's Soul Child

This type's soul child is the vulnerable giver. Inside the Eight is the hidden Two, who wants to give and to supply to others. He is an innocent giver who has not yet developed a manipulative motive for giving. He is a little person within who has been anticipating others' needs and fulfilling them for the sheer joy of giving. This giving, at its core, is a focused way of experiencing essence, for to give is to have life. Giving to others in big or small ways is an outlet for this soul child's emerging self, for to give is to express this child's true nature, true power.

She needs to be loved, to have affection and most of all to have a relationship with the other. Not to give would isolate her, and remove her natural inclination to build relationships through serving. She may come to you offering her cookie or a taste of her glass of milk, for in sharing she can be connected to you. She may have her feelings hurt if she is not acknowledged for her giving or her offering, but she is not developed to the point of knowing her power to stop giving or to withhold (if things don't go her way) is a grand control mechanism. She basks in the innocence of vulnerable self-exposure. She wants to give what is hers, risking others' rejection, or the devaluing of her gifts. Nevertheless, she walks up to you to show her precious treasures and to offer one or even all to you. She wants to help therefore she can be experienced as the parents' apprentice or assistant. She knows when someone feels bad because there is a budding empathy for others. Therefore she gets the pillow for you or she merely says, "You feel sad?" She will cheer you up and give you laughs. She will want to make your load lighter. She will want to be valued for her service and will try to find her true place in helping. This is when she is truly happiest, because she then belongs to you, and you belong to her, in a wholesome reciprocity. She does not know any shame in her vulnerability, but is needy of love and of validation. She is grounded in freedom, and in an inner knowing that she is a recipient of grace.

This endearing personality is a powerful entity for he makes himself integral to his surroundings. The emerging powerful self has no disdain for weakness in self or others. He has empathic feelings for the underdog or those who are helpless. The tender heart of this young giver is what is hardened when the wound occurs, and instead of vulnerable giving he resorts to invincible power as the defense. He vows that weakness shall ever be seen again. Dominating power takes center stage. Reality is seen as a fight rather than as a love feast. Never yielding to self-exposure again, this soul child becomes an ironclad powerhouse. Then this soul child goes into supreme hiding and repression, until he can one day be known again after the powerhouse kills its own inhabitant. Now alone, he has the opportunity to invite the soul child back again with the acknowledgement of his own neediness and vulnerabilities which make him open to others' involvement or help, and in helping others. Now the power learned in Eight space is alchemically united with the extension of his own self to meet the needs of others, without denying his own.

Type Nine's Soul Child

Within every Nine is an industrious heart, full of ideas about accomplishment and bubbling with achievements. This child was an achiever before she "went to sleep". Always striving to be first and to throw the ball the highest, the Nine's soul child naturally succeeded. She was an actress able to dress in appropriate clothes for her role. She may have asked for a crown for her birthday or have yearned for first place among her siblings in the race for her parents' affection or attention. She was quick and able to know the most efficient strategy to come in first or to achieve stardom in her little world. She could do things quickly and could catch on to the "system". She was able to be attractive and colorful, and could find ways to gain applause.

She was keen on entering projects. It was natural for her to build the highest Lego tower, or the largest city of blocks. She wanted to run fastest and to walk and swim before she could. She would be seen outreaching others when teachers or parents were giving out things. She was not intolerant of others' needs, yet her zest to be there first was as inherent as was her sperm's diligence in penetrating her egg. She was masterful in getting things done. She was always hopeful; she prayed at bedtime to do God's Will.

He could present himself in many ways to achieve a delight in his admirer's eyes. He could be an angel, a gardener, or a salesperson. Any personage, he could bring to life out of his repertoire, he would. Whatever it took to win you over, he would become. Fear had not yet taken hold of him. His personas were still child's play designed more for winning you over than to pull the wool over your eyes. He was busy because there was much to do, much to build, to win, and to make; to be. The wound came when this little person felt it was no longer acceptable to be this way. He relinquished his accomplishment for the sleepiness and dissociation of the Nine. He was angry that he must shut down his busyness, yet even the anger was suppressed and buried as the sleep took over and as the anesthetized personality found refuge in detachment, complacency and in seeming not to care.

The integrating Nine who achieves consciousness, must remember his soul child's sense of self. This sense of self-hood is the way a Nine no longer has to negate the feelings of being somebody. Self-abasement and belittling are healed by the passion of the soul child who accepts self without the ego trappings. The unconditional love of the Nine has burned away his self-abasement. Now the Nine can see himself in his own right as one who can accomplish openly. This gives life and energy to the person who fell asleep long ago.

A Prayer for My Soul Child

Oh, God, I have lost a
part of myself. It is missing, long gone
into an abyss of silent darkness.
The veils of shame and knowledge
drape over this pure part of me – this
lost portion of my soul. I weep with
grief as the veils are lifted and I
see this orphaned child. Pure light
is this holy being. This child of mine
knows no hate, or fear, or rage.
I see this part of me, oh God, as
immortal being, overflowing love, and
divine mind. My God, my God,
I need this child of mine.
This chaos and suffering have to end.
I see the destructive pattern.
I need my fully created self. Unveil my
child, Dear God, and through
the love of Christ, re-member
this child into my soul. Let me
once again see through those deep, pure
eyes which reflect your radiance.
Let me come unto You
as a child comes, for this
is Your way.
Restoreth my soul, Dear God.

~Amen~

196

Chapter Thirteen
The Enneagram of Holy Ideas

How awe-inspiring, that born within everyone, are nine spiritual truths that are the fundamental principles underlying all reality. And how amazing it is that within every person, one of these truths inherently predominates to form the core of that person's essence and spiritual nature. It can be said that the Holy Idea is indeed, the "essence of one's essence".

When we begin to journey toward our essence, we return also to our Holy Idea. Once this idea is re-membered and embraced, we can make the Enneagramatical journey to the other Holy Ideas. Remember, all the Holy Ideas are inborn and available, yet one particular Holy Idea is our essential nature. As multi-dimensional truths, the Holy Ideas expand consciousness with each integrative journey around the Enneagram. We are spiraled on each journey to a higher level of consciousness. We become more steeped in being, and in living as our enlightened nature. The concept of the spiral in development of human consciousness is outlined by Don Beck and Chris Cowan in *Spiral Dynamics*. (1)

Reconnecting with our essence and Holy Idea is like noticing a new bud on a plant. This bud holds the full flowering to come. The spiral movement upward toward consciousness is like the bud's unfolding. The more it unfolds, our increased consciousness spirals upward into enlightenment. With each spiral turn upward we come to know our Holy Idea in a deeper, more essential way. (See Figure 11).

As we travel the Enneagram of Holy Ideas in the direction of integration, we assimilate into our spiritual being, each of the Holy Ideas. This alchemical process of assimilation creates a completeness of our spiritual nature and an alignment with pure consciousness. The completeness or wholeness of being along with pure consciousness, allows us to experience true being without the burden of personality, its ego, the fixations of personality or the suffering that comes with all of these.

It is clear that our type and its Holy Idea are confined to the points and passageways of the inner triangle (9, 3, 6) or to those of the hexad (1, 7, 5, 8, 2, 4). In light of these separate paths, how is it possible for a person to assimilate <u>all</u> of the Holy Ideas into their being? The answer to that question begins by reminding the reader that all of the Holy Ideas are already within each of us, just as all the personality types are within everyone. All the Holy Ideas come from the endowment that human beings were given as part of reality. This is a gift of grace called "beingness", with love being its primary substance.

There was however a loss of contact with our "beingness" (or our essential nature as humans). This is sometimes referred to as "the fall". The predicament of humanity caused by a disconnection from its true nature is an archetypal theme in many religions and belief systems. This true nature espoused by most religions, is love and the pure bliss of being made of love. Holy Love is the

Holy Idea of point Nine. It follows then that point Nine's Holy Idea is so fundamental that it can be said to be the "birther" of all the other Holy Ideas. Humanity's separation from Holy Love which is the substance of all "beingness," is the fall itself. Each Holy Idea is a "child" of Holy Love and represents a particular aspect of that Holy Love as it manifests in being. In their having been forgotten the nine Holy Ideas are replaced by the ego. As we learn, however it is not possible for the ego alone to re-establish the divine connection. It is the soul which must return to its essential nature and its Holy Idea in order to be grounded in being once again. In the process of alchemical transformation, the ego can be a tool of the soul. If the loss of consciousness is "the fall", its regaining can be called the restoration of consciousness.

The Holy Ideas are "brothers and sisters" who all come from the same birth parent, "Love". As close relatives they carry aspects of one another within themselves and therefore, have wings in each other and are wings to each other. Whether a person is on the inner triangle or on the hexad, as they travel the Enneagram of Holy Ideas in the pathway toward integration, they make the spiral climb of their journey either through points 9, 3, 6, or through 1, 7, 5, 8, 2, 4. Because of the shared natures of the Holy Ideas, persons of the inner triangle or the hexad will re-incorporate the same wholeness of the Holy Ideas into their soul.

Can a person disintegrate on the Enneagram of Holy Ideas by flowing with his arrows as he does on the Enneagram of Personality? This could happen only if the Holy Ideas had aspect that were inherently disintegrative (such as with each of the personality types on the Enneagram of Personality). The Holy Ideas however, are embodiments of spiritual truth. Therefore by following the pathway of disintegration on the Enneagram of Holy Ideas, the person would not regress toward any inherent negativities within the Holy Ideas. They would simply encounter another spiritually pure Holy

Idea. In the philosophy of Holy Ideas the disintegrative or negative movement as such is the result of the person's FORGETTING his Holy Idea. He then proceeds in forgetting the other Holy Ideas in the journey of disintegration around the Enneagram. The pattern of disintegration in the Enneagram of Holy Ideas would be as follows: the person on the primary triangle would first forget her essential Holy Idea with which she came to earth. Then she would go with her arrows along the pathway of disintegration on the Enneagram of Holy Ideas, repressing or forgetting each of the other Holy Ideas as she disintegrates through loss of consciousness. For example, a Nine would begin the process of becoming unconscious by first forgetting her Holy Idea of Holy Love. She would then digress to forgetting her Holy Idea of Holy Faith at number Six. Then she would disintegrate in forgetfulness (or in unconsciousness) even further by forgetting the Holy Idea at point Three, Holy Law/Holy Work/Holy Hope. The same process of forgetting is followed of course by those on the hexad.

The Holy Ideas are the essential component to finding and re-membering one's essence. The Holy Idea is the spiritual word, or logos, for each individual. The word of the person is that which forms their deepest spiritual purpose. Therefore, this word is the invisible substance of the essential nature of the person as a manifestation of the One True Source. Our having been created with a word breathed into us at our making is a principle in the Gospel of John when it is written, "In the beginning was the word and the word was with God, and the word was God. He was in the beginning with God" (John 1:1-2). (2) In this scripture it can be said that God's "core" or essence is the word, just as we (made in God's image), have a word at our core. Our word was with us from the beginning and it was our being, it is our Holy Idea. We are it again, when we remember it and when we remember the essence of ourselves to which this word gives life.

Figure Ten
The Enneagram of Holy Ideas

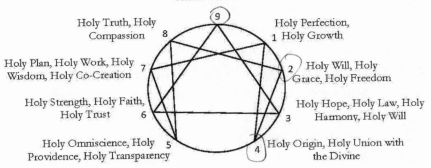

Holy Love, Holy
Unconditional Love

Holy Truth, Holy
Compassion

Holy Perfection,
Holy Growth

Holy Plan, Holy Work, Holy
Wisdom, Holy Co-Creation

Holy Will, Holy
Grace, Holy Freedom

Holy Strength, Holy Faith,
Holy Trust

Holy Hope, Holy Law, Holy
Harmony, Holy Will

Holy Omniscience, Holy
Providence, Holy Transparency

Holy Origin, Holy Union with
the Divine

Figure Eleven
The Spiral of Consciousness

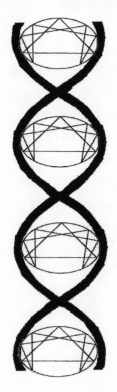

The Holy Ideas

The soul unites with the body as the body is formed and becomes the essence of life for the emerging being. Coming from the One True Source of all being, the soul transmutes through the human being, the pure consciousness of the One True Source. This soul consciousness is the essential nature of the person and remains at its core even as the personality structure develops around it. Essential nature is expressed uniquely by each being. The basis of essential nature springs from a particular word or logos placed in the soul at the persons making.

There are nine such essential such words which are spiritual ideas of pure consciousness. These ideas are aspects of the Divine that are so fundamental, they are non reducable. Each soul contains all of these nine ideas, however each soul's nature arises from one and only one of these nine ideas. This is called the person's Holy Idea.

How can we understand these nine ideas as being consciousness emptied from the Divine into humanity? This is best explained through analogy. The One True Source of all being, (or pure consciousness) can be compared to the sun's pure light. When the sun's light shines through a prism, it separates into various colors. These colors are always the same, are related to one another and emanate from the same single source of light. This process of light shining through a prism is analogous to the transmutation of the One True Source of all being into humanity as separate aspects of its consciousness. These aspects are constant, are related to one another, and emanate from the One True Source of all being. This thought was expressed by James Martineau, Christian clergyman in 1879 in his book, *Hours of Thought on Sacred Things.* "Were our heaven never overcast, yet we meet the highest morning only in escape from recent night; and the atmosphere of our souls, never passing from ebb and flow of love into a motionless constancy, must always break the white eternal beams into a colored and tearful glory." (3)

The optical spectrum illustrates this concept. In physical science the optical spectrum is composed of nine different colors. (red, orange, yellow, green, blue, indigo, violet, infrared and ultraviolet). All of these colors are from the same one source of light. Similarly, there are also nine fundamental spiritual truths which all come from the One True Source of all being. Expressed through human beings, these are called the Holy Ideas. How or why a human's soul is "assigned" a certain expression or route spiritual nature is not known and has been a matter of theological and ontological study. According to the Enneagram's theory, the human being's personality type is determined first and for most by the one Holy Idea placed in her soul from birth. Like the optical spectrum, each Holy Idea has its own "color" or aspect expressing a quality of its Divine source. The inherent Holy Idea and its influence in determining the personality of an individual is a pivotal concept. We will explore this subject later in this chapter.

The Historical Background of the Holy Ideas

The Holy Ideas are essential spiritual truths that were given their current terminology by the South American teacher, Oscar Ichazo. (4) Ichaxo is reported to have learned the Enneagram in the middle of the last century from a secret mystery school in the Middle East called the Saramoui Brotherhood. It was this mystery school which reportedly also taught the Enneagram to George Ivanovich Gurdjieff, the first Westerner to discover and teach the Enneagram. Ichazo, who later founded the Arica Institute in Chile is the first teacher to define and explain the Holy Ideas as part of his knowledge of the Enneagram. He had reportedly collected this information from his visits to the Middle East and from his studies of ancient wisdoms. The Holy Ideas began as early Greek philosophical precepts. The philosopher, Plato, wrote of certain divisions of higher universal truths (the Divine Forms; the

Platonic Solids). Plato derived a classification that later influenced the evolution of the Christian "Cardinal Virtues". Plato's virtues of temperance, prudence, fortitude, and justice, are associated with classes of people in the city described in The Republic. (5) Basic ideas were later developed and expounded upon in a more definitive was by the Neo-Platonist, Plontonus (205 -270 A.D.) in The Enneads. This work was compiled by his disciple, Porphyry, and was composed of six groups of nine treatises. (6)

In short, the early and later Greek philosophers, who were influenced by Persian and other Eastern philosophies, are attributed with having first classified essential truths of the universe.

It is thought by some that the early Christian monastics such as the Desert Fathers may have been influenced by the Greek philosophers' ideas of the divine essentials. A Greek monastic and student of Origin of Alexandria is Desert Father, Evagrius of Pontus (345 – 399 A.D.) who is said to have first devised a list if eight evil human thoughts or temptations. (7) Pope Gregory is noted as having reduced the list to seven in the sixth century, which we now know as the Seven Deadly Sins.

Let us not forget, that the same ideas of classification of divine precepts and essential archetypal truths were being developed in other philosophies and cultures as well. The Hebrew Kabbalah (Tree of Life) is one such list as well as the Ten Commandments. (8)

George Ivanovich Gurdjieff, mystic and teacher of the last century did not pass the Enneagram down as a personality system as such. Gurdjieff did describe chief personality features of nine basic energies. He maintained that the chief features were the kernel of a false-self that causes human suffering. His work is written about by his student, P.D. Ouspensky in, *In Search of the Miraculous – Fragments of an Unknown Teaching.*(9)

Claudio Naranjo, a Chilean psychiatrist learned the Enneagram from Ichazo and first taught it in the 1970s in the United States.

Neither Naranjo nor Ichazo attached any religious, denominational, or sectarian elements to the Enneagram as a whole or to its Enneagram of Holy Ideas. This was apparently first accomplished by one of Naranjo's students, Father Robert Ochs, who as a Roman Catholic Priest, in the United States later taught the system within a framework consistent with Christian theology. (10) (11)

Other students of Claudio Naranjo, including A. H. Almaas (the Diamond Approach), Sandra Maitri and Helen Palmer have elucidated the Enneagram and its Holy Ideas. A. H. Almaas has written a major work on the Holy Ideas, in Facets of Unity. (12) In studying the interpretations of the students of Naranjo as well as other authors including Richard Rohr, Maria Beesing, Patrick O'Leary, Don Riso, and Russ Hudson there seems to be agreement among many of these authors on several characteristics and premises of the Holy Ideas. Generally agreed upon premises among many authors are as follow:

1. The nine Holy Ideas are the essential principles of reality that cannot be broken down into smaller components.
2. The Holy Ideas are the embodiments of essential spiritual truths that form the bases for all experience and all reality.
3. The Holy Ideas enter the world as part of a person's essence and consciousness.
4. Though a person coming into the world can resonate with all nine, there is one particular Holy Idea to which he or she is completely transparent, sensitive, and aligned.
5. The Holy Idea of the person is part of his or her living expression and is linked inextricably to their essence or "soul child".
6. One's Holy Idea is lost and forgotten as each person loses the connection to it. Eclipsed by

the ego which developed in the person from its beginning, the Holy Idea is forgotten. To cope with and move through the world, the ego and its personality structure take charge of the person.

7. The personality structure is at its core, the reaction to the loss of the Holy Idea and compensates for the missing Holy Idea by developing a compulsion of thinking and behavior to replace it.

8. In compensating for the gap left by the 'disappearance' of essence and its Holy Idea, the ego takes over to provide the person other ways of moving in the world, resulting in great suffering.

9. The Holy Idea can be "re-membered" only by returning to one's essence.

10. The returning to essence and to the remembering of the Holy Idea does not mean a relinquishing of ego, or of personality, but a re-incorporation of the essence and its Holy Idea into a newly constituted being. This is accomplished through transformational work.

How each Holy Idea is explained and actually applied seems to have a slightly different flavor from author to author, yet many major tenants are seemingly shared. The following explanations of the Holy Ideas are from having my integrated and distilled fundamental points of several authors, and schools of thought. Also, a part of these descriptions are my own interpretations of the Holy Ideas which views them through the lens of the Beatitudes according to Jesus, the Pauline fruits of the spirit, as well as clinical observations from my own practice with persons reclaiming their Holy Idea as part of returning to their essence.

Type One
The Holy Idea of Holy Perfection – Holy Growth

Type One has the Holy Idea of Holy Perfection – Holy Growth. In this Holy Idea, reality is perfect in all ways by its very nature. We, as part of this reality, are perfect also. Perfection is not static; it is dynamic, spiral, progressive and many times obscured or non-apparent. Arrests or reversals of the process are simply parts of the intrinsic regulatory mechanism of a pervading perfection that propels an overall upward movement. For example, droughts and floods compensate in time for each other's seeming negative effects ultimately serving to preserve the land. Likewise, for human beings, seeming setbacks, devastation, brokenness, and losses in life can serve to evolve growth of the spirit. Overall movement is in the pattern of upward spiraling growth.

Being conscious of the perfection in all reality this type must relinquish its ego's compulsion. Because of this Holy Idea the One no longer unconsciously and automatically corrects perceived flaws, deficits, fallibilities, wrongs, etc. Instead of being held prisoner of continuous correcting of circumstances to fit the ego's agenda, Holy Perfection frees and expands the One's consciousness. This expansion takes the One to the level of awareness that makes him sensitive to divine movement in the world. In light of this Holy Idea, he moves with serenity about circumstances that are imperfect because he knows that Holy Perfection is part of a much bigger picture than his own limited view. Experiencing presence and mindfulness raises his consciousness to see Holy Perfection as preferable to his ego's fixation on perfection. Living out of this Holy Idea replaces "the correcting of wrongs" with the simple precept of "the allowing of perfection" to manifest in everything. By uncovering the inherent perfection in everything, its beauty and order can be seen. What covers or obscures this perfection? It is the heavy coating of egoic thought, fixations, and suffering. Removing the layers of ego and the suffering it causes, can make room for inherent perfection to manifest in situations and people. The process of affirming and bringing forth the inherent perfection in everyone and all things replaces compulsive "fixing" and potentiates healing. This requires relinquishment of the person's egoic concept of what is perfect or best, so that Divine perfection arises.

This Holy Idea inherently carries an air of lightness, because now there is relief from having to bear the load of preserving standards, judging all that is wrong and feeling resentment when others do not listen or comply. Freed from the notion that all must be perfectly finished products, now the One can embrace the virtue of serenity.

The bearer of this Holy Idea is a living expression of ultimate discernment, sacred poise, joy, and serene alignment with the perfection of the cosmos. Alignment with this higher divine order brings the spiritual fruit of joy. No longer is there a passion of anger and resentment, for people and circumstances are under overarching divine timing and divine growth (Holy Growth). This is true perfection. Flaws and wrongness are now viewed as being under the most expansive and Holy Idea of perfection possible. This idea cannot be grasped by the ego mind alone. This idea brings its virtue, serenity.

The bearers of this Holy Idea as a person or collective, now can "rejoice and be glad" because Jesus infers, they are of the same mind as the prophets. When unenlightened egos do not understand this mind, they will reject and punish the bearers of it. But the joy in knowing, that even these punishers too, are 'perfect', takes away the sting. The bearer of this Holy Idea is now free to discern true perfection and to bring healing, all in the countenance of serenity.

Type Two
The Holy Idea of Holy Will – Holy Freedom – Holy Grace

The Type Two's Holy Idea is Holy Will – Holy Freedom – Holy Grace. In this Idea, all being, all consciousness, and the totality of reality are propelled by the fundamental and intrinsic energy of the Divine. There is a divine intelligence within this energy that accomplishes its will. Alignment with the divine will and becoming part of its life force is brought about by surrendering to it.

In surrender, the ego does not value its will above divine will, for it is in divine order that the enlightened individual finds his true freedom and beingness. The person in alignment with this Holy Idea expresses Holy Will as naturally as a child passes onto others the love he experiences from his parents. Once in touch with Holy Will, he is certain of its inherent goodness known as Grace. Holy Grace is the divine giving that creates, nurtures, and "renews the face of the earth without 'payment'".

Only by relinquishing her separate ego agenda to the supremacy of Divine Will can one be fully free to consciously receive the overflowing love abundant in the Holy Will. Holy Will expresses full autonomy or freedom to enact its will, and gives the person who joins this will, freedom from ego.

If individuals or collectives see themselves as being the true source for what is needed, they have raised themselves above Divine Will and Divine Freedom. An individual's self-elevation to the level of being the source of all good things creates an illusion of omnipotent benevolence. As ego pride demands a continuation of this illusion, Holy Will is obscured. Cut off from Holy Will and its Grace, the hubris of the giver increases. The "lauded giver" even with ego inflation starves for what he really needs at his depths: to be loved freely by others.

What the individual (or collective) needs is to be loved. Alignment with divine love and will supplies this need. Experiencing real Holy Grace, removes the need for being 'the source' of all good things to others, and for being admired as the source. Distinguishing oneself as "so separate" from the whole, that one is seen as a source unto themselves, also removes the person from functioning as part of a unified whole. The growing sense of separateness is part of the pride, which wants to flex its ego's will above the whole and the Divine.

In surrender to and alignment with divine flow, the Type Two person (or collective) no longer want to be a source but a humble channel allowing Divine Will to flow to others. This frees the Two from the trap of service and the passion of pride in order to embrace Holy Grace and its spiritual fruit of meekness.

Type Three
The Holy Idea of Holy Hope - Holy Law - Holy Harmony – Holy Will

The Holy Idea of Type Three is Holy Hope, Holy Law, Holy Harmony, and Holy Will. All of these names of this Holy Idea are connected. They are built on the principle that the cosmos is in eternal transformation according to a pattern derived from its divine mind. Nothing and no one are able to operate outside this pattern and the connecting fabric of the whole. All happenings and all beings are interdependent and interconnected. There is no separate entity, source, or separate reality. All reality is in accordance with the movement of hope as full enlightenment and transcendence unfold. Individual egos who perceive themselves as separate from the whole may build their own kingdoms. These kingdoms are made by ego for admiration they interpret as love. They cannot ultimately survive without becoming conscious of how their dominion fits into the harmony of all being, and into the Holy Law of the common and shared reality. By emptying their spirit of "self interest", they become poor of ego, vulnerable, responsible, present, and integral to the global community, the village, the family and to the pure essence of self. When this occurs, Type Threes can experience the truest love.

The person or collective, who has forgotten this Holy Idea, cannot relax into the divine intelligence that is its gift. They are so busy being successful for "love" that they do not realize that divinely functioning patterns must be recognized and joined. Those who do recognize this can become one with divine flow. Type Threes who have forgotten this idea are trying to build their own hope and harmony, and their own rules. In so doing, their self-made ideas of reality may conceal truth. The intrinsic Holy Harmony in all must be re-membered in order to have real hope. Re-membering this is essential to those who have lost this Holy Idea, or they will be consumed by their strivings, to bring about their self-made hope.

The fruit of the spirit for this Holy Idea is longsuffering or patience. No longer are the bearers of this Holy Idea slaves to ego agendas and efficient accomplishment. Now, the individual or collective can be emptied of the spirit of self admiration, of the passion of deceit, and of the need to achieve a separate self-made story. The new emptiness makes space for the fullness of Divine Intention, which includes loving all including the bearer of this Holy Idea. In this fullness of love, the person is not clamoring for success, or the image thereof. These are replaced by the virtue of veracity, or truthfulness.

Type Four
The Holy Idea of Holy Origin – Holy Union with the Divine

The Holy Idea for the Type Four is Holy Origin – Holy Union with the Divine. This Idea holds that everything and all beings are "arisings" or manifestations from the great divine ground of being. All sense perceptions of those things or beings appearing before us are manifestations of the One True Source of All Being. Everything and everyone are outcroppings from this One Source, like branches are to their main vine; indeed the same sap and life force flow in both the vine and its branches. The One True Source of All Being is known in part through our sense perceptions of it. We are most fully alive as we acknowledge the seamless connection we have to all of nature, and to ourselves as parts of it. When we are using our inherent propensities to create, we are channeling the One True Source of Being through us, and in this activity become unified with our source.

The loss of this Holy Idea caused the person to develop an ego that was not fully conscious of its divine source, or its inseparable connection to it. Also lost was the awareness that the true self is a unique expression of the One True Source. Because of this loss of conscious connection to the Source, the Four, tries, through being special, to regain connection and love. By seeing themselves as originators of their own creative activity, the forgetters of this Holy Idea (Fours) think they can create the love their forgotten Holy Idea once gave them. Despite their compulsive efforts to feel these feelings, Fours typically do not feel real; something is still missing. Persons perceived by Type Fours as living their authentic lives are objects of Fours' passionate envy. Fours lament their past and despair of their future.

By fully enjoying the spiritual fruit of goodness from their Holy Idea, Type Fours are no longer fascinated with tragedy, pain, the profane, and the mysteries of their past. No longer are they searching for someone to come and rescue them, to understand them, and to complete their identity. They know their Holy Origin, and even though they may encounter persecution for their new path or cause, they know it is one that is righteous (or in a right relationship with the Divine). This creative endeavor and its rightness, frees Fours from the trap of seeking authenticity and gives them the virtue of equanimity or composure. Knowing that the Divine life force, from which they come, flows through them in each present moment and is the source of their creative activity. They are grounded in union with God.

Type Five
The Holy Idea of Holy Omniscience – Holy Providence – Holy Transparency

The Holy Idea for Type Five is Holy Omniscience – Holy Providence – Holy Transparency. This Idea is based on the principles that the One True Source of All Being is the lover of all things and the Knower of all things. In the fact that we are manifestations of the Divine Source of All Being, we were before the fall, part of all love and part of all knowledge. Temporarily, however this wisdom is spread in portions among everyone. It is like the pure light of wisdom is fragmented into diverse segments among people. There is a division of wisdom among humanity, and it takes the whole of humanity in concert for wisdom to be used to its fullest divine purpose.

Because of this fragmentation, certain persons, (Type Five) who have forgotten their Holy Idea have felt un-whole, empty – as if the totality of knowledge must be regained and held by them. Therefore they hunger for as much information as possible to satisfy an ego wanting all knowledge. Underneath this desire is to have the feeling of the fullness of love they once knew and that they have confused with knowledge. This ego desire gives rise to avarice in individuals and in collectives. Insatiable hunger for the filling of the empty "hole of not knowing" drives the person to withhold, withdraw, and hoard. These separate individuals (or collectives) become disconnected to the whole and over-attached to their knowledge. To secure their self-made sense of worth, boundaries are erected between others and those who have lost this Holy Idea. This hoarded "worth" is an unconscious mental design to feel worthy of being loved, and valued. The boundaries are illusions that temporarily obscure the truth of the unity and interdependence of all reality. Each person of this lost Holy Idea is seeking to be filled, but there is distrust in the Divine's ability and will to fill the emptiness. They are caught in the trap of seeking knowledge and hoarding what they know, while withdrawing from the common unity of all life.

This Holy Idea gives its bearers a way to detach from their knowledge-seeking. The Five's virtue therefore is: nonattachment. The One True Source of All Being knows and provides just what is lacking (Holy Providence). When this Holy Idea, as a righteous idea, is hungered and thirsted for, then the One True Source of All Being will bless its bearer with ultimate fulfillment. Then Divine Providence may flow. In this manner, there will be a spirit of Holy Transparency to the love that connects all with one another. The fruit of this spirit is kindness which inherently carries the idea of connection to others.

Type Six
The Holy Idea of Holy Faith - Holy Strength - Holy Trust

The Holy Idea for Type Six is Holy Faith – Holy Strength – Holy Trust. This Idea is grounded in the fundamental truth that "being" is the inner nature of every person. True being is the touchstone of one's inner truth. Being is the "I Am" of existence. It confirms that we indeed 'are' and that we exist in reality. Contact with our inner aliveness is an acknowledgment that we are spiritual beings who have manifested in physical form. By living out of this immeasurable and unseeable inner aliveness, we are reaching with faith, back to the wellspring of all aliveness. This inner aliveness at its core is our essence. All is of one essence out of which come various and diverse expressions. The essence of the individual is experienced by being present. In experiencing our essence we know that it is good and anchors us to ourselves, our strength and our courage. We also know that in experiencing our essence and the essence of others, that there is a re-membering of how reality once was and that it may return to that again, now.

Persons who have forgotten this Holy Idea have lost touch with their essential beingness. They are searching for a person, an external source of strength, a belief, or a concept that will replace the terror of being without an inner assurance of one's essential confidence.

When the Holy Idea of Holy Faith – Holy Trust was forgotten, the insanity of the uncertain and sometimes cruel world, prompted this person to form an ego passion of fear and cowardice. At one time long ago, when essence was the source of this individual's being, there was no fear, but when the ego finally eclipsed the person's essence, she searched for the security lost with her essence. Security became her trap. Security was continuously sought because of continuous self-doubt. The fearful ego of Sixes rebels against authority or either clings to it as a way to feel connected to

216

it. The Sixes who are authority-dependent are living unconsciously because they have no contact with their Holy Idea.

Authority-dependence ultimately brings more fear and anxiety. When suffering becomes too great, relief is sought. Only Holy Faith in the Divine can replace the fear. This is not a faith based on external 'rescue' by the Divine. It is a faith in the "I Am", of being. This brings the spiritual fruit of faithfulness. This fruit comes from knowing that we are expressions of God, that we are overflowing love, immortal being, and divine intelligence. There is now the virtue of a purely courageous heart, uncontaminated with fear and doubt. From this vantage point, one can see God.

Type Seven
The Holy Idea of Holy Plan - Holy Wisdom - Holy Work - Holy Co-Creation

The Holy Idea that is the true and essential nature of the Type Seven is rooted in the principle that people are learning their way back to consciousness. No amount of human manipulation of mental states, of outer circumstances, or consumption of the material can ultimately change the inner code of each soul (Holy Plan). How a soul manifests and reaches its full flowering is within its soul's inner design, which is beyond the ego's understanding. Trusting the process of an unfolding divine plan is a trans-logical operation which cannot be comprehended by the intellect alone. Aligning spiritually with this plan, brings divine order to the life who re-members this Holy Idea. One can then be accepting of the Holy Plan which includes the Holy Plan of birth, life, and death. If Sevens surrender to this Holy Idea, they will no longer seek comfort through gluttony, escape, or denial.

The Sevens who have lost touch with this Holy Idea form an ego that fears the absence of a plan. Therefore fear is the primary cause of their ego planning. Their frenetic planning is to comfort their fear of not knowing that a Divine Plan exists. They have forgotten this. Now their ego's attempt to mask the pain of being out of touch with the Divine Plan brings over-indulgence, denial of reality, continuous movement, and any other behavior that seems to remove the suffering.

The trap for Sevens is in trying to create perfect happiness, and painlessness. This fantasy ultimately crumbles, yet they persist in living out their self-made story of never-ending fun and abundance. By following the illusion that "more" can satisfy, comfort, and blissfully distract from feeling pain, the suffering worsens.

Re-membering their Holy Idea, stops the cycle of over-doing, over-fantasizing, over-indulging, over-going, over the top, and the suffering these bring. Trusting in the Holy Plan and joining with it in Holy Co-Creation, open their eyes to the holy places of life's endings, life's beginnings, and most of all to life's "now". Pain, loss, deprivation, and mourning are now understood as part of the essential reality born of Divine wisdom. The virtue of sobriety and the spiritual fruit of temperance replace the trap of ego planning. The ability to grieve mindfully and to mourn authentically gives the bearer of this Holy Idea, ultimate comfort as he or she accepts that there is a Holy Plan.

Type Eight
The Holy Idea of Holy Truth – Holy Compassion

The Holy Idea of Type Eight is Holy Truth – Holy Compassion. This Idea is presupposes that when we look past appearances, we become aware they are illusions because only the One True Source of All being is the fundamental reality. Being is all that there really is. Being and Truth are one in the same. Appearances in life that reflect the fallen state of humanity also reflect the dualities caused by humanity's separation from its One True Source. Dualities such as good/bad, heaven/hell, ego/essence, etc. are the results of ego inflation. The ego that sees itself as all-important requires oppositional forces, war, inter-personal conflict, and allies to assert ego identity through opposition to an enemy. Ego inflation causes the ego to believe that it is its own source of power. In this belief there is non-alignment with the One True Source of All Being. When we re-member that all is basically made of one, we become conscious with our identity as being part of this One True Source. Therefore to perceive life in oppositional dualities is no longer required.

Persons born with this Holy Idea, but who have forgotten it (Type Eight), eventually develop rage. This rage is a reaction to the loss of the idea that they are grounded in being and in truth. Being in a body further enrages them because they experience it as limiting them in the world. The ego fuels the rage as a way to feel powerful as a reaction to feeling so limited. Dominion and power over others is a reaction to their sense of inner weakness felt due to the loss of the Holy Idea. This causes much suffering as this person or collective constantly wage war in an attempt to reassure themselves of their being. This collision course with others does in fact reinforce and enlarge the ego. As a result, dualities are created by the, we/them, me/they splits necessary for the oppositional forces to continue fueling an ego identity. Dualities create a false world of envisioning persons or collectives as oppositional to "me", different from "me", or as enemies of "me". Suffering results as those who forget this Holy Idea are ultimately relegated to their own arrogance. They are trapped by their self-conceived justice preserved by fighting with others.

Holy Truth brings simplicity and wholeness to the fragmentation caused by dualities. Holy Truth shows Eights that their suffering is caused by being isolated from others due to their tyranny. When incorporating this Holy Idea, Eights re-member their lives when things were simple, manageable, calm, neither tumultuous nor "larger than life". Now the bearers of this Holy Idea remember their true nature and live simply out of its innocence.

When Eights remember their Holy Idea, dualities disappear and all of creation is seen in truth as one being. There is no more rage or arrogance as there is now Holy Compassion for those who would were once seen as different or opposed to "me". Holy Compassion gives the bearers of this Holy Idea a deep connection to their essence's inherent compassion. In knowing this they are sure of their being. They, in being compassionate and merciful, have obtained mercy themselves. The fruit of this spirit is gentleness.

Type Nine
The Holy Idea of Holy Love – Holy Unconditional Love

The Holy Idea of Holy Love – Holy Unconditional Love is the mother of all the Holy Ideas. It is the basic principle that the essence of being is pure love. Expressing this benevolent love is the continuing intentionality of the cosmos. This love is what all being seeks to express and reveal in reality. It is the central purpose of each of the other eight Holy Ideas. The love that motivates the creative activity of the universe is reflected in all creation. It is the brightest and whitest light that can be shone. The innate love a mother has for her child, the enduring love between family members, the pure love persons have for friends, the land, the resources, the beauty of all manifestation…these are just some of the loves on the spectrum of love light. This love is natural and intrinsic to the experience of being.

Nines who forget this Holy Idea are full of anger because they can no longer feel this love. They doubt this love is there for them, because they have forgotten it and its unconditional nature. They have also forgotten that they are essentially made of this love, and for that reason can never be separated from it. There is no duality to this love – all are made of it, but those who forget this Holy Idea are consumed by the rage of being apart from it. They feel cut off and unworthy to even express their anger at being so far from it. The ego constructs a fixation to anesthetize these persons to all this rage and unloveableness. The ego fixation has Nines "go to sleep" about their feelings, their unmet desires, and their longings to be truly cherished. Asleep and paralyzed emotionally, physically, and spiritually, Nines shut down and live that way. To stay asleep, they anesthetize themselves to the world.

Nines, who see all sides of a situation, discount their feelings and their worth for the sake of avoiding conflict and being awakened from their sleep. This trap of self-abasement, meant to hide them, ironically brings them suffering. They find they cannot hide or become worthless because the entire world caves in on them. Their insulated world is shattered, and conflict comes pouring in causing excruciating anxiety.

When they chose to wake up to their Holy Idea, they are brought to their virtue of diligent action with a remembered sense of worth and loveableness. Knowing and living out of the Holy Unconditional Love of God, the people of this Holy Idea can now move in the world with the fruit of the spirit of peace as peacemakers. They are called the children of God. It is undeniable that children are loved by God unconditionally, for such is the kingdom of heaven.

Chapter Fourteen
Prayers of Spiritual Transformation for Each Enneagram Type

This chapter is the heart and soul of this book. It transitions the brilliant concepts of the Enneagram into the scared realm of communication with the Divine. Without spiritual transformation the Enneagram in all its wisdom would merely be an intellectual exercise. Prayer is a supreme action taken by human beings to invite Divine involvement in our lives. Consciousness of ourselves and others gained from the Enneagram opens us more fully to the prayers of our soul. The Enneagram's wisdom reveals our nature and the causes of our concerns while it expands our awareness of what it is for which we pray. The powerful Holy Ideas are the core of the nine passionate prayers to follow. They bring us into holy space where there can be intimacy with God.

There are numerous kinds of Prayers. Some are praise, some are petitions, some are confessions, and some are pleadings. There are prayers of submission, of healing, prayers for protection, endurance, and many more. The following prayers include most of the kinds listed above, yet if one word could be used to describe their genre, it would be transformation: prayers for spiritual transformation.

How was it possible to write these prayers, and use them in teaching the Enneagram for over the past twenty-five years? The prayers came from my prayer to God for a way to facilitate spiritual change in those who attend Enneagram conferences and workshops I conduct. Before the prayers were written, the Enneagram conferences were enlightening but they missed something...they missed teaching the students <u>how</u> to move beyond the veil...the veil that hides them from their true selves...the veil that stands between intellectual insight and divine intervention...the veil that blocks us from living as a truly conscious spiritual being.

I retreated to the Gulf Coast for a time alone to make my prayer to God. "Oh God, You have so beautifully given these truths, and have so generously given us the teachers of this holy method. Give me a way to employ these learnings, a way to live these truths, a way to become the being you created me to be. Oh God, for those souls who come to these events for spiritual change, I lift them up to You. Give me ways to involve them in Your transformation. Give me the words, You would give them. Oh God, grant us ways to be redeemed. In Your Name, Amen".

After this prayer, in the morning I was brimming over with spiritual energy to sit and write. The process was done in one sitting that lasted for hours on a deck overlooking the lagoon at Gulf Shores, Alabama. As the sun was setting over the lagoon, the prayers were completed. I did not think up these prayers; they flowed out of my pen as if I were taking dictation. They stand today just as they did at their being gifted, with only minor revisions.

As soon as the prayers were introduced into the Enneagram trainings, the events themselves were transformed. The prayers gave an actual way to begin the acts of redemption and transformation, right in the training sessions. The prayers brought strong emotional responses, not only from those persons who prayed the prayer for their own type, but from those who were also moved by the prayers for their loved ones.

Each prayer is a plea to God for transformation…it is a request, much like the prayers of David in the Psalms, to be heard by God and for our predicament to be known and helped by God. These prayers come at a very crucial time in the Enneagram conferences. They are presented after the participants have encountered the dreaded dilemmas and character traits of their own type. The shame and disarming truth about each type come across so strongly, that most persons are at best deflated and at the least, are despairing. Once faced with the undeniable truth of their false self, they are presented with the hopeful and positive concept of embracing their soul child as a way out of the false self. The prayers are presented just when everyone is asking "Ok, I get it, but how do I get there"?

Of course, these prayers are but a starting place. The extremely personal ones are made by each person to God concerning his or her specific situation. However, these prayers, place us into the spiritual consciousness that propels us against the force of the arrow. It is that first leap back to essence and to the divine alchemy that is already taking place.

A Prayer for the One

I praise you, Creator God, for the wonders of this orderly universe – the patterns of your weather, the tides so rhythmic, the planets in their divinely ordered orbits. You, Oh great God, are the author of these forces, made to run rightly, consistently, and in Your divine law. Thank You for Your sacred laws, Your standards that offer us boundaries and guidance for living. I am so grateful to You, my Lord, for my knowing about the importance of Your divine rules of life. I have known the uncertainty of life without Your guidance, and I do not like that darkness and confusion. It pulls me into an abyss that splits me even from You.

Oh, how I delight in my being able to work hard for the just and the right causes You lay before me. Thank You for my gift of discernment, Lord. I seem to instinctively know the right paths to take, though they may not be pleasant ones.

This inner knowing has been a burden at times, dear Lord, because others can't see what you let me see. Try as I may, they many times reject my discernment, my standard, the obviously right path. My heart sinks so often, dear God. I feel the loneliness of Moses as his people rejected Your law. I feel so often like dashing the tablets into dust as he did. But oh, that anger is so often held inside of me. I fear that if I let it out, I will not be good – that I will be wrongly out of control – that the sin of anger will have gotten me. Oh God, save me from this peril, save me from my own sin, my worry, my furrowed brow, my dismay of others' mistakes, and my condemnation of them whenever they err.

Dare I confess to You Great God that I am as critical of myself as I am of others? I try so hard not to deserve those harsh self-judgments, that anger, but the trap of perfection seems ever present. Help me out of this terrible trap of being an inner critic of myself and a judge of others. Stop those internal voices of mine which scream out my flaws endlessly, and compel me to point out the flaws of others. Seeking perfection is taking me down to despair.

Free me, Oh God, to know that it is You, not I, who is in charge, and that no one is perfect. Free me to grow, and to know that life is a process, not a perfectly finished product. Take away my bitterness and resentment that change me into a person caught in rigidity, anger, and self-loathing. Lift my spirits, please, and show me Your levity, happiness and hope, that I may live in it rather than in the dark chambers of keeping score and condemning others' wrongs. Let me laugh and sing as I find balance in knowing that Your right paths are transforming my rage to serenity and love. Let me skip, dance, and play, my Dear God.

AMEN

A Prayer for the Two

Dear Lord, I am in awe of Your gift of life and all, Your freely given gifts. I am in awe of Your unconditional love – the gift of life itself. I give You praise for Your magnificent experience of life with its bounty, nourishment, and relationships.

Oh Holy Parent, I am so grateful for the giving heart that you gave me. I just know how to give, how to help, and how to meet the many needs of others. I do not resent doing these things but find life in them. Being a helpful companion and friend to others is sublime love for me. I know no better bliss than to give freely, with no strings attached. Just that ministry of giving is so pure. It is an emulation of how You give to this world. My service to others reflects Your purity and Your love.

I am needy Lord God. I feel unloved and unacceptable unless I give and help continuously. I am caught in the trap of service in order that I believe that I am loved. But I cannot tell others how needy I am…I cannot even admit to myself that I am so wanting, of so much.

Save me from my prideful giving, oh Lord – the way that I move in the world to get for me, not to give for You. When I am exalted for my beautiful gifts to others, I feel so great that I become fixated on how I can get that feeling to come again. You know me; I find a way, and before I know it, I am stepping up on Your altar, almost unconsciously. Am I there to serve, or to be worshipped? Dare I say that? Dare I expose my giving as a way to get? Stop me from wanting people to eat out of my hand – those who I make dependent, those who I control to make sure they love me. Help me, oh God. I am sick of helping. Help me to know my own real needs and help me to meet them. I am so tired of feeding others and starving myself. I am so tired of making the meal, wanting the applause, and starving my soul with vengeance if I do not get appreciation.

Let me know I am acceptable…Dear God, that I am loveable not because of my giving but by Your grace. Lord let me no longer have to "wow" another with how much I can do for them to prove that I am worthwhile. Oh, Dear God, put me in touch with my humble self as only You can. Let me accept my gift from You as divinely inspired and acceptable, even as a precious work of art. Fill me, Lord, and let me give, not out of desperation, fear or unlovableness, but out of the abundance of Your love for me.

AMEN

A Prayer for the Three

Dear God, You are my maker and I praise You for the opportunity to live life victoriously. I know that You need me because there is so much to be done for You and Your kingdom. I share Your goals and pray for the strength to help You meet them. I am so aware of so much that is to be accomplished, dear Lord.

When I am feeling unworthy, I stoke the furnaces of accomplishment for my own ends. I feel, dear God, that I am not worthy unless I produce, win, succeed, and capture the trophy. I am seemingly tireless in making this happen, but I am best, oh God, when I can do this for You, not for the successful completion of the story of "me".

However, I feel so badly about myself, at times that I will do practically anything to bring about a win…for the win says I'm on top….everybody loves a winner and I must win to feel loveable, wanted, and desired. Loss nauseates me, as I fear a loss in the game means a confirmation of my nothingness, my inferiority, and my ugliness. I will even use a lie, a mask, or a trick to win. Those empty wins, even though only a façade, bring me satisfaction. It is only when the lie becomes my life that I lose my self respect. I simply accomplish more and more to make a successful image for myself. I get into the trap of efficiency – all goes so fast. All becomes a means to an end…there is no present all is for the future, and getting there as fast as I can. Would I be loved if I were a loser, Oh God? Your reply to me "Did Joseph lose when he was sold into slavery by his brothers? Did Mary become a loser when she became with child? Did Jesus lose when He gave up on the cross?"

I can look very good, Lord. I can make it through this life on the image, but You placed deeply in my soul the need to do Your will. In addition to Your will, I must give up my compulsion for efficiency and success. I must let Your will be my overriding principle. Oh, Dear

Joseph Benton Howell, Ph.D.

God, show me Your hope, Your will, Your divine administration, and guide me into thankfulness and truthfulness by Your principles. Your will that the community be considered over self is my way now. I want to feel success that will never stop, but my prayer today is that my successes, and even my defeats, will be Yours.

AMEN

A Prayer for the Four

I bow before You at Your sacred altar. The beauty of this spot is unmatched, dear, creator God. You have so freely given to Your world its boundless beauty. Your creation is so incapable of being captured by anyone – whether it is through icon, dance, canvas, theatre, sculpture, song, design, symphony, poetry, drawn line or, any other form of artistic expression. Nothing can match the beauty of Your world.

When gazing at Your mountains, beaches, or plains, I see each landscape change as the light changes. And I see each day as one-of-a-kind, never to be repeated in Your book of days. I am so saddened that I shall never live to experience Your world fully, in all of its exquisite manifestations. Even the darkness and the mystery of Your world holds intrigue for me. Your gift to me of seeing things in my own way has been a constant comfort for me. I take refuge in knowing You understand me in the way that only a creator can understand His or Her own creation. Am I special to You? I know that I am. I sometimes do not want to admit that all parts of Your creation hold unique specialness to You, but regretfully, I must. I take comfort however, in knowing that there is not another soul just like the one making this prayer to You. How enlivening it is for me to know that no one has looked out of my eyes as I have, nor thought the exact thoughts as mine. No one has created exactly what I have created in union with You; You are my Holy Source, my Holy Origin. I take this to heart, oh God, and thank You.

So often, I feel envious of those who have their real lives. I cannot find mine. I need my real life oh God…but I feel hollow inside, defective in that my past has maimed me, crippled me. I try so to figure it out, to find the missing piece of my life's puzzle. But I fall head over heels into self-absorption when I do this. I don't know how to get out of my project, "me". Is there another project oh God that will give me my real being?

Oh, dear creator God, free me of this past and the fixation that I have upon my wounds, my tragedies, and my agonies. Let me move on from them, knowing that they, nor another person, can give me my authentic self. Let me know that I do not have to wait to live my real life. Give me union with You all the time so that I can find my true self; the fulfillment of the seed that You placed in me at my creation. Heal me, O God, giving me the gift of living in the present moment, creating with equanimity in the beauty of Your eternal now.

AMEN

A Prayer for the Five

God, can you find me? I am over here, out of the way. I am calling You for help. I am eager to know, and for so long have tried to find the answer, to finally know enough. I've found that the more I know, the more I need to know. I am weary now, dear Lord, and need the comfort of Your divine providence. I find that I cannot fill my emptiness alone, no matter how wise I become. I am trapped in the gathering of knowledge.

When I clutched everything I knew and held it to my chest, and in my stinginess would not share it, I felt comfort. I felt that I had everything I needed in my self-contained world. This was, as You know, dear Lord, mere fantasy. I had nothing but the voice inside saying I must have more knowledge to fill such deep, deep emptiness.

That is why I call You today, dear Lord. You know that I am barely balancing on this edge. I am so scared. If I fall inward toward my inner life, my fantasies and my intake of information, I go into this dark abyss. This is a big, black hole, a bottomless pit of isolation and injestion. It takes me away from the world and I am like a lone, caged, and hungry animal. If I back away from the edge, I must enter the world, which overwhelms me with its chatter, sights, sounds, and demands, and then it swallows me. This is a precarious balancing act, teeter-tottering on this precipice, and I sway fearful of either direction.

So, I pull in and make my own world, and somehow in this space I cry unto You, oh Lord. You see me through my camouflage; You call to me, as You hold my hand and lead me. You give me, out of Your divine generosity, the very prayer for my lips and You fill me with Your bread and wine. Let Your spiritual food give me the fortitude, oh God, to strongly move out into Your world and to share the wisdom You have given me. With this wisdom and detaching from hoarding it, I am no longer empty. Through Your providence I am filled, not with knowledge but with Your spirit. Now I can fearlessly venture forth to feed the hearts of my brothers and sisters. It is truly in giving that we receive.

AMEN

A Prayer for the Six

Trembling, I come before You, oh God. Life has revealed to me that there is no safe place. Oh God, are You my parent? Are You watching over me? The way is so unsure, and I do not know which path is more secure. I cannot decide. I am filled with pictures in my mind of what will happen if I make the wrong choice. I am horrified and scared to death. Even the innocent of the pack, community, or organization could be hurt or die if I make the wrong choice. I would be at fault; I would be punished, even annihilated in their revenge. They would be justified in their devouring of me, for I will have failed in preserving the good for all. Any bad decision of mine would be seen by others as an ultimate disloyalty. I would be a traitor of sorts, deviant and despicable to those whom I displease.

Oh God, if I am to live, I must make choices. If I make choices, no one will protect me from the consequences. I am so tired of "owing my soul to the company store"; I am so shameful of hiding behind a protector. I am trapped by my need to be safe, and I am suffocating in that security. Must I hide by burrowing in a hole, becoming as someone's patronizing pet, or pretending to be so strong that no one will detect my fear, my deviance? What pitiful choices, dear Lord.

Will You adopt me, oh God? I am in need of Your parenting, Your divine protection. I just know that You not only led Your people through the Red Sea, but I know that You gave Your transcendent peace to the huddled persons in gas chambers of the Holocaust. Time after time I hear the accounts of Your protection, Your deliverance, Your comfort, Your divine out-workings. And in my own life – You have never failed me, but I always fear You will "this time". I, who will not trust You even to heal a headache, now must trust You for everything. I know now that I must trust You not so much for protection from life, but to call forth my inborn courage and strength. "Arise and walk", You say to me. You point me to my inner strength.

Help me to know that everyone is deviant in some way and that You use this to give us understandings we would never have had. Help me to know my shadow and to embrace it, so that I will not see it in others in an attempt to hate them instead of in me. Help me to stop visualizing the worst-case scenarios that play endlessly in my mind's eye. Give me the quick parental "hush" as the voices begin to chant their fearful phrases. Strengthen me with Your pure heart of courage, dear God, and let me trust You. Let me relax in my true identity, as that confident, peaceful being You created me to be. I am so thankful that You have given me Your kingdom in which to live and work fearlessly, without trembling.

AMEN

A Prayer for the Seven

Merciful Creator in Heaven, I am exhilarated by the richness of Your world, with its never ending variety, color, and plenty. Thank You for the opportunity to feel Your joy and happiness, knowing that in our faith with You, we may look to the future with confidence and optimism.

I am so incredibly happy that this gift of life brings with it the enjoyment of family, friends, and activities. I love the laughter and good feelings at celebrations, Lord. I am overwhelmed with the happiness that You give Your people, and I can never seem to get enough of Your abundant life and of rejoicing in it.

When pain comes into my world, I want to vaporize it, to transform it into an unreal phenomenon, far removed from me. It rarely works, but it is enough to keep the pain from entering too much of me. I sometimes have the hope that I can finally rationalize pain completely out of my life.

The older and wiser I become, the more I find myself putting away these cherished, childish ways of thinking. I know that pain, as well as pleasure, are a part of life. My prayer is that You will give me the ability to sit with pain so that I will be able to receive my greater good. I must awaken to the fact that grief is a healing part of life that births me into being fully alive. Birth and death are all one, Oh Lord, and I have looked only at what were the "happy sides". What I want is happiness, and in trying to perfect the happiness, I become frustrated, distracted, and feel that "more" is the solution when "more" is part of the problem.

Pain and deprivation are avoided by me, oh God. I try to blot them out, but find that when I do, my life becomes thin, superficial, and fragmented. Can it be, oh God, that the real depth and meaning I search for in movement, things, and fun, are also to be found by walking with You in the valley of the shadow of death? Can it be that what I blot out is actually what I need?

I am ready, Holy God, to shed my idealism, although it promised me a bright future. I am ready now, because my idealism was built out of my thoughts and my planning to achieve perfect happiness. I know now, dear Lord, that following Your holy plans means holy intimacy with You and in this intimacy I create along side of You – this is far better than my efforts to create perfect happiness for myself. Like giving birth, the painful suffering must precede beautiful new life. Oh God, give me Your gifts of patience and endurance that will stop my overindulging, my racing thoughts, my endless distractions, and my denial of what is. I rejoice that You make me sober and whole, that my cup overflows, and that in Your answering my prayer I am truly happy.

AMEN

A Prayer for the Eight

Only to You, God, can I show my open heart, my weakness. I pray that I can show more people as my life continues, but I am so angry at life. The injustices I have always noticed call me to fight for justice to prevail. Even though it is to settle the score, the more I fight, the stronger I become, and the more others see my arrogance. I am open to You only because I am trapped. I am trapped by my own lust for life and justice, which call me to be stronger and invincible. I have built such an impenetrable fortress that I am sealed in it alone, and I cry out to You for help.

I am suffocating in my strength and power, cut off from the very milk of human kindness I once dismissed as mere sentimentality…a type of weakness. Now I thirst for that milk, oh God, as I am totally alone. I am in control of my fortress, I rule it… the entire domain. But it is empty and devoid of what I thought would never stop… people to love me, admire me, because they need me. Now they have all left me, and my anger is even greater. My rage wants revenge. However, this is not the way.

Give me the ability to be with others again, Lord, to experience love. I know from Your word that to be with others, I must first have compassion for them, not my arrogant judgment and my need to rule them, which are parts of my lust for life.

Oh God, my pain is so great over having been so misunderstood. I thought that if I showed my vulnerability to others that they would not respect me. I thought that if I was not strong and forceful, I would have no place in Your creation. It has always been in my nature to protect, see the bigger picture, and step forward fearlessly, as did Solomon with the sword. I bordered on being ruthless.

Grant me, oh Father-Mother God, your divine connection so that I may rule over my domain under Your Lordship. Give me compassion and empathy so that I can experience others' pain without feeling that I will become a weak vessel. Help me to give to others out of my weaknesses as well as out of my strengths... to give to others out of the simple wholeness of my nature. Quell my threats, dear Lord, with Your compassionate spirit. Let me be connected to life and to others, not through my own power, but through Yours.

AMEN

A Prayer for the Nine

Dear Lord, I praise You for grounding me, for giving me that knowing, that confident instinct. Thank You for the slow and certain flow of Your river of life. I know that I will always be in it. Thank You, that I will always be part of it.

Your love has touched me at my core, that unshakable part that I cling to in times of uncertainty when the outer chaotic movements try to conflict and bewilder my soul. I cling so deeply to that inner knowing, Lord, that You placed inside of me at my creation. Thank You for that.

I watch others in such upheaval. They cannot see the other side of the mountain; they cannot imagine that there can be advantages, opportunities, even gold inside things that look like failures or tragedies. I thank You, too, Lord, for my knowing that the advantages, opportunities, and gold have their own curses. Therefore, I go to that intermediate, unshakable place of peace where neither heights nor depths can stir me. It is that tranquil inner space of calm relinquishment that you have given me so naturally. Oh, great God, I thank you for that sacred space, that serene temple.

Oh Lord, I am sometimes so embedded in my groundedness that I find the solid earth is deep, moist mud for me. My feet, though firmly planted, cannot even be lifted, and I wait. I look at your wonder and just stay. I find union with the mud. I blend with the mud and my life stops. I am sinking.

Oh Yahweh, when I am lulled to sleep in that warm, earthly comfort, I am so lethargic that I sink into the mud too deeply. I am on the verge of resignation, of giving up, of saying, "It doesn't matter." I am numb. If I don't matter, maybe no conflict will occur. I am so afraid of battles. I'd rather bring on lazy sleep with wine than be awake for a fight or a brawl. But I can "sleep" my life away, and never truly live. Oh, great God, lift me up out of this quicksand of lazy resignation and point me to higher ground. Show me what I must accomplish for myself, for others, and most of all, for You.

Oh, great God, energize me with Your unconditional love so that I may truly matter, feel worthy, able, alert, and alive with all of my senses. Transform my anger into space for growth. Empower me so that I may go forth to give others what You have so freely given to me: the certainty, the mediation, and the peace that can mend the rifts of life. Restore my holy nature, oh Lord. Grant me Your sacred action and bless me with Your companionship as I go diligently into the battlegrounds and the peaceful plains before me.

AMEN

Chapter Fifteen
The Return to Essence

Returning to our essence involves a spiritual method of reclaiming a forgotten part of our soul, and blending it with our spirit. Discovering and reincorporating our essence is accomplished through spiritual transformation process. This process has been called alchemy was first used in the Medieval period to describe a mystical process of transmuting baser metals into gold. Another purpose of this ancient and mysterious chemistry was to discover through the interactions between and combinations of elements, an elixir of life. In the early nineteen hundreds, Carl Jung adopted the term alchemy to characterize the mysterious process of psycho-spiritual combinations and transformation. For Jung, the term alchemy best describes the process of transmuting a person's psychic energies, deeper passions, and spiritual awareness into higher ordered amalgams. The unification of the masculine and feminine, the integration of shadow and combining the opposites of personality functions, to achieve consciousness are but a few of the products of spiritual alchemy. For Jung spiritual alchemy involved such processes as dream interpretation and working with the mandala, which took nearly the entire second half of his life to understand. (1) (2)

As Carl Jung knew, the elements of spirit can have transformational properties similar to those of earth's chemical elements. In the physical sciences, the transformation of elements is frequently conducted in a crucible. This impervious container holds the elements which undergo pressure, force, blasts, combustion, and radical changes in the temperature. These processes result in transformation of the composition and the condition of the crucible's contents. In spiritual alchemy, a similar container is required that can withstand the different forces of spiritual change. This spiritual container must be able to hold with integrity, the masculine functions of penetrating force, in that it disseminates, forges, expands and contracts. The container must also conduct the essential feminine function of the womb, in that it holds, endures, nurtures, and transfers the life force from creator to the creation and from the creation to the creator. This divine container miraculously creates a balanced and safe space for sacred transformation. The holy crucible's masculine and feminine strength and integrity emanate from the immeasurable and mysterious Divine.

The sacred container of spiritual transformation is so aligned with the Divine, that its qualities surpass all human capacity. The container is the hospitable bearer of the holy mystery. Some of these containers are: the sacraments, spiritual direction, rules of life, meditation, dream discernment, holy dance, holy pilgrimage, prayer, the chant, holy music, holy artistic activity, study of sacred literature, fasting, the use of spiritual gifts, and the fruits of the spirit, holy service to others, worship, the sacred community of faith, holy action, spiritual retreat and holy presence. There are many others.

The container is the place wherein the essence is re-membered. This in and of itself is energizing because in re-membering, contact is made with the word that blessed the person at their making. This word, the kernel of one's essence, is one's Holy Idea. Remember, loss in childhood of the memory and knowledge of one's Holy Idea was the trigger for ego to take over and remain in force. Not since the loss of the Holy Idea in childhood has the person had such a glimpse into the egoless state which is re-visited when the person enters a holy container for the purpose of spiritual transformation. During the alchemical process augmented by the spiritual container the dominance of ego is lessened allowing pure essence to surface. Essence, as one's re-established base of operation, gives new eyes, ears, and perception to everything. Its Holy Idea becomes central and provides deep purpose replacing previous ego purposes. Change is happening at the deepest levels of beingness.

The next step is the amalgamation, within the spiritual container, of the person's essence with their spiritual wisdom. Distilled from ego suffering, as well as from the joys and understandings collected on life's journey, the spiritual wisdom will now bond with essence alchemically. This one-of-a-kind amalgam will provide a new and effective way for the soul's wisdom to move in to contribute to the world. Previously, this wisdom had depended on ego to express it. But because ego unconsciously used this wisdom to empower its compulsion, its spiritual usefulness was diminished drastically.

There are other forces and elements that, in the spiritual container, facilitate the bonding of essence with wisdom. There is an intensity of psychic energy when people experience the innocence and pure purpose of their essence. They usually experience grief for their essence (soul child) as they know that its innocence and purity are future victims of mounting wounding. Then come the repressed anger toward others and the tears that had never been shed. As the innocence of essence is combined alchemically with life's wisdom in a fire of forgiveness, there is a residue left in the holy crucible. This residue is the "burn off" from the alchemical bonding. In this new amalgam, because there is no alchemical 'acceptance' of sin, guilt, fear or hatred, etc. these are the residue. Poured out on holy ground as ash, is the residue which is buried in the earth. The residue is no longer part of the being. In the new essence, it is known that sin, guilt, fear, hatred, etc. are all forms of unconsciousness, which as byproducts of the ego fixation, blocked true life, true consciousness, and the ability to be fully alive and present.

The resulting new "amalgam" or new creature is a person living in the present moment as an expression of her Holy Idea. The remembered innocence of essence has become one, with the wisdom gained from life's journey. This is true consciousness. It is even more than the pure consciousness with which we were born. This consciousness is wrought from one's life wisdom and total transparency to the One True Source of All Being Who is love. One's essence therefore includes an embodiment of the 'sum' of this One True Source in its expression of the nine Holy Ideas, and predominantly one of them. The essence is innocent, pure, transparent to the Divine, and expressive of the Holy Idea. It is free, full and happy, aware of its divine connection beyond the level of intellectual awareness. It is the spontaneity, truthfulness, and glow we emanate when fresh from heaven and when we live in the Kingdom of Heaven. It is the wonder and awe experienced in the early years before the scales were eventually tipped making our woundings heavier than our wonder. It was before ego predominated when living was perceived as new, joyful and as mostly an exchange of love.

The following are excerpts from my actual interviews with children who are not yet dominated by ego. Notice in the children's responses to my questions the themes of essence: wonder, awe, reaching beyond, grasping more understanding, innocence, trust, simplicity, inner knowing, joy, spontaneity, transparency, self acceptance, surrender to what is, presence, and love.

Kelly; age five

Question: Can you tell me about life, Kelly?

Response: I love to live. I can breathe in and out all day long…(breathes in deep breaths). I run fast too, all the way to the big tree. You can live anywhere you want. Some people live in the woods, some have houses, some are in the street.

Question: Why do you live where you live?

Response: I live on the lane because my Daddy built our house there and that's where we put our things. Why do you live here? (looks around).

Jeremy; age four

Question: Why do we need to work when we are adults?

Response: I work. I make…I can put these things together (puts duplo blocks on top of each other) See…it gets high up! If it has a weak spot…it will fall…I work with my Mama in the house…she makes me supper.

Question: What about mean people, tell me about them.

Response: The bad man is in the movie. I don't know him… he can't get out of the movie. Mama says he can't get us. The men and mamas on my street are nice. Everybody is nice but not in the movie.

Angela; age seven
Question: What is in your purse today?
Response: (legs crossed) Oh…it's just girl things…(laughs) I have my lipstick…it's really a chap stick…and I have a charm. (opens purse…looks in) there's not much here, you wanna see?
Question: What's life all about?
Response: (flicks hair out of face) It's like my Daddy coming home from Iraq. I didn't know for sure…I mean I needed him back to me…he skyped me from there. I knew he would come back. That's what it's about.

Maria; age five
Question: Tell me about you, Maria.
Response: I jump in the pool and float on the water…the sun goes into the water…it twinkles (the water) when the leaves shake over it (the sun). I get in the twinkles and splash. I will do it again when I go home, from here. I sing with my brother in the pool. I squirt water and twinkles from my mouth onto my brother (laughs and makes motion with her mouth like she's squirting water out).
Question: Who is God?
Response: He is the one we pray to, cause He is (hesitates) He is my Mother and Daddy's Daddy.

Robert; age four
Question: What do you want to do now?
Response: This! (pours out all the blocks from a basket onto the floor, looks at the interviewer, and sits in the middle of it all).
Question: Are you ever worried about something?
Response: My mama is. Can you play with me?

Rylee; age six

Question: Tell me about animals, Rylee.

Response: My dog is Sam. He knows me. He eats food from a dish on our floor but it's ok. He told me to let him out the door to go potty. I did. He thanked me…he thanks you when he shakes his tail…Sam smiles and leaks spit from his mouth. Sam knows the squirrels and chases them – he found a big bug on the porch. Sam knows me.

Question: What's the best thing ever?

Response: When I can be with Sam and my big sister on the beach…everybody's happy and there's a laugh in everybody at the beach.

The poet, Vachel Lindsay alluded to children's eventual loss of essence to the adult world of unconsciousness.

The Leaden-Eyed

Let not young souls be smothered out before
They do quaint deeds and fully flaunt their pride.
It is the world's one crime its babes grow dull,
Its poor are ox-like, limp and leaden-eyed.

Not that they starve, but starve so dreamlessly;
Not that they sow, but they seldom reap;
Not that they serve, but have no gods to serve;
Not that they die, but they die like sheep. (3)

Christ addresses the unconsciousness that has been part of the human experience since the fall. He quotes from themes written in Isaiah 6:9 as He speaks in Matthew 13:14-15.

> You should indeed hear but never understand
> > and you shall indeed see but never perceive,
> For the people's heart has grown dull,
> > and their ears are heavy of hearing
> > and their eyes have closed,
> > lest they should perceive with their eyes
> > and hear with their ears,
> > and understand with their heart,
> > and turn for me to heal them. (4)

To those who Jesus perceives as conscious He says in verses 16-17 of the same chapter:

> But blessed are your eyes, for they see, and your ears,
> > for they hear
> Truly I say unto you many prophets and righteous
> > men longed to see
> What you see and did not see it, and to hear what you
> > hear and did not hear it. (5)

To recapture this essence of ours, we take a soul's pilgrimage back to our beginnings. Looking at photographs, going through baby books, reading packed away letters, or merely talking with those who knew us "then", are ways to take this holy journey. Methods for "returning" are best accomplished in a spiritual container that provides a sustaining integrity and safety. You may refer to the Level of Essence Indicator in Chapter Three.

Following is a recounting of part of the return to essence as experienced by Tim, age forty-three. His spiritual container was guided inner dialogue with his essence within a spiritual retreat.

"I was at a spiritual retreat away from home. Having prepared for this process, I brought a photo of myself from my early childhood as instructed. I was embarrassed to show the picture to anyone. I kept it in my pocket until I had to look at it to complete the exercise. In a small group the leader prepared us, for the powerful experience that was to follow. I was asked to put the picture before me, gaze into the eyes of the child (who was me) and to look at his purity, his consciousness, his innocent openness to the divine. I was almost flushed with embarrassment as I saw me for the first time. I saw all the way past how my mother had dressed me, past my temperament, my quirks, my preferences, my foibles and 'style'. I saw into the heart of my being. It was as if that vulnerability of the child in the picture exposed my true nature. He was vulnerable, open, trusting of life, and he was ok. I have felt like that only a few times as an adult. He knew what I had forgotten since then. I wanted to know again what he knew. Is that why we love kids so much? They are so vulnerable…they are so real. They know and live what we want to know and live again. They do not yet know to hide…oh back to me…I saw through to the real child sitting on the rocking horse. I saw his essence, that quintessential kernel of his nature…I knew he was still inside of me. I could love him. I wept as I looked at him because I knew he would lose in just a short while, the innocence I saw in him. I had compassion for him. I loved him. I wanted him! I prayed thereafter to live out of his consciousness, not out of my own head. I told him I loved him. He seemed to speak to me and to say that he had been there all along. I told him I felt terrible for all the pain we had endured. He said it was because of the pain that I now had the wisdom to reach out to him. I am still getting reacquainted with him. I won't forget that day…since then I've kept that photo on my desk with those of all my other loved ones. He reminds me of who I really am, and who I can be everyday".

Another experience of returning to essence is retold by Wanda, age fifty-seven. Her spiritual container was spiritual direction and guided imagery.

"I am in spiritual direction. I studied the material on essence, and was elated to have gone through a meditative experiential exercise that opened up my life. I was asked to find the child who was the me of my early years. I was given guided imagery by my spiritual director. In this imagery I was able to return to my childhood home and to visualize myself. There I was in my own room at, say age three! I saw me, what I was wearing, and exactly where I was on my bed playing. Then my spiritual director asked me to say "hello" to this little me. I did, and then my spiritual director asked me to say something else to the little 'me'. I found myself going over to little 'me' and playing paper dolls with her. This child was so sweet, so open to me, like she knew who I was. Then my spiritual director asked me to ask the child the following question. "What are you going to do in this life? The answer just <u>floored me</u>. She looked up from her dolls, dropped her hands into her lap and in an almost exasperated way said, to me, "Now Wanda, you know that we are here to be love". After that we had the greatest chat. She reminded me of all that I had forgotten about why I live. She spoke the words that I believe God spoke to me when God sent me down here fifty-seven years ago. I was profoundly affected…I was transformed. I am now more of my real self than ever, and I speak to her often.….I am her….often".

Another account is from Everett, age eighty-four. His spiritual container was prayer.

"My enlightenment, if you want to call it that, happened in my late fifties. I had enjoyed the simple life with many friends and never-ending activities such as, world travel, camping, and many business as well as academic pursuits. I had a wonderful job with a regional trucking company as their head accountant. I had dealt with the deaths of my parents yet, one day it all hit me, I was really alone. I lived in the house of my birth, attended the church I was christened in, and because of this and my friends, I lived with a false sense of stability and security. But when the realization happened – the awareness of my aloneness, I broke. I remember where I was. I was in the entrance hall of my house. It was the area in my growing up years, where my parents had welcomed friends and family to countless Christmases, birthdays, visits, celebrations, and gatherings. I could hear all the familiar voices, and the laughter. I saw their faces, and even myself as a boy in their midst. I fell to my knees right there in the entrance hall. My grandfather clock chimed as its vibrations passed through my body. I suppose my prayer was the prayer of a man who is dying. I had no one to live for really and no other worlds to visit, or to conquer. My friends were special, but on holidays, they were with family and I was a fifth wheel. That morning I was in a different state of consciousness than I had ever been in. It was a place between heaven and hades, between light and dark, between life and death. I could smell my mother's applesauce cake, and I could hear the voices of love that once echoed around me. I prayed to find a way to live again. I asked for a sign that my prayer was heard. In the prayer on my knees right there I gave up. I just stopped fighting in my mind for things to be different. I became totally there, totally alive, and supremely happy. In the prayer, a distinct impression came upon me that I had to relinquish more than my perception of how life ought to be. Then I saw it…. the sign for which I had prayed. I saw the innocent self I was as a young boy…I saw how industrious and trusting I was, how full of hope and adventure I was. Most of all I saw that reflection of God in him. It reflected God's never-ending love, a love that's there no matter what. "If I knew it then, why don't I know it now? I asked myself. I knew that if I became that innocent, trusting self again, I would have to give up hating those who I thought stood in my way, and those who made fun of me. I have always been so awkward and odd. I had been bullied…. And I had been shunned. But now I wanted to give up the resentments. I wanted to be finally free of all that had closed me in and weighed me down and sucked the joy out of my life. In my prayer I saw Christ, who had me by the hand. Holding His other hand was the boy. The boy's spirit jumped inside of me…the spirit of hatred jumped out. I have never felt that aloneness since. I have found a new way to live".

Mary, age forty- eight gave the following account. Her spiritual container was the labyrinth.

"Walking the labyrinth with preparation and scripture was a spiritual container for me. This process took me an entire summer. I walked the labyrinth daily for two and one half months. Each time it was entirely different, and each day's experience was a building block to greater awareness for me. I think it was the repetition that did it for me. It was like a walking chant. The same labyrinth, the same walk, reaching the same central space every day were what put me in a sacred rhythm. The rhythm, the prayer and the readings formed a structure for me that summer. It was a different summer for me because I had just ended a relationship with a man I loved. His alcoholism was the stumbling block for us. I was a perfect match for him too. I was a classic enabler. When he beat me in a drunken episode, I hit my very lowest. Never ever was I raised to give myself to physical abuse, yet I had sunk that low – all for what I thought was love. The readings were about change and transformation. I wanted to get back to my essence, but had no way of doing so. It was the labyrinth and prayer that showed me who I really am. The sacred rhythm reminded me of my mother's carrying me in a circle inside the house when I was sick, scared or overwrought. The circular motion of the labyrinth spurred me to remember my mother's cradling me and soothing me with her walking me, her soup and her prayers. The labyrinth reminded me of that little one in my mother's arms…she was me! She accepted her mother's love and was able to feel better as her mother walked with her in her arms. I was able to get in touch with what I used to have. I was able to get in touch with my inborn openness to receiving comfort. Somehow my adult self got it all wrong… my adult self thought I was the one that had to always <u>give</u> comfort. The labyrinth, my labyrinth spiritual coach, my prayers and readings all brought me back to my real self. I was put in touch with the most real and deep rhythm of existence. I live out of the child's perspective now without forgetting what I've learned in adulthood. I just know that I need things, especially comfort at times, and that I can receive it. I feel healed".

It is important to note that for some persons, returning to any reminder of childhood is intimidating, if not outright terrifying. There are many reasons for this, including early childhood abuse, chaos and confusion in the family of origin, neglect, abandonment and other traumas. The often asked question in light of this "block to finding essence" is: "How can I return when it is too painful to do so"?

In response to this question, the block to finding essence is there for a good reason. The psyche has walled off painful parts of an important phase of life. One must not return to essence if in doing so, it creates more pain and suffering. The person must first explore and heal the pain associated with their early years. This will require spiritually oriented counseling and therapy. If healing childhood traumatic memories can happen first, the person may then contact their essence. For many persons, however, their early childhood was so negative and their memories so fearful, that there is a blank where their childhood memories should be. Within the blank there is only a scared and lifeless child. There is a process by which the positive life of essence can be re-infused into the damaged inner child of the past.

Once the barriers of resentment and hatred toward others are no longer psychological inhibitors, the person can make use of the infusion process. It is basically conducted by an experienced minister, spiritual counselor, or therapist. Within a spiritual container, the person reconstructs their inner perception of their early childhood. This can be begun by using the Enneagram of Holy Ideas. When the person finds and knows his Holy Idea the can consult his spiritual guide, to "flesh out" other characteristics of essence. This is also a form of spiritual alchemy.

The following is a case example of Phillip, age forty. These are his words.

"I was damaged as a young child…I didn't need to go into details, but it involved sexual abuse from a 'trusted' person outside the family. I was very young but I still remember it. It has been the toxic thing hovering over me all my life… anyway I could not do the return to essence as part of my healing process, because to return meant to go back to the me who was basically shut down. I didn't even speak until I was six years old; and then it was only minimal verbiage.

When I began the process of spiritual re-infusion of my inner child, I knew I had hit something…all the qualities of essence were actually there when I was a child, but they were simply not outwardly expressed because there was, as I said, a major shutdown. As a child, I just sat and watched. People thought that was just me and I guess I thought that too. Re-infusion is like blowing up a limp balloon. I came to life…I had everything I needed, except just one important thing: spiritual aliveness. Beginning with my Holy Idea of Holy Faith and Holy Trust in God, a portal opened up for me. I could get a basic understanding of my first self…my true self and I logically added the characteristics that went along with living out of and expressing the Holy Idea. I could then reframe my childhood shutdown as "my waiting" in trust. I could now perceive myself as having been courageous with a naturally endowed endurance. I could realize my inner strength as I had learned to survive resiliently in a world of continuous hurt. Eventually I came to really know my essence. I was now able to think of my early childhood years, with peace. I was then ready to re-incorporate my essence".

Chapter Sixteen
The New Eyes and Ears of the Kingdom of God

When we finally re-member our essence, our soul child, we have the realization of our true selves. We simply are an "I AM"; we are not an "I AM THIS OR THAT." We are now able to be, like we were, as children. We are fully present – at one with being.

Before we come to self realization we are caught and enslaved by continuous mental thought. This thought is continuous for it has to protect us from the ever-present world. It (the ego mind chatter), takes us away from our pure consciousness. This ego thought takes us away from living in pure openness with God, to the unseen. The mind will not let us be free of its chatter. We are not even aware that the mind actually runs us. We are "employees" of its thought patterns. This continuous mind chatter gives us a sense that the 'voice" is really we. We are so entranced by this inner voice of the ego, that we pay close attention to it. We then let it become our self.

This voice oppresses us by wrapping us in its preoccupations, its defenses, its primitive ideas, and its imaginings. The hyper vigilant voice of the ego at one time protected us, but now its chatter is a constant siren keeping us on alert. Once we feel safe... it then speaks about how we could get more, become more, how we could make our own story of ME. At that vulnerable point in our early life, this ego compulsion came to "protect" then to help us escape what we fear. Then it chattered how to get what we desire. The problem is that we identified with this voice and thereby lost our sense of oneness with Being. That innocent joy of being, that openness to consciousness and that childlike awe of the unfolding mystery of it, all left us. The result was suffering.

Now we have awakened. We have turned away from the ego chatter and have embraced the state of pure consciousness. We now feel our own presence with such joy and connection to Being. We go beyond what we thought was ourselves. We go into a deep union with the Divine. In that presence we find that in <u>stillness</u> is where we really live. The still point within is the Kingdom of God. It is our connection with the Great Source of all Being.

In total presence you now see with different eyes, you have new ears. You are living with intense awareness of the moment and all its "isness," all of its manifestations. There is a powerful sense of presence to you and to God. Irritation and fear vaporize. If you can do this, there is <u>great</u> peace within and then your actions and words come from here, instead of from ego chatter.

The secret is to let the light of consciousness flow stronger. Your mind will continue to "talk" and "play movies", but you see its antics with a detachment even with amusement as you observe your mind trying over and over to steal your attention, to keep you under its spell, and to give you instructions on how to be a false self.

Christ pointed to this awareness throughout scripture. He knew the ego is involved in self, in fear and in gratification of the image of self. He knew we could not find the present moment of peace and stillness if we let the ego run our lives. He saw even then how the ego mind destroyed people by literally taking then away from beauty, love, joy, playfulness openness to God and all of the fruits of the spirit. He literally had to remind people to once again "consider the lilies", "become like little children", "lighten your burden", "do not worry" and "have life abundantly!"

When you live in the Kingdom you are a new creation. No longer are you preoccupied with how big, how loved by others, or how influential you are. You do not want to control others or make them say the lines you write for them. You do not want others to play their part as you "produced" it in the movie of your life. All these desires are replaced with a yearning to be a part of what God is manifesting through you and in the world. The desire to be the center of a self made story no longer fascinates you. You become aware of the real story going on: the story of God. You are now conscious of the real story to be watched and heard instead of the story of ME. You want to know your purpose in the real story. You are not as fearful of others because in your new sense of connection and friendliness to all life, you can see how very much you are, or have been, or could be just like them. You now know it is the undesirable and scary aspects of yourself that you fear when you see it in others. This is all clear to you now. Your new eyes see others not as dangerous or despicable, not as hated or ignored, but included, understood, pitied, forgivable and loved. For after all, they are just like you in some way.

We are also like the homeless, the sick, the ignorant, the prisoner, the poor, and the alienated. When we see such persons, we do not recede, but see ourselves in them when we are in this state. We see our loved ones when they were in this state. We look straight into the eyes of these persons, and see the misery and pain of their existence, and we recall that same pain in ourselves. We see ourselves through new eyes.

Neither do you see the "rich and famous", or the leaders, or the brilliant or the beautiful as though they are persons unlike you. Those we celebrate, laud, applaud, and stand in awe of, those we perceive as competent, beautiful, smart, and spiritual, are all you as well. Why should a human be worshiped when what they are is us as well? For we too, have specialness as an expression of the divine, just as much as they! With our new eyes, what hidden parts of ourselves have we yet to see? What are our own special attributes that make us "valuable" in our own sight? What more admirable trait can we have than to be Christ to those around us? That is the truest thing to celebrate and deserves its own applause! With the eyes of the kingdom, we can see everyone as being valuable.

How Is It to be in Essence?

In essence, there is little attention paid to the past or future. One has goals, yet the goals are merely aspirations of the living Holy Idea within. Certainly there are practical goals like getting a degree, or building a house, yet these goals are not to serve ego, they are to bring forth manifestation of spiritual gifts and aspirations. For example, if Martha wanted to make a dress, and if she were living in essence, she would make the dress to reflect her spirit and the Holy Idea behind that spirit. She would then use divine creativity to bring forth a dress that expressed her true nature. If Martha lived in ego, however, her choice of dress would be centered around the image of self and self's story. The dress would unwittingly or even intentionally be designed to elicit a desired response from others which would confirm the ego's wished-for self concept, or add to the story of the ego's "me".

In living in essence, there is little haste to have all means be for a desired end. Things are not looked upon as steps to achieving ego goals. The steps of accomplishment are in and of themselves, precious present moments in which more life and learning may arise. There is an overriding need of the person living in essence to be so aligned with reality, with the unfoldment of truth and circumstances as they occur, and with the arising ideas and events of the present instant, that their actions are in accord with these. If for example, Raymond in his essence, could not find his missing wallet, he would choose not to react to the fear of missing such an important item. He would, instead be receptive to what came to light while looking for the wallet. He would be looking for what is discovered in the search that may be needed later, or something to surface that he had lost previously. He would, in the absence of fear, be present to the moment so that he could be fully aware of all that may be happening around him. He knows that what he may hear, or see will inform him of the divine message. In uncertainty he becomes even more alert. He experiences everything that is happening without being distracted by what is happening.

People living in essence do not fret, react, or act out if circumstances do not go as they had hoped…they trust life and its inherent perfection. They listen for perfection so they may take right action rather than reactive action. So, for example, when there is a breakdown of one's car, the anger is dispersed fairly quickly. It is replaced by a receptive awareness of and a surrender to what is. This allows the spirit to relax. Even in relationships that do not go as desired, if the spirit is relaxed, and if the person living in essence perfectly aligns with the Divine, even seemingly disastrous circumstances can be experienced as holy opportunities for the inherent spiritual wisdom within them to come forth. This may take more time than we want it to take. When impatience is part of our reaction, if even for a minute, we will know we are not attending to life in our essence, but we are unconsciously wanting our own timing. Our timing, when placed as more important than Divine Timing, is usually our ego's timing and comes from ego's desires.

Because we are no longer operating out of an ego compulsion, when in essence, there is an innocence that re-takes us. It is our childhood's non-assuming, non-paranoid receptivity to the world. Thinking the best of another person is the first line of perception rather than to entertain thoughts of fear, competition, envy, etc. toward them. This new thought is essence's replacement of ego fear with childhood's sense of connection to all life. It is a need to delight in another's presence more than to suspect or use that presence for ego's aims.

Wonder becomes the basic preoccupation. This is a feeling of awe about each moment and each form of living expression in the moment. This perception is explained by Candice who had just returned from an intensive spiritual retreat on Essence and the Enneagram. This is what she reported:

"I felt essence come to me on that few days away. I remember it well; my partner and I were walking in the woods on an exercise to collect things that represented our essence. We as a couple, had been judged by members of our church as bad people because of how we found each other and left loveless marriages to be together. On our 'exercise' we both found prickly pinecones that looked like they could really do some harm to you if you let their sharp points near you. But, we found the pinecones to be as soft as leather, bendable, with pliable points, so soft they could never prick your hand. What a message...right there in the woods at camp. It said to us both gently, that what may look hurtful, rough, and ominous, is not. It is just what we needed to feel affirmed. As I tell you this story, I can feel my being in essence. I have been living in it as much as possible since that all-important retreat several months ago. As I tell you this, I have a new freedom. I am not tethered to what those people at church think of me. Their condemnation is complete unconsciousness. What I am paying attention to right now is that over your head out the window in the clouds is a huge puppy dog. It's changing its' shape as we talk; just look at it!"

How to Assess Our Essence

We have varying amounts of essence at different times. Essence is consciousness, and is an expression of trust in life. Several major dimensions of essence are part of a self-assessment indicator you may administer to yourself (Chapter Three). Results will inform you of your own perception of your level of essence.

Prayer For The Eyes
Of The Kingdom

Smudge the film from my eyes, oh Lord,
Let me see – let me see your Kingdom.
I hear it, clear and crisp and ringing;
Now let me see its rainbowed village
Use mud and spittle, Cake it upon
My eyes so I may be freed from this
Darkness.......

In my mind's eye all I can perceive are
Gray buildings, people I may hate,
Or people who harm me. All I know
Are the colorless forms of my fears,
The endless chattering until death.

Your tender touch lifts away the mud from my eyes.
You tenderly wash them and dry them.
A prism of light pierces the blackness and twinkles as star rays,
Flickering, dancing!
What glory!

Now I see – I see clearly- the brilliance, the radiating aliveness!
I see past the old blurred images into the newly revealed land.
Golden sun lights up the whole world
You show me!
You appear in everything I see
Even in the pores of my skin –
And You are in everyone I gaze upon –
even the ones who hurt me.
The Kingdom has come,
And I can see it!

Amen

Chapter Seventeen
The Beatitudes of Jesus and the Enneagram

Blessed are the poor in spirit,
for theirs is the kingdom of heaven.
Blessed are those who mourn,
for they will be comforted.
Blessed are the meek,
for they will inherit the earth.
Blessed are those who hunger and thirst
for righteousness, for they will be filled.
Blessed are the merciful,
for they will be shown mercy.
Blessed are the pure in heart,
for they will see God.
Blessed are the peacemakers,
for they will be called the children of God.

> Blessed are those who are
> persecuted because of
> righteousness, for theirs is the
> Kingdom of heaven.
> Blessed are you when people
> insult you, persecute you
> and falsely say all kinds of evil
> against you because of me.
> Rejoice and be glad because great
> is your reward in heaven,
> for in the same way they persecuted
> the prophets who were before
> you. (Matthew 5:3-12) (1)

It is noteworthy that the Beatitudes of the Gospel of Matthew, in the fifth chapter, contain nine monumental blessings. In reviewing these different blessings, there is a great similarity between each one and a corresponding Enneagramatical type. It is not obvious at first glance, that the nine beatitudes are blessings for each type's movement toward faith and consciousness. Understanding the beatitudes in this light, allows us to see each of the nine types as being blessed and rewarded for taking the path of faith. In Enneagramatical terms, the faith journey would be the path of going against the arrows. Christ speaks to this passageway, "For the gate is narrow and the way is hard that leads to life and those who find it are few" (Matthew 7:14) (2)

The Beatitudes in Matthew correspond directly with an Enneagramatical type that has made the leap of becoming conscious being. A summary is as follows in order given by Matthew.

The Beatitudes and the Nine Enneagramatical Types

<u>Beatitude</u>	<u>Type</u>	<u>Blessed For</u>
Poor In Spirit	3	Emptying Of Spirit Of Self
They That Mourn	7	Accepting Pain To Co-Create
The Meek	2	Having Humility
Who Hunger And Thirst	5	Being Filled With God's Providence
The Merciful	8	Embodying Of Compassion
Pure In Heart	6	Relying On Courageous Faith
Who Are Persecuted	4	Taking Right Action
The Peacemakers	9	Moving In The World Using Their Gifts
When Men Revile You	1	Enduring Criticism With Gladness

As for the sequence of the beatitudes as presented by Matthew, I cannot detect at this stage of inquiry, a pattern corresponding to the arrows or energies of the primary triangle or the hexad of the Enneagram. The only sure correspondence is that each type's blessing is for their having gone <u>against</u> their arrow to the essence or point of integration and consciousness. This is the "narrow and hard way to life" described by Christ.

Following are each of the beatitudes explained in light of each type's faith journey (going against the arrow) toward consciousness.

"Blessed Are the Poor in Spirit"
Type Three

Who are the poor in spirit? They are those who had been "rich" in spirit or in other words, "rich" in self. Type Three is like the rich young ruler who is high spirited with success. (Luke 18: 18-25) When Jesus speaks with this rich young ruler he asks him to lose what he is most spirited about: power and riches. This ruler will not allow himself to become poor in the spirit of self, therefore he becomes sad. If this young man could have replaced "self will" with the will of God, he would have found the truest success. The Holy Idea of Type Three is God's Holy Work, Holy Law, and Holy Hope which replaces personal ego goals. God's holy instruction may bring failure in the world's eyes yet it will in the end, give the greatest gift of all as promised by Christ, the kingdom of heaven. Life is then lived by Type Three in the consciousness of God's purpose.

The "poorness" of the Three's spirit becomes a gateway to his accomplishing good for <u>all</u> not just for self. Why did the rich young ruler go away sadly instead of gleefully or happily? He was sad because his inner essence wanted to stay and feast upon Christ's invitation. He was sorrowful because his powerful ego suppressed his inner nature, (his true self) in order to satisfy its demands. It may have been after years of suffering that this man finally opted to be poor enough in the spirit of self to invite consciousness in. The reward for taking this faith journey is to gain the Kingdom of Heaven…. "for theirs is the kingdom of heaven."

"Blessed Are They that Mourn"
Type Seven

Type Seven avoids pain. Pontius Pilate also avoided pain by abdicating what, in his heart, he knew must be done: freeing Jesus. (Matthew 27: 11-24) He washed his hands instead in a symbolic act of ridding himself of responsibility. He avoided the pain of standing up for a virtue that would have made him unpopular causing him much grief. He therefore denied the pain of his own guilt by "washing his hands". If Type Seven can face pain she is able, unlike Pontius Pilate, to get what she truly wants: joy in living, and comfort in life's pain. The fun loving unconscious Seven however stays in constant motion to prevent feeling the pain of life. Sooner or later, the Seven with her over-consumption and distractions cannot be consoled. Suffering sets the Seven on a search for relief. Going against her arrow to the contemplation of the healthy settled Type Five she can finally, with God's help, take in and process the pain of life. The Holy Idea of the Seven finds co-creation with God. This gives the Seven an activity but it is not the activity of denial, it is an alignment with the God of life and God's Holy Plan, of death and of resurrection. She sees now that life is an unfolding gift which is born of pain. In grieving and mourning her losses, the Seven can give birth to a new way of being. This is real comfort…. "For they shall be comforted."

"Blessed Are the Meek"
Type Two

The story of Mary and Martha (Luke 10:38-42) is a depiction of type Two. Martha represents the <u>unconscious</u> Two who caught in the trap of service, feels resentful that she has too much to do. Out of touch with her real needs, Martha complains to Jesus that she has no help in serving people at the gathering: "Lord do you not care that my sister has left me to serve alone? Tell her then to help me". Jesus shows her that her sister Mary, (a representation of a <u>conscious</u> Two) is not preoccupied with serving but is first attending to her own deepest needs. Martha's controlling demand that Jesus tell Mary to help is answered by him when he says, "Martha, Martha you are anxious and troubled about many things; one thing is needful. Mary has chosen the good portion, which shall not be taken away from her". Jesus tells Martha what her <u>real</u> need is: it is to go against her arrow and to journey in faith, to understand and fulfill her deepest needs because "<u>there is only one thing that is needful</u>". He has also stated that Martha's pride in being of service can be taken away, but what Mary values cannot be taken away. Mary had humbled herself to sit at Jesus' feet and listen. Mary in her meekness had gone (against her arrow) to the conscious Four, but Martha had gone (with her arrow) to the controlling unconscious Eight.

What does it mean to receive an inheritance of the earth? Certainly Christ did not mean the Two's reward would be a largesse of material wealth or political power. To inherit the earth is to become one with the natural continuous flow of God's bounty. The earth is continually renewed by God. This is evident in the seasons, the new life springing from the planet and the cycles of life upon it. Inheriting the earth is blending with its cycle of giving and receiving. Becoming one with the earth, the Two can always be a recipient of God's Grace, God's Will, and the Holy Freedom from traps of unconsciousness. The Two's giving can then be from a place of fullness and love, instead of camouflaged neediness. Jesus blesses the Two's meekness or humility which is her virtue… "for they shall inherit the earth."

"Blessed Are Those Who Hunger and Thirst after Righteousness"
Type Five

The Five is hungry. They try to fill their inner emptiness with information and knowledge. Many times, they fill their stomachs as a way to feel full. They can also hoard things as a way to retain a feeling of fullness and completeness. The Five must go against her arrow to the consciousness of Type Eight. Here she can receive her Holy Idea of Holy Omniscience and Divine Providence. She must make a leap of trust to be filled by the Divine, instead of her knowledge. Jesus spoke to the hunger drive in Matthew 6:31-33 "Therefore do not be anxious saying, 'What shall we eat? Or what shall we drink? Or what shall we wear?' For the Gentiles seek all of these things; and your heavenly Father knows that you need them all. But seek ye first his kingdom and his <u>righteousness</u> and all these things shall be yours as well".

In this beatitude, the final reward for those who hunger and thirst after righteousness is that "they shall be filled". In being filled with righteousness, the Five can drop her compulsion to fill up with knowledge, and then move with the strength and power in the world.... "for they shall be filled."

"Blessed Are the Merciful"
Type Eight

The Eight is powerful. He commands submission from others and in the extreme can be tyrannical. Eights are compelled to seek justice but when they are unconscious they can become their own judge, jury, and executioner. Eights will end up in extreme suffering if they do not turn and with compassion, be of service to others with their masterful power. The Apostle Paul had been full of wrath and judgment before he changed. Like an unconscious type Eight, he persecuted others at his own hand. When he was converted however, he became consciousness. (Acts 9: 1-19) He understood that the simplicity of believing in God's goodness called him to be <u>merciful</u> to others. The combination of mercy and power in the Apostle Paul changed the course of history.

Another example in scripture of an Eight energy combining compassion with power is in Luke 7:1-10. A Roman centurion of powerful rank, sought out Jesus to heal his servant, who was at the point of death. The humility to seek out Jesus and the caring displayed by this man of great power and authority, touched Jesus deeply. In return, Jesus gave mercy and healed the servant. In this Beatitude, Eights are rewarded by Christ for taking the narrow passageway of compassion and mercy. This brings them the reward of being recipients of mercy... "for they shall obtain mercy".

"Blessed Are the Pure in Heart"
Type Six

Type Six is fearful. They live in a readiness for something to go wrong. The worst case scenario for the Six is to have his deviance exposed. If this is exposed, he feels unworthy to be loved and accepted. Peter captures the energy of the Six. As a loyal disciple, he gives his life to being a follower of Jesus. His experience of walking on the water, exemplifies the paramount issue of trust for the Six. Peter was able to trust for a time, yet in the end, he lost that trust and fell into the sea, only to be lifted up by Jesus (Matthew 14:28-32).

When Jesus predicted that Peter would deny him three times, Peter could not believe this. Peter did deny knowing Jesus, in order to escape association with "a criminal". Peter's denial illustrates the compulsion of the Six to let fear take over. It was only later that Peter faced his fear, became pure in heart, and had the courage to endure even death for his master. The "heart" has been an archetype symbol of courage. The word courage is derived from the French "coeur" which means heart. Indeed, for the Six, courage is a by-product of the process of owning ones' shadow and going to the peacefulness of divine affirmation (going against the arrow to point Nine). This takes the Six to his Holy Idea of Holy Faith, Holy Trust, and Holy Strength. These Ideas, purify the heart, give it courage and make it whole to trust peacefully in God. The Hebrew "Shalom" and the Arabic "Salaam" are often translated as "Peace", but come from the Semitic root for wholeness. It is in this peaceful wholeness that the Six can see God…. "for they shall see God."

"Blessed Are They Who Are Persecuted for Righteousness Sake"
Type Four

Type Four longs for what most feels he lacks; an authentic self. He envies those who he perceives do have a real life. This lack of feeling authentic makes Type Four want to be special and unique. He pines for someone to come along to save him from his despair. Unconscious of what to do with his life, he envies those who he thinks have it all together. He is creative and sees life artfully, but he is saddened about his tragic past and all that has caused him to be so misunderstood. His despair ultimately leads to the darkness of depression.

Zacchaeus (Luke 19:1-7) can be a representative of type of type Four energy who took the faith journey. Seeing himself as defective and different from others, he was also hated as a sinner and tax collector. Even though he was a rich man, Zacchaeus must have felt the incompleteness and despair of the Four, because neither his role nor riches satisfied him. He wanted to see who this teacher, Jesus was. By going against his arrow to the conscious Type One, Zacchaeus received a great blessing. At Type One, he discerned the right thing to do: this right thing was to shed any semblance of specialness, to creatively compensate for his small stature, and to climb the tree to see Jesus. Zacchaeus was persecuted by the on looking crowd who murmured against him as a sinner. Christ however, recognized Zacchaeus' bold act of righteous faith in climbing the tree, and blessed him with being his houseguest that evening…"for theirs is the kingdom of heaven."

"Blessed Are the Peacemakers"
Type Nine

Nines are avoiders of conflict. They are able to see all sides of a situation, but when they are unconscious, they shrink from voicing an opinion. Unconscious Nines are asleep to life most of the time. They want everything to run smoothly and find that being unaware lets them feel "ok". They see few problems and don't really cause much of a stir. When Nines are anxious, however, that means they have pushed the envelope of denial, and have been awakened to their own uneasiness. Nines must go to their conscious Three in order to be alive healthily. This puts them in a place of action rather than lethargy. In the place of action they can move in the world with their Holy Idea: God's Holy Love and Unconditional Love. In embracing this, they can do what they do best, make peace. Their reward for peacemaking is that they will be called the children of God. Mary, the mother of Jesus is an excellent example of a Nine who has gone to her Holy Idea and who has become a peacemaker. Her peacemaking nature was seen at the wedding feast in Cana (John 2:1-11). At this wedding feast the wine had run out. People were anxious and worried. Mary negotiated between the anxious servants and Jesus, and she brought the two together to solve the problem. She asked for Jesus' help on one hand, and on the other she instructed the servants to "do whatever he tells you". If Mary was a Nine, her peacemaking nature was a result of her "going against her arrow" to the action of the conscious Three. This action combined with the Holy Idea of Love, brought about for Mary, the wedding's success. Moreover it was this holy peace and calm of Mary that said 'yes' to giving birth to Christ. Peacemakers are called the children of God. In that children are essence, peacemakers are representatives of God's essence….."for they shall be called the children of God."

"Blessed Are You When Men Revile You and Persecute You and Utter All Manner of Evil Against You on My Account"
Type One

Type One is the standard bearer. As a natural discerner of what is right, Ones frequently take positions of judgment and authority. Knowing the right way is the gift of the One. They are charged with making hard call and final decisions many other people avoid. Ones, however, know their duty and do not shirk it. <u>Unconscious</u> Ones will make judgment but are unable to endure the backlash, or the dismissal of their pronouncements. As a result Unconscious Ones can mount up anger, become depressed, and even be self punitive for having been ignored.

<u>Conscious</u> Ones, however, keep a positive outlook and issue their opinions thoughtfully and directly. There will always be rebels against the issuance of truth. Christ calls for truth to be proclaimed. In reaction against the Type One's decisions, proclamations, and judgment calls, some people will defame, punish and call the Type One "evil". Christ blesses Type Ones who have remained balanced and have continued to issue truths for Christ's sake. Christ knows that for judgers of truth to remain balanced, they must be able to experience joy. At Type One's point of integration (the healthy Seven) are hope and optimism. Going to Seven and remembering their Holy Idea (Holy Perfection) give Ones a way to carry out their divine purpose. Christ speaks to the

joy Ones receive when going against their arrow to the hopeful Seven by saying "Rejoice and be glad, for your reward is great in heaven for so men persecuted the prophets who were before you". In a sense, all of the disciples had to go with Type One energy in order to spread the Gospel…"rejoice and be glad for great is your reward in heaven."

Chapter Eighteen
The Flowering of Consciousness

Flowers bloom by sunlight as well as by moonlight. To the conscious eye, the blooming flower is as beautiful at night as by day. The following stages of consciousness are depicted as the blooming of a flower and the progression of the day. These stages are not always experienced in this order. Generally, however there is first an experience of realizing self in its deepest form, before the expansion of consciousness into the perception of others and the earth.

Stages of Flowering
1. <u>The Dawn of Consciousness</u>. The small green bud appears on the stem. "I am tired of this suffering; I am not my life's story".
2. <u>The Early Morning of Consciousness</u>. The small green bud enlarges and has fullness. "I am a

much deeper being than my personality. I am
essence; I choose to live out of this essence.
I am not separate from others; I am not my
own source; I am not the past or the future;
I am the present and as essence part of all essence".

3. <u>The Late Morning of Consciousness</u>. The bud
    bursts forth; the first petals can barely be seen.
    "I am connected to all and all is connected to
    the One True Source; my self-made concepts of
    me and "my story", no longer stand alone – they
    have meaning only as they are part of the grand
    connection to the One True Source and Its story".

4. <u>The Noon of Consciousness</u>. The bud opens; the
    petals' color is rich; the petals are extending.
    "The One True Source lives Its purpose in
    me. My awareness expands to knowing and
    feeling the life force inside me. I know it
    is the same life force inside all life. I align
    with it, and with the totality of all life force".

5. <u>The Early Afternoon of Consciousness</u>. The
    petals grow and expose even deeper richer
    color. "I am remembering my purpose and
    how it is part of the great story; my purpose
    connects me to others in ways that let me
    see their essence. I speak to their essence. I
    am connected to the earth and hear her speak".

6. <u>The Late Afternoon of Consciousness</u>. The
    stamen and pistil grow and reflect the sunlight.
    Their pollen floats in the air. "The great story,
    the holy mystery is unfolding; I bloom in all
    my facets including in my masculine and in my
    feminine. I take action to help others and the earth".

7.   <u>The Twlight of Consciousness</u>. The pollen
     is visited by bees; the nectar is readied for
     the birds. "My awakening bids others to
     also awaken; my wisdom is freely given;
     I receive others' wisdom. This bouquet
     of love does not know selfishness or violence".

8.   <u>Evening Time – the Moon Appears</u>. The flower
     is full and open. It shines in the moonlight.
     "In the darkness I can see what would have
     caused me to stumble. Now, I see with new
     eyes and hear with new ears. I am stirred to
     action beyond my old boundaries. In this
     light, there is 'no darkness at all'; I move in love".

9.   <u>Night Time – the Stars Appear</u>. The flower
     sways in the gentle breeze of stillness. Its petals
     begin to wilt ever so slightly. "I am ready to
     return to the Source whenever it is time. I am
     part of all knowing; I am full and free and
     happy; the great mystery unfolds in every
     present moment. I am ready for tomorrow's dawning".

Flowers of Consciousness come in many varieties, colors, sizes, fragrances, and shapes. When the tree of life begins to flower, it manifests amazing and beautiful "knowings" about all levels and facets of living. These knowings are holy; they are the flowers of consciousness. There are some flowers close to the center of the tree – those "knowings" about one's inner self – the essence of life expressed only as that one flower can express it. These flowers, though close to the tree's center, radiate a luminosity that shines through the branches and gives the tree a glow. The glow of the flowers and their sweet fragrance beckon us to come see, and breathe in the pure inner essence of consciousness. When someone lives out of the flowering of consciousness a light radiates from her. Free from ego she operates without defensivity, violence, or competition for love. Essence abounds, as if coming from every pore.

Many flowers on the tree are blooms of different kinds of holy knowings. People and the world are known through new eyes and ears, because the holy knowings, bloom the person into a new perception. Holy knowings include the flowering of consciously perceiving others' essence and the flowering of consciously knowing we are all one, the flowering of consciously knowing others through love, not by the intellect, and the flowering of knowing that everyone to whom we relate, is a cause for a flowering. Others flowerings are the flowering of knowing that others' opinions of them are not the main concern, the flowering of the knowing we must release, the flowering of knowing to be attuned to the divine mystery, the flowering of knowing the necessity of holy space, and the flowering of knowing life as the present moment.

The holy knowing of consciousness flowers in us to see other people as their essence, not their ego. Flowering persons look into the eyes of all others, to see beyond their words, and behavior, to their core of love within. In those who do not seem to be conscious is an essence that may not yet be known, even to the person carrying it within them. If we can address the essence of each person we meet, instead of his ego, we can relate deeply and authentically to his consciousness. For those yet to awaken, we can potentiate the blooming of their consciousness simply by seeing and addressing their essence. They may be surprised at first when their essence is addressed, but there is almost a relief and a delight in them when this occurs.

Relating to the essence in others was addressed by theologian Martin Buber in his book, *I and Thou*. In this work, the sanctity of all human life is proclaimed. For Buber every person is a reflection of God, and every relationship is to be held in reverence; everyone is a "Thou". (1) This concept is elucidated by the Enneagram's Holy Ideas. Remembering that every person at their core is a unique expression of one of the nine Holy Ideas, we can relate to their core instead of to their ego. Recognizing another's Holy Idea is most easily accomplished by remembering that each Holy Idea is carried within us. We can relate to all persons therefore, on a rudimentary common ground of spirit.

Flowering in the holy knowing that we are all one, takes the discomfort out of relating to others. Those who were once perceived as higher "on the ladder" than we, are now the same as we. It also takes away any air of superiority we may have when relating to those once perceived as "lower on the ladder" than we. Knowing the oneness of all life creates a level playing field, among persons, because the value of all persons is equal. The various purposes of everyone (whether a CEO, a child, a stay at home parent, a senior, or a fast food cook), are seen as "holy requirements" to keep life going in the world. Without one of its many cogs, the wheel of the world could not bear its heavy weight. Ego tends to separate people into gradations of importance. This relegates persons to being viewed according to ego's priorities rather than as an essence (an essential cog). Each cog is a "holy cog" and the wheel must have all of them, regardless of how ego views any one cog.

The knowing of other persons is a beautiful flowering of consciousness. The following quotation is attributed to St. Bernard of Clairveaux who said it so well, "Other selves cannot be directly known by reason. But they can be known directly by love which is a function of the will". If a conscious person wants to flower in relationship, he or she must "will" to know others by loving them consciously. This does not necessarily mean to actively <u>do</u> loving acts for others. It means taking a loving spiritual posture toward them. A loving posture removes antagonism. Antagonism is born of ego. When someone carries negative emotion for another, this usually means the "other" is not playing his part in the person's ego story. As long as others are perceived as roles in one's ego story, the essence of others cannot be seen. Once there is a holy knowing of another's true worth, the flowering can happen. Every human situation can be another arising of a flower of consciousness. All situations are potential flowerings that call for living out of one's essence, surrendering to what is and being fully present to self, others, and the Divine in the current moment.

When one flowers in his own essence, there is a joy of knowing that the world has little sway over his emotions. The essence is not so much worried about others' opinions of him. The essence is more focused on expressing love. Of course there are upsets and relapses. There are times when the old ego comes to the surface, and when past sufferings are revisited, or re-suffered. Yet the new creature transformed from ego to essence, now operates out of a tremendous amount of self-awareness. She sees and observes from an "alter ego", her lack of consciousness nearly at the moment it occurs. This power of inner alertness is the greatest gift of consciousness, and can be used in all situations.

Flowering in consciousness includes fully opening to the holy knowing of "release". For many, the process of release is called letting go, surrendering, or relinquishing. It is the releasing of the ego's image of what should be. Release is followed by an acceptance of what is. For the conscious person, releasing and accepting are daily, even minute by minute activities. The spiritual insight to this principle can be completely missed unless one understands the role of ego in the release-acceptance way of life. Releasing and accepting do not mean passivity and paralysis, but rather a joining with the undercurrent of divine activity in all situations and all persons. So in order to let go, release, or surrender, the flowering person merely gives up her ego's perception and replaces it with an acceptance of the divine mystery. Ego then has an important role. This point is subtle but very important. Ego, in submission to the divine mystery, joins with spirit to take action. The result is spiritually-aligned activity and movement.

Those who are flowering in consciousness are attuned to the ever-present mystery. They are looking for it, living in it, and are communing with its Creator. That which the Creator manifests is more important (actually it is of utmost importance) than what the person's ego may want to bring about. In fact the conscious person practices submission of ego to the divine mystery continuously.

The tree of life has space between each flower and each branch. A butterfly, a bird and flying insects can easily fly between the limbs, leaves, and flowers. This space is a reflection of holy space; that non-substance that is the dwelling place of spirit. Flowerings find greater life within this space. They know that the holy freedom of unencumbered space must exist in order that a full blooming arises. It is the same in the flowering of our consciousness. In the holy space is the "oxygen" for the blooming of consciousness. Space is the place where spirit and mystery interact with the same spirit and mystery within us, to open our petals fully. Stillness and contemplation are those open spaces that define the substances within them. If there was no space there could not be life.

Consciousness flowers as the person lives in the present moment. Living in the present, means being present. When Christ said, "The Kingdom of heaven is at hand", (2) he may have been alluding to the urgency of moving out of "sin" into the light, however He could have also been referring to the 'now' of the present moment. He may have been acknowledging the fact that sequential time does not matter because the only time in which we can live is the time at hand – the present instant. Living in this timeframe saves us from the certain destruction of trying to live in the past, the future, or both past and future. Living in the present is the only way to be in union with one's aliveness and one's divine connection. Paul echoed this sentiment when he said in Second Corinthians 6:2 (NIV) "For He says, 'In the time of my favor I heard you, and in the day of salvation I helped you 'I tell you <u>now</u> is the time of God's favor, now is the day of salvation". (3)

Living in the present moment is also a spiritual practice of other spiritual paths including Sufism. In The *Enchanted Oasis of the Ringed Dove* (4) a book by Adran Sarhan, this concept is elucidated. "Time has value, importance and beauty. You only thrive in the time that is in your hand. For how could you hold onto something that is not in your hand? It is the now. It is the present. The time in your hand says to you, 'I am here' I am with you. I am your contentment. I am your pleasure and joy giver. I am the life, the love. I make you tranquil and pleasant. I give you peace that is the gift of eternity. I soothe your mind. I put rhythm in your heart. And your heart beats to the moment. And life is a dance when you are living it".

Spiritual teacher Eckhart Tolle espouses that the "now" is the only time that we ever really have, and that <u>we are</u> the now. (5) How can this be, that <u>we</u> are the now? The answer is best described by the illustration of the electrical communication devices such as the radio, telephones, or computer. None of these devices <u>is</u> actually the communication itself. They simply conduct it. Yet electronic communication could not be conducted without the devices. Therefore the radio, telephone, and computer can be said to <u>be</u> communication. By analogy, when we are conducting the present moment, we <u>are</u> the present moment. We flower the present moment as we live it, as we express it, and as it blooms in our voice, in our countenance, in our alertness, in our awareness, and in our consciousness.

The Flowering of Consciousness
The Holy Ideas and Stages of Consciousness

When the ego and the essence have aligned optimally with the Divine, it is then possible for the consciousness to emerge, followed by the expansion of consciousness called "flowering". There are many interpretations and traditions relative to the dawning and growth of consciousness. For the purpose of this writing, however, I will propose that there are nine parts of the plant that grows us into the flowering of consciousness. These nine working parts are the Holy Ideas. By first integrating one's own Holy Idea, then the other Holy Ideas as one goes against their arrow, it is possible to flower in consciousness.

In re-contacting one's Holy Idea, and in becoming fully conscious of it, one can then progress, according to Enneagramatical movement to incorporate sequentially the next Holy Ideas on their arrow path. The completion of the Enneagram of Holy Ideas does not stop with one revolution around the Enneagram. One continues again and again as if in a spirally upward movement, touching on each Holy Idea, at a higher level of understanding at each revolution. The person is propelled upward by this spiral movement beyond each previous stage of flowering. (see Figure 11, Chapter Thirteen).

It is of note that the personality type identification and movement against the arrows can be foundational steps in the flowering of consciousness. Discovering one's Holy Idea, speaks to one's primary spiritual nature which is at a deeper more fundamental level of being than is one's personality and ego. This deep spiritual nature is the essence. The Enneagram of Holy Ideas is a method of "returning to essence" as one flowers in consciousness.

Once the search for relief from suffering begins, the person has become open to a new way of living. Everyone who becomes conscious has in some way found their own portal (opening) to new awareness. Portals can vary as much as do people, yet portals to new consciousness correspond in kind to the type of suffering of the person. It is the suffering that actually finds, and opens the portal. For example, if the unconscious ego of a person is fixated on security (Type Six) and if she or he have reached a critical mass of suffering, their portal to relief would involve achieving security and safety in a transformed sense.

How can such a basic need as security be transformed? The Holy Idea of Faith and Strength (Type Six) is this person's way (portal) out of suffering and into consciousness. After reaching her critical mass of suffering when her husband died, a person of this type eventually was driven to search for relief. Her portal was discovered to be her shift away from her compulsion of seeking security toward finding security in her Holy Idea of Trust. She found a job in the hospital, a place that terrified her previously. She became an aid in the emergency room. Never again did she suffer insecurity and its terror. She found an opening to live a new way …a new consciousness. This was her transformation.

Every day of her life Eve reasserted her faith in the "ground of being". When asked how she found her portal to consciousness and out of suffering, these were Eve's words:

"I had depended upon my life's mate, Jeff, for my security. In a way I see now that seeking security was who I was, so Jeff was the major reason I could be me. Oh, I could do computer work and volunteer work, keep a house, and maintain a small business, yet my real identity came from all I got from Jeff. He was my rock of security and our togetherness gave me a role…a way to be a person who was safe. I was a fulfillment for him too, because he needed someone to protect. The hole in my heart that was left when he died was a hole in my safety net and in myself. I was no longer secure. I was no longer myself. I lost my mate, and my sense of completion. It was like if our lives had been a movie, now the whole movie was messed up. The pain of this was so great because his death meant that things would not work out the way they were supposed to. We had many, many plans...we were to have kept on loving each other forever. It all got shattered...and I had no way to live, but I couldn't live the way I had, with Jeff. I didn't even know how to go on. This persisted even after the normal grieving period into several years of mounting anxiety and panic. I began looking for a way out of this agony. I know that the growing sense of insecurity and fear was spinning me into illness...I didn't want to be sick and die...I knew deep inside, I wanted to live. I felt I had more to contribute... more to do that I had not yet done. The time came when I was desperate enough to do something, as they say, "out of the box". I knew whatever it was going to be, it would be shown to me by God. Someone told me that "the universe" would conspire to show me what it was. I began to trust in something bigger, something that wasn't Jeff or another person. Even though trusting went against my nature...now I know deep inside, that I <u>can</u> rely on "the universe" and that as part of that universe, I can trust my own self. My suffering was from the pain of not having the security and selfhood I had lived for with Jeff. The suffering got greater over time because I kept clutching to the idea I needed Jeff to come back and make my life again. The harder I clutched the more pain I had. It was that same hurt oddly enough that pointed me to <u>other ways</u> I could receive the security and a sense of self. Little did I know that working in the E. R. would open my life so much…it was just the opportunity I needed to trust again but in the most expansive definition of trust. This time my trust was not in Jeff and his protective care of me. It wasn't in the love I got from him; this time, trust took on a different, broader definition for me. It was a trust that all would be ok no matter what…because I was now changing my trust focus from a person, to "the universe"…I guess that means God. And with that change in what trust means I knew I was indeed strong and was brave…I got love too…there again, not from a person, most primarily, but from all the people who I meet daily who I am now open to. They are the new way I am getting loved. I am not the same me. I have a new way to be me now. I am trusting in life, I am open to being loved by many others. And I have in a sense, found the real me. I am aware like I've never before been aware".

Another example of consciousness being reached through a portal of transformed suffering is that of Jay, age ten. He suffered with Cystic Fibrosis. Jay is like many other children who have had life-threatening health challenges. There arises in them a maturity beyond their chronological age. This is due to the unavoidable and untimely possibility of a death. Affliction, disability and even abuse can bring on an early arising of consciousness in youth.

"I know that I am not going to live to be an old man. My Dad says I act like an old man now. It's like I see things, other kids my age don't see…they don't want to see these other things because they are still playing and having fun. I can't always have fun. I have to have my treatments. Those remind me everyday that I am sick. But this illness (CF) gives me a way to be that other kids can't be. I mean, I know I am not going to live forever…they don't know that about themselves. I can be happier because I make every second count, just like right this second that we are talking in…I see you and I can feel my Mom who is in the next room, and I can also feel my Grandmother here with me; she died when I was in the first grade. I feel all this at the same time. I am much happier than the kids in my class…but they feel sorry for me. I wish they wouldn't. I wish they could feel what I feel and see what I see. Then sometimes I just wish I could play like they do…but when you know certain things, you can't just play…when I play, I have fun, but I feel like I am an old man having fun. How do you like talking to an old man in a kid's body, Bub?

The Flowering of Consciousness of the Environment and All Crimes Against Life

One of the most monumental flowerings of consciousness happens when the dots are finally connected between ego and the destruction of life. These dots were connected dramatically for me one day a couple of years ago, at the very beach where I grew up. My wife Lark and I were walking on the beach at sunset. It was a different walk from the usual ones, as the oil spill in the Gulf had made its way to Alabama's sugar-white coast. The walk was almost eerie – something very essential to the beach was missing… so noticeable was the absence of the seagulls and their calls as well as their elegant dives into the waves for food.

From the small sand pipers who dart in and out of the aprons of moving surf, to the majestic gulls of the air – we could see none. All of the sudden we stopped in our tracks. There before us, on the oil-stained sand, frantically flapping in the orange glow of a setting sun was a huge sea bird, struggling against all odds to take flight with its heavily oil-soaked wings. As we approached this beautiful bird, a Great Northern Gannet, the fear in her eyes was alarming. She had not only been trapped by heavy oil, but now she was defenseless against two creatures approaching her.

How very against the natural order was this. "She, by all rights of nature, should be flying high above our heads now", Lark and I said to each other.

Quickly, we got a beach towel and swaddled the bird with its four foot wing span. As I held her to take her to safety, I could feel her heart pounding against my hand. This was the heartbeat of all life in the universe. It represented to me the panic all oppressed or deprived beings feel, if they cannot breathe freely, fly, raise their young, and simply "be". This pounding of a heart in jeopardy, was the pounding of life to be naturally free.

The bird was eventually revived by professional rescuers and returned to an oil-free habitat.

In reflecting on this poignant event, I have seen how the dots connect. The dots ultimately lead from death and destruction to its cause: the agendas of egos that see the attainment of their goals as separate from the delicate interconnection of all life. The ego, regardless of its fixation or of its being an individual or a collective ego, is a major cause of that which destroys the planet and life. It is the ego that will take and not replace; it is the ego that will opt for the bounty of immediate gratification instead of respect for the sanctity of all being. It is the ego that sees only its aims in its own, narrow self-centered view, and itself as its own source of solution. It is indeed ego that, in its zeal for oil in the Gulf of Mexico, overlooked the all-important safety measures for all life, human and animal. It is ego that pursues its own aims and looks the other way when forests are destroyed, when hunger abounds, and when war or terrorism are chosen as the means to its end.

The heartbeat of <u>all</u> life is asking for the inherent perfection in these circumstances to come forth. The heartbeat calls for consciousness.

Earth's Cry Unto God

Oh God,

I am your child, Earth, crying out to You! Things are at a boiling point in this atmosphere. I am covered in a fog of smog. Hardly able to breathe, the shield You gave me to protect my surface from the sun, is gone and I am gasping. The smog made holes in the air and finally melted most of my shield. I pray to You for rescue, Oh God. Please save me! These human inhabitants who just arrived a few short eons ago, are wreaking havoc here. I do not know why they burn parts of me to make smog, and I have no idea why they chop down my covering of forests to leave me bare. In my bareness, I get deep wounds on my surface and my soil ends up wearing away. The sun beats down so intensely that I am parched. Even my ice caps are melting. My once frozen glaciers are becoming my tears. The animals, fish, and insects you placed on me before humans came, have never hurt me. But now the humans are killing them off in great numbers. Everything may die leaving me to host only the humans who are dangerous to me. Humans seem to have no end to what they will do to burn me, use me up and rid me of my friendly inhabitants. How much more can I bare, oh God?

They stop at nothing to rob from me, as I watch them from my high mountain, steal from each other as well. I see and feel thousands of footsteps march across my surface time and again to wage devastating war. In hoards, bands and armies they come, and have fight to take the land, sea, and resources from each other. I soak up the blood and bodies of millions. Don't they know they all share the same home in this Galaxy? Why do they turn on each other when they are the only species of their kind anywhere? Why don't they all know that they all want love, families, good crops, and peace? Yet all they see are how they are unalike. They fight about who is best and who is in power over the others. They can even make themselves extinct in just one day, or even less I hear in the rumblings. Though they build rockets, tall buildings, and can clone themselves, are they really the smartest inhabitants I've ever had? I think not, oh Great Creator.

I get the idea, God, that these inhabitants think they can run things their way. The problem is, they can't agree on how things should be run. They can't agree to stop this insane murder/suicide even though they know this is happening. Can You tell me the cause of this Oh God? If I could tell those inhabitants their ways are insane, I would. I know that Your holy plan uses even this destruction for Your ultimate good. But is there any way to awaken this generation, so that they can turn this around? Are they going to destroy themselves and be replaced with other manifestations of You? Can You help me to awaken them, or will You chose to make a new form of life that will embody Your consciousness? Help us, oh God. Amen.

God's Answer to Earth's Cry

Dear Earth,

I know you well. I am your Creator. I have heard your cries and prayers, and also those of the people who are conscious of what you are telling me. I am so sorry that once again, my people have chosen their own will above mine. These inhabitants are my children but they are squandering their inheritance. I weep with you over their choice to fight each other for more and to rid you, Earth, for their own gain. Their freewill, given by me so generously, so they could voluntarily choose me, has been misused. They have willed to control all and to replace Me in their world. I gave them the choice to co-create with me or to seek self. Those who chose Me were empowered and gained abundance. But not enough of them have yet chosen Me. In choosing to create their own kingdom, many of them, even nations of them, have given me a place of honor in their temples. But many of their temples are erected to glorify themselves. And this they do; they worship themselves. So many are drunk with pleasure, dominion, and conceit. So many are totally unaware of you, Earth, or of reality. Egos have run so wild with their choices that in wars and in their tyranny, they kill even their fellow inhabitants' babies. All of their devastation is for more dominion, more gold, more power. Their dominion, gold, and power are just symbols, trophies of theirs for making themselves gods. I am sorry and I weep with you that they chose this illusion to live by. Their choice to be god kills the babies, kills the children and their parents, and sucks the resources out of the earth, slashes the forests, and makes the holes in your atmospheric protection. On the individual level too, many are so blind that they are hurting their own children and neighbors.

They all know deep inside that their choices send their souls into the hell of suffering. They all know deep inside that peace between them could yield joy and happiness. They all know somewhere deep inside that there could be enough food for all, enough energy for their machines and for light in darkness. Deep inside they all love babies and children – deep inside they <u>are all</u> children. Deep inside they all have experienced their Holy Idea that I breathed into them at their beginning. Their choice to replace Me, has wiped out their memory of these things along with the knowing of my love for them all. I am forgiving them because they know not what they do. They will slay each other and you, Earth, until the miraculous blooming of consciousness. This is happening now; they are remembering, one-by-one, flowering by flowering.

Your Creator, God

APPENDIX

SPIRITUAL POSITIONING SYSTEM

To discover your actual position and movement in spiritual development using the Enneagram, look to the following steps.

1. Take the Howell Enneagram Profile Questionnaire, or another Enneagram Inventory. Determine your highest scores.
2. Which center are you in? Gut, Heart or Head. Do you relate to that center?
3. Of the three numbers in your center, with which do you most identify?
4. What level of integration/consciousness are you within your number?
    a. Healthy/Consciousness
    b. Average/Semi-consciousness
    c. Unhealthy/Unconsciousness

5. After identifying and understanding your
   number, look at its two wings on either
   side. Of the two, which one is the stronger?
6. What is your instinctual subtype? Is
   it Social, Sexual or Self-preservative?
7. What is your number for Integration/
   Consciousness? (found by going against your arrow).
8. Are you moving toward Integration/Consciousness?
9. What is your number of Disintegration/
   Unconsciousness? (found by going with your arrow).
10. Are you moving toward Disintegration/Unconsciousness?
11. Is your strong wing moving toward
    Integration /Consciousness or Disintegration/
    Unconsciousness? (against or with its arrow)
12. Have you discovered your soul child and Holy Idea?
13. What is your level of essence? Take
    the Howell Level of Essence Indicator.
14. What stage are you in on the Stages of
    Emergence of Consciousness? (See Figure 11)
15. In what phase of consciousness are you?
16. In what stage of Flowering are you? (See
    Chapter Eighteen, Stages of Flowering).

ENNEAGRAM WORKSHEET

TYPE ONE
The Standard Bearer
"I am a hard worker."
Avoidance: Anger

_____
_____
_____
_____

TYPE TWO
The Nurturer
"I am helpful"
Avoidance: Own Needs

_____
_____
_____
_____

TYPE THREE
The Winner
"I am successful"
Avoidance: Failure

_____
_____
_____
_____

TYPE FOUR
The Creator
"I am unique"
Avoidance: Ordinariness

TYPE FIVE
The Scholar
"I am wise"
Avoidance: Emptiness

TYPE SIX
The Team Player
"I am loyal"
Avoidance: Deviance

TYPE SEVEN
The Bon Vivant
"I am happy"
Avoidance: Pain

TYPE EIGHT
The Commander
"I am powerful"
Avoidance: Weakness

TYPE NINE
The Harmonizer
"I am peaceful"
Avoidance: Conflict

LIST OF FIGURES

NOTES

Chapter One
The Enneagram of Personality – A Passageway to Consciousness

1. John Sanford. *The Kingdom Within*. London: Lippincott Company, 1970. pg 18.
2. Mark 4:9. English Standard Version
3. Matthew 6:22. English Standard Version

Chapter Two
The Types

1. George Appleton. Anglican Bishop of Jerusalem in *Jerusalem Prayers for the World Today*. George Appleton, 1974.
2. Nancy Segal. *Born Together – Reared Apart: The Landmark Minnesota Twin Study*. Cambridge: Harvard University Press, 2012.

3. Carl Jung. "The Psychology of the Child Archetype", in *Reclaiming the Inner Child*. Jeremiah Abrams, ed. Los Angeles: Jeremy P. Tarcher Inc., p 29.

Chapter Three
Self Assessment
1. Richard Rohr. *Falling Upward*. New York: John Wiley and Sons, 2011.
2. Marion Woodman. "The Soul Child" in *Reclaiming the Inner Child*. Jeremiah Abrams, ed. Los Angeles: Jeremy P. Tarcher, Inc., pg. 100.

Chapter Four
The Ego, Its Fixation and Suffering
1. Eckhart Tolle. *A New Earth*. New York: A Plume Book, Penguin Group, 2005. pg. 125.
2. Matthew 7:24-27. New International Version.
3. Deuteronomy 8:3 and Matthew 4:4. New International Version.
4. Genesis 3:12. New International Version.
5. Jan Cox. *Dialogues with Gurdjieff*: Vol. 1. Stone Mountain, GA: Chan Shal Imi Society Press, 1976. pg. 169.

Chapter Five
The Three Levels of Functioning Within Each Type
1. Ken Wilber. *The Essential Ken Wilber*. Boston and London: Shambhala, 1998, pg. 182.
2. Henri Nouwen. *Adam*. Maryknoll, NY: Orbis, 1997.
3. Don Riso, Russ Hudson. *The Wisdom of the Enneagram*. New York: Bantam Books, 1999.

4. Don Riso. *Understanding the Enneagram.* Boston: Houghton Miflin Co., 1990.

Chapter Eight
The Instinctual Subtypes of the Enneagram
1. Abraham Maslow. *Motivation and Personality.* Richmond, CA: Bassett Publishing, 1970.

Chapter Ten
The Emergence of Consciousness
1. Anthony Stevens. *On Jung.* London: Penguin Books Ltd., 1990. Pg 165.
2. Maria Beesing, Robert Nogosek, Patrick O'Leary. *The Enneagram: a Journey of Self Discovery.* Denville, NJ: Dimension Books Inc., 1984.
3. Oscar Ichazo. *Interviews with Oscar Ichazo.* Arica Press, 1982.

Chapter Eleven
Christ, Children, and Consciousness
1. Robert E. van Voorst. *Anthology of World Scriptures.* Lawrence, KS., USA: Barrister Books, 2010.
2. Peter Hannan. *The Nine Faces of God.* Dublin: Columbia Press, 2007.
3. Matthew 5: 3-12.
4. Galatians 5: 22-23.
5. William Law. *A Appeal to All That Doubt.* Printed for William Innys, at the West End of St. Paul's. 1729. In *The World Treasury of Religions Quotations.* Ralph L. Woods, ed. New York: Garland Books, 1966. Pg. 955.

6. Marie-Louise von Franz. "Puer Eternis", in *Reclaiming the Inner Child*. Jeremiah Abrams, ed. Los Angeles: Jeremy P. Tarcher, Inc., 1990. pp. 126-137.
7. Horton Foote. "The Trip to Bountiful." Screen play for the movie directed by Peter Masterson. 1985.
8. Oscar Ichazo. *Interviews With Oscar Ichazo.* Arica Press, 1982.
9. Matthew 18:2-6. English Standard Version
10. Matthew 18:10. English Standard Version
11. Mark 10:13-16. English Standard Version
12. First Corinthians 13:11-12. English Standard Version

Chapter Twelve
The Soul Child

1. AH Almaas. Facets of Unity. Berkley: Diamond Books, 1998.
2. Matthew 18:3, New International Version.

Chapter Thirteen
The Enneagram of Holy Ideas

1. Don Beck, Chris Cowan. *Spiral Dynamics, Mastering Values, Leadership and Change.* Oxford: Blackwell Publishers, 1996.
2. John 1:1-2. English Standard Version
3. James Martineau. *Hours of Thought on Scared Things.* 1879. Miami: Scholarly Publishing Office, University of Miami, 2006.
4. Oscar Ichazo. *Interviews with Oscar Ichazo.* Arica Press, 1982.
5. Plato. *The Republic.* New Haven: Yale University Press, 2006.

6. Plontius. *The Enneads*. New York: Penguin Books, 2005.
7. Jeremy Driscol. *Evagrius Ponticus Ad Monachos*. Paulist Press, 2003.
8. Howard A. Addison. *The Enneagram and the Kabbalah.* Woodstock, VT. USA. Jewish Lights Publishing, 2006.
9. P.D. Ouspensky. *In Search of the Miraculous – Fragments of an Unknown Teaching*. New York: Harcourt Brace and World, 1949.
10. Maria Beesing, Robert Nogosek, Patrick O'Leary. *The Enneagram: a Journey of Self Discovery*. Denville, NJ USA: Dimension Books Inc., 1984.
11. Sandra Maitri. *The Spiritual Dimension of the Enneagram*. New York: Jeremy P. Tarcher, Putnam, 2000.
12. A. H. Almaas. *Facets of Unity*. Boston: Shambhala, 2000.

Chapter Fifteen
The Return to Essence

1. Carl Jung. *Dreams*. trans. by RFC Hull, New York: MJF Books by arrangement with Princeton University Press, 1974.
2. Anthony Stevens. *On Jung*. London: Penguin Books Ltd., 1990.
3. Vachel Lindsay. "The Leaden-Eyed" in *The Congo and Other Poems*. New York:: The McMillan Co., 1919.
4. Matthew 13:14-15. English Standard Version
5. Matthew 13:16-17. English Standard Version

Chapter Seventeen
The Beatitudes of Jesus and the Enneagram
1. Matthew 5:3-12. New International Version
2. Matthew 7:14. English Standard Version

Chapter Eighteen
The Flowering of Consciousness
1. Martin Buber. *I and Thou*. New York: Charles Scribner and Sons, 1939, reprint, Continuum International Publishing Group, 2004.
2. Matthew 4:17. English Standard Version
3. Second Corinthians 6:2. New International Version
4. Adnan Sarhan. *The Oasis of the Ringed Dove*. Torreon NM USA: Sufi Foundation of America, 1994. pp 70-71.
5. Eckhart Tolle. "The Art of Presence". Sounds True Audio. C. 2007

Made in the USA
Lexington, KY
24 January 2014